ADOBE® CS3 WEB WORKFLOWS

BUILDING WEB SITES WITH ADOBE CREATIVE SUITE® 3

JOSEPH W. LOWERY

Wiley Publishing, Inc.

ADOBE® CS3 WEB WORKFLOWS: BUILDING WEB SITES WITH ADOBE CREATIVE SUITE® 3

Published by
Wiley Publishing, Inc.
10475 Crosspoint Boulevard
Indianapolis, IN 46256
www.wiley.com

Copyright © 2008 by Wiley Publishing, Inc., Indianapolis, Indiana

Published simultaneously in Canada

ISBN: 978-0-470-26127-9

Manufactured in the United States of America

10 9 8 7 6 5 4 3 2 1

Limit of Liability/Disclaimer of Warranty: The publisher and the author make no representations or warranties with respect to the accuracy or completeness of the contents of this work and specifically disclaim all warranties, including without limitation warranties of fitness for a particular purpose. No warranty may be created or extended by sales or promotional materials. The advice and strategies contained herein may not be suitable for every situation. This work is sold with the understanding that the publisher is not engaged in rendering legal, accounting, or other professional services. If professional assistance is required, the services of a competent professional person should be sought. Neither the publisher nor the author shall be liable for damages arising herefrom. The fact that an organization or Website is referred to in this work as a citation and/or a potential source of further information does not mean that the author or the publisher endorses the information the organization or Website may provide or recommendations it may make. Further, readers should be aware that Internet Websites listed in this work may have changed or disappeared between when this work was written and when it is read.

For general information on our other products and services or to obtain technical support, please contact our Customer Care Department within the U.S. at (800) 762-2974, outside the U.S. at (317) 572-3993 or fax (317) 572-4002.

Library of Congress Cataloging-in-Publication Data

Lowery, Joseph (Joseph W.)

    Adobe CS3 web workflows : building web sites with Adobe Creative Suite 3 / Joseph W. Lowery.

        p. cm.

    Includes index.

    ISBN 978-0-470-26127-9 (paper/website)

1. Computer graphics. 2. Desktop publishing. 3. Web sites—Design. I. Title.

    T385.L694 2008

    006.6--dc22

    2008008487

Wiley also publishes its books in a variety of electronic formats. Some content that appears in print may not be available in electronic books.

For Margot, the hardest-working daughter in school biz

ABOUT THE AUTHOR

Joseph W. Lowery has been writing about computers and new technology since 1981. He is the author of the previous editions of the *Dreamweaver Bible* and *Fireworks Bible* as well as *CSS Hacks and Filters* (all published by Wiley). He is also the author of *Dreamweaver 8: Beyond the Basics (Lynda.com)*, *Joseph Lowery's Beyond Dreamweaver*, *Dreamweaver MX 2004 Killer Tips* (with Angela C. Buraglia), and *Dreamweaver CS3 Recipes* (with Eric Ott), all published by New Riders. He has also written books on HTML and using the Internet for business. His books are international bestsellers, having sold more than 400,000 copies worldwide in eleven different languages. Joe is also a consultant and trainer and has presented at Adobe conferences in the United States and Europe, and at ThunderLizard's Web Design World. He is currently the vice president of marketing for WebAssist, the leading provider of Adobe extensions.

iv

PART **01**
Photoshop to Dreamweaver

PART **02**
Fireworks to Dreamweaver

PART **03**
Flash to Dreamweaver

PART **04**
Photoshop to Bridge to
Fireworks to Dreamweaver

APPENDIX
Additional Workflows

CREDITS

Executive Editor
Chris Webb

Senior Development Editor
Kevin Kent

Technical Editor
Jim Babbage

Production Editor
Liz Britten

Copy Editor
Mildred Sanchez

Editorial Manager
Mary Beth Wakefield

Production Manager
Tim Tate

Vice President and Executive Group Publisher
Richard Swadley

Vice President and Executive Publisher
Joseph B. Wikert

Project Coordinator, Cover
Lynsey Stanford

Compositor
Patrick Cunningham

Proofreader
C.M. Jones

Indexer
Jack Lewis

Cover Image
© Jupiter Images

CONTENTS AT A GLANCE

vi   PART **01**   PART **02**   PART **03**   PART **04**   APPENDIX

Photoshop to Dreamweaver   Fireworks to Dreamweaver   Flash to Dreamweaver   Photoshop to Bridge to Fireworks to Dreamweaver   Additional Workflows

TABLE OF CONTENTS

CHAPTER 03: FROM COMP TO LAYOUT

PART 2: FIREWORKS TO DREAMWEAVER   98

CHAPTER 04: COMPOSING WITH VECTORS   102

viii

PART **01**   Photoshop to Dreamweaver

PART **02**   Fireworks to Dreamweaver

PART **03**   Flash to Dreamweaver

PART **04**   Photoshop to Bridge to Fireworks to Dreamweaver

APPENDIX   Additional Workflows

PART 3: FLASH TO DREAMWEAVER

x

PART **01**
Photoshop to Dreamweaver

PART **02**
Fireworks to Dreamweaver

PART **03**
Flash to Dreamweaver

PART **04**
Photoshop to Bridge to
Fireworks to Dreamweaver

APPENDIX
Additional Workflows

APPENDIX A: ADDITIONAL WORKFLOWS   306

INDEX   316

INTRODUCTION

When you think of all the work that goes into building Web sites, you realize that the Web is multimedia incarnate. Today's Web is an amalgam of images, illustrations, animations, and video—all gathered neatly and delivered to the site visitor in a coherent package. Who creates all those component parts and then weaves them together in an attractive, organized design? You do, the modern Web designer. And how do you do it? With a wide array of tools such as those bundled together in the Adobe Creative Suite 3 Web software bundle.

There are a great many books out there that focus on each of the component parts of Adobe CS3 Web. I know; I've written a good number of the ones targeting Dreamweaver. However, there are precious few—if any—that tackle the bigger picture, the one that Web designers face every day: How do I use these tools together and how do I use a tool that I'm not really familiar with? That's the two-pronged goal of *Adobe CS3 Web Workflows*: to describe the workflow from one product to another and to detail essential techniques in each program, so you can get your work done.

I've long been fascinated by workflow. I remember in the early days of the Web I was talking to some Photoshop users at a publishing conference and asking how they converted their print materials to Web sites. One fellow described how he measured the screen—literally, with a ruler pressed up against the screen—and then transferred those measurements to the table-based layout. Most of the others around him agreed that they used the same technique. Suffice it to say we've come a very long way from there. However, the pathways are not always well lit, and the specific destinations may be overwhelming for the first-time visitor. I wrote this book to shine a light on the workflow process and give folks a leg up when they're just trying to complete a job but have to master multiple sophisticated rich tools along the way.

WHO THIS BOOK IS FOR

Designers come to the Web from all different perspectives. Some started in print, while others are photographers, animators or even, amazingly enough, Web designers. Few, however, have mastered all the tools contained in the Adobe CS3 Web software or, for that matter, used them all together. This book is for everyone who is coming from one place and trying to create better Web sites.

- If you're a Photoshop user who is struggling with CSS-based layouts, this book is for you.

- If you're a Fireworks devotee whose design shop has standardized on Photoshop for bitmap manipulation, this book will help you get up to speed.

- If you're a Dreamweaver designer whose boss has gotten Flash video fever, this book delivers what you need to got noticcd.

- If you're a designer just starting out who wants to learn how to get the most out of the major investment in software you just made, this book is *definitely* for you.

Depending on where you are in the design spectrum, you may find different parts of the book more useful for you than others. Feel free to skip from one part to another or focus on a particular chapter if need be. The parts and chapters are highly compartmentalized so you can get what info you need quickly and easily.

WHAT THIS BOOK COVERS

As the title indicates, this book covers Adobe Creative Suite 3 Web software. Adobe offers two versions of all of the bundles, Standard and Premium. For the most part, this book is more applicable to the Premium version, which includes Photoshop CS3 Extended, Dreamweaver CS3, Fireworks CS3, Flash CS3 Professional, Contribute CS3, and Bridge CS3, among other programs. However, Standard users will find pertinent material in more than half of this book (Parts II, III, and most of IV).

HOW THIS BOOK IS STRUCTURED

There are four major parts to the book, each designed to examine a specific workflow:

- Part I covers the Photoshop to Dreamweaver workflow with a focus on building your comp from the ground up in Photoshop and designing in Dreamweaver.

- Part II is Fireworks to Dreamweaver–centric and highlights some of Fireworks's unique graphic abilities as well as specialized tasks in Dreamweaver such as building Web standards compliant, CSS-based navigation.

- Part III explores using Flash and Dreamweaver together. Flash video is a primary focus along with basic— but still essential—techniques for using the timeline. The Dreamweaver section details how to integrate your Flash movies for maximum impact.

xiv | PART 01 | PART 02 | PART 03 | PART 04 | APPENDIX

Photoshop to Dreamweaver · Fireworks to Dreamweaver · Flash to Dreamweaver · Photoshop to Bridge to Fireworks to Dreamweaver · Additional Workflows

- Part IV covers a longer workflow: Photoshop to Bridge to Fireworks to Dreamweaver with key stops along the way that describe how to heal and otherwise correct photos, tag images for quick retrieval, comp out a form with symbols, and implement a form with full AJAX-driven validation.

- Appendix A gives an essential overview to a number of other workflows, including Dreamweaver to Contribute, Illustrator to Photoshop to Flash to Dreamweaver, and Fireworks to Flash to Dreamweaver.

Each part has a part opener that gives a 10,000-foot view of how the flow works between the chosen products. Review these sections to get a quick grasp of how to move from one tool to another. The chapters provide more in-depth, step-by-step details of working with each of the tools themselves, while keeping an eye on the overall workflow. Sprinkled throughout the chapters are sidebars labeled "Core Techniques," each dedicated to helping you quickly grasp what you need to know to achieve a specific goal in a specific program or working with groups of products.

WHAT YOU NEED TO USE THIS BOOK

You'll need to have a copy of Adobe Creative Suite 3 Web Premium (preferred) or Standard on either a PC or Mac. I do most of my work on a PC, so the figures are all from the Vista OS—my apologies to my Mac comrades. However, the programs act nearly identically on the two platforms and, where appropriate, I indicate both PC and Mac keyboard shortcuts. You'll also need the exercise files as noted in the next section.

WHAT'S ON THE WEB SITE

Please visit the Web site for this book at www.wiley.com/go/adobecs3webworkflows to download the complete set of exercise files. There are exercise files for each chapter (10 in all), all compressed into a single zip file; there is also one additional zip, which contains an example AVI video for use in Part III. Digitized raw video that has not yet been converted to Flash video format is quite large, even compressed and best downloaded separately.

WHO YOU GONNA CALL?

Feel free to drop me a line if you get stuck, need some clarification, or just want to offer up some random praise. My email address is jlowery@idest.com, and I answer all my email: sometimes slowly, but always surely.

PART 01

Chocolate Dipped Design

Home

Web

Print

Contact

Page title - and subtitle

Lorem ipsum dolor sit amet, consectetuer adipiscing elit, sed diam nonummy nibh euismod tincidunt ut laoreet dolore magna aliquam erat volutpat. Ut wisi enim ad minim veniam, quis nostrud exerci tation ullamcorper suscipit lobortis nisl ut aliquip ex ea commodo consequat. Duis autem vel eum iriure dolor in hendrerit in vulputate velit esse molestie consequat, vel illum dolore eu feugiat nulla facilisis at vero eros et accumsan et iusto odio dignissim qui blandit praesent luptatum zzril delenit augue duis dolore te feugait nulla facilisi.

Heading goes here

Lorem ipsum dolor sit amet, consectetuer adipiscing elit, sed diam nonummy nibh euismod tincidunt ut laoreet dolore magna aliquam erat volutpat.

Lorem ipsum dolor sit amet, consectetuer adipiscing elit, sed diam nonummy nibh euismod tincidunt ut laoreet dolore magna aliquam erat volutpat. Ut wisi enim ad minim veniam, quis nostrud exerci tation ullamcorper suscipit lobortis nisl ut aliquip ex ea commodo consequat. Duis autem vel eum iriure dolor in hendrerit in vulputate velit esse molestie consequat, vel illum dolore eu feugiat nulla facilisis at vero eros et accumsan et iusto odio dignissim qui blandit praesent luptatum zzril delenit augue duis dolore te feugait nulla facilisi.

Heading goes here

Lorem ipsum dolor sit amet, consectetuer adipiscing elit, sed diam nonummy nibh euismod tincidunt ut laoreet dolore magna aliquam erat volutpat.

Lorem ipsum dolor sit amet, consectetuer adipiscing elit, sed diam nonummy nibh euismod tincidunt ut laoreet dolore magna aliquam erat volutpat. Ut wisi enim ad minim veniam, quis nostrud exerci tation ullamcorper suscipit lobortis nisl ut aliquip ex ea commodo consequat. Duis autem vel eum iriure dolor in hendrerit in vulputate velit esse molestie consequat, vel illum dolore eu feugiat nulla facilisis at vero eros et accumsan et iusto odio dignissim qui blandit praesent luptatum zzril delenit augue duis dolore te feugait nulla facilisi.

PHOTOSHOP TO DREAMWEAVER

For the longest time, Web designers lived in a schizophrenic world. On one side, Adobe Photoshop ruled the artists' roost with the most powerful graphics program available. On another side, Macromedia Dreamweaver was the Web professional's choice for clean code output and feature-rich visual layout. Not only did these two programs not work together easily, but their parent companies actively competed against each other with rival products. While some designers kept to one company or the other, there was a constant drumbeat from those who craved the best of both worlds.

With the release of Adobe Creative Suite 3 Web, the disparate worlds of Photoshop and Dreamweaver were united. For the first time, Photoshop and Dreamweaver were available in one package—and, best of all, engineered to work together. Web designers everywhere can now benefit from the enhanced workflow and smoothly move from comp to Web page or from Web layout to graphics editor and back again.

There are two major pathways between Photoshop and Dreamweaver. First graphics saved in Photoshop's native file format, PSD, can now be opened by Dreamweaver. Dreamweaver converts the Photoshop file into a Web-ready format (GIF, JPEG, or PNG) through a user-controlled interface titled Image Preview.

The other path from Photoshop to Dreamweaver lies through the clipboard. A selection copied or cut in Photoshop can be pasted in Dreamweaver and doing so invokes the Image Preview dialog for optimizing the exported image.

Given the iterative nature of the design process for most Web designers, it is essential that the workflow between Photoshop and Dreamweaver be a two-way street. Once a Photoshop-generated image is placed in a Dreamweaver design, it can be sent to Photoshop for further modification. Again, the clipboard serves as the conduit from Photoshop to Dreamweaver; however, the altered graphic is automatically saved with the previously chosen Web-oriented settings, so there is no need to repeat the export process.

In the following chapter, you'll begin by creating a *comp* (a.k.a. a composition) in Photoshop. Designers new to this program will learn numerous essential techniques including working with layers and extracting a figure from its background. On the Dreamweaver site, the basic operations—such as establishing a site and creating a new page—will be enhanced with the development of a Cascading Style Sheet (CSS)–based, Web standards–compliant layout. Subsequent chapters in this part of the book will cover the integration of both Photoshop-created foreground and background images into the Dreamweaver design.

THE FLOW: PHOTOSHOP TO DREAMWEAVER

As noted earlier, there are two distinct ways for moving graphics from Photoshop to Dreamweaver. Here's an overview of the first approach (see Figure I-1):

1. Create your graphic comp in Photoshop.
2. Save any individual component (primarily foreground images) as a native Photoshop (PSD) file.
3. Open PSD file in Dreamweaver and convert it to Web-ready format.

FIGURE I-1

The second method (Figure I-2) requires the following steps:

1. Select desired image in Photoshop.
2. Copy or cut the selection to the clipboard.
3. Paste the clipboard in Dreamweaver and convert the image to a Web-ready format.

FIGURE I-2

To modify an image placed in a Web page in Photoshop (Figure I-3), you'll follow these steps:

1. Select the image in Dreamweaver and, from the Property inspector, choose Edit (the Photoshop icon).
2. Image opens in Photoshop for modifications.
3. Select and copy the modified image.
4. In Dreamweaver, paste the copied image.

FIGURE I-3

NOTE

The example Web page used in this part was inspired by www.macaroondesign.com, created by Yul Moreau. Yul is freelance Web designer as well as Senior Graphic Designer at Business Interactive.

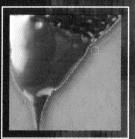
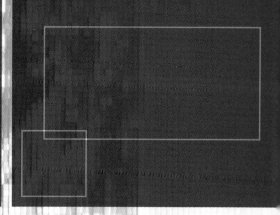

Adobe Photoshop is rightly well known for uses in digital photography, print preparation, and even, with the introduction of Photoshop Extended, medical imagery. Although lesser known, Photoshop's Web capabilities are equally robust. Factor in the ubiquity of Photoshop in design houses around the world and its newly introduced Dreamweaver connectivity, and you have a tool ready to create a comp for almost any Web site.

Given its full-featured implementation as a graphics editor, it's no wonder that Photoshop is often overwhelming to those new to the software. This chapter—and the others following it in this part—takes a learn-by-doing approach. Here, you'll build up a sample composition in Photoshop to be converted to a Web page in Dreamweaver. As you move through the design process, you'll encounter core techniques essential to working in Photoshop. The core Photoshop techniques covered in this chapter are:

- Working with layers
- Making a selection
- Extracting images from the background

Later chapters in this part build on the design foundation you put down in Photoshop and extend your work to its ultimate goal: a Dreamweaver Web site.

CHAPTER
01
CREATING THE COMP

INITIALIZING THE COMP

While there is no direct interaction between Photoshop and Dreamweaver detailed in this chapter, that doesn't mean there is no workflow between the two. Part of any design process is the initial visualization of the project and, whether you sketch out your ideas on paper or in a graphics tool, it's always good to consider your end result. If your site requirements demand an HTML-based site rather than a Flash-based one, your design direction is going to be influenced by what's possible with modern Web standards–compliant implementations. For example, a race car spinning onto the middle of your homepage and then zooming off to reveal the previously hidden content is probably better suited for a Flash presentation, even though it could possibly be done with advanced JavaScript techniques.

When considering a design for an HTML-based page, it's a good idea to keep these questions in mind:

- Where are the natural divisions in this design that will translate into a CSS layout?

- Which figures are in the foreground and can be inserted as `<img>` tags?

- Which graphics are best displayed as background images and defined in a CSS style?

As I go along, I'll point out where these considerations would occur to me so you can get a sense of how to apply them to your own work.

The example comp created during this exercise is for a fictitious Web design company called Chocolate Dipped Design. You can start the comp in Photoshop by creating a new page:

1. From Photoshop's main menu, choose **File ▶ New**.

2. When the New dialog box (Figure 1-1) opens, enter **Chocolate Dipped Comp** in the Name field.

   Although not critical, it's a good idea to name your pages upfront when defining them in Photoshop. The name appears in the document title bar, which is handy when working with a number of open files. Moreover, the

NOTE

Throughout this book, I use the term HTML to refer to both HTML and XHTML-coded pages. XHTML is the most recent incarnation of the HTML language and incorporates a standards-based coding approach; the default document type (or doctype) for Dreamweaver CS3 is XHTML 1.0 Transitional. As HTML encompasses all variations, you'll find it used consistently in these pages.

name becomes the suggested filename that appears in the Save dialog box—a minor timesaver, true, but in the often hectic world of Web design, every little bit helps.

3. From the Preset menu, select **Web**.

The Web preset provides a variety of common Web page sizes, including 800 x 600 and 1024 x 768, in addition to the standard sizes for Web banner ads such as Leaderboard and Wide Skyscraper.

4. From the Size menu, choose **1024 x 700**.

FIGURE 1-1

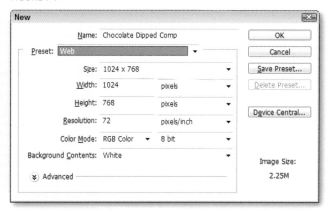

What size Web page is often the first decision a Web designer faces. The answer depends on a number of factors, primarily related to the client's needs and experience. If the visitor logs in from a previous or existing site, you'll be able to get an idea of the screen resolution employed by your client's audience. If the vast majority is using a lower resolution, such as 800 x 600, you'll need to work within those restraints. If, on the other hand, a significant proportion is viewing the site with 1024 x 768 or higher, you can safely increase your design space to those dimensions. The trend in computing is definitely toward larger monitors with higher resolutions, but it's always vital to put the client's interest first.

5. Leave Resolution set to **72 pixels per inch** and Color Mode to **RGB 8 bit**.

These default settings reflect standard monitor output.

6. From the Background Contents menu, choose **White** and click **OK**.

What color you start your comp with is a personal choice; some designers prefer transparent over white. I typically choose white because that is the default background color for rendered Web pages.

7. Choose **File ▶ Save As**. When the Save As dialog opens, navigate to a folder to store your images or create a new one. Keep the suggested name as well as the default options and click **OK**.

Photoshop opens your new document full size with the magnification set to as close to 100 percent as possible given your program window size. You can change the magnification as needed by using the Zoom tool.

SETTING PREFERENCES

To better allow you to work the way you want to work, Photoshop has a full complement of preference settings: ten entire categories of them, in fact. Although Photoshop offers a great number of optional settings, when you are creating Web comps, there is one change that is highly recommended. Web pages are presented primarily in a pixel-based medium, and it's a good idea to switch Photoshop's basic unit of measurement to pixels. This setting instructs Photoshop to display all positioning—on rulers as well as X and Y coordinates in the Info panel—and dimensional—width and height—information the way browsers render the page: in pixels. Additionally, Web designers should set the type unit of measurement to pixels. While print designers used to working with points may be thrown off their game, pixels are one of more frequently used units of measurements in CSS for text.

To establish the proper preferences for working on the Web, follow these steps:

1. Choose Edit ▶ Preferences ▶ Units & Rulers (Windows) or Photoshop ▶ Preferences ▶ Units & Rulers (Mac). See Figure 1-2.

2. From the Rulers menu, choose **pixels**.

3. From the Type menu, choose **pixels**.

FIGURE 1-2

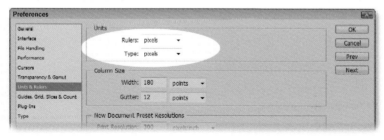

4. Click **OK**.

NOTE

If you worked with previous versions of Photoshop to create Web designs, you may be wondering whatever happened to ImageReady. ImageReady, a Web-oriented bitmap editor previously paired with Photoshop, has been discontinued. For similar—and arguably more advanced—functionality, turn to Adobe Fireworks, part of the Adobe CS3 Web suite and covered elsewhere in this book.

WORKING WITH LAYERS

I remember the first time I opened an example file from an experienced Photoshop designer. The image before me was a relatively simple-appearing logo with a curved framed and highlighted lettering. Okay, I thought, he's got text surrounded by a rounded rectangle against a textured background; I suspected the figure was comprised of 4, maybe 6, separate objects total. I opened the Photoshop Layers palette to take a look at how it was made and almost fainted when the 43 different elements were revealed. Layers are essential in Photoshop.

Every object—whether text string, rectangle, or digital image—is placed on its own layer in Photoshop in the Layers palette. Layers are stacked above or below one another and easily rearranged if necessary. You can hide or display layers or lock them against further editing. As you'll see later in this chapter, layers can even have effects applied to them.

Layer groups are used to keep the potential multitude of layers orderly. A layer group is represented by a folder icon and can contain other layer groups as well as layers. Layer groups can also be hidden or locked as needed.

While both layers and layer groups can, and often are, created on the fly, it's a good idea to prime the canvas as it were and create your basic structure. You can start by creating the three primary layer groups:

1. Choose **Window ▶ Layers** or, from the docked palette group, click **Layers** to expand the Layers palette (Figure 1-3).

FIGURE 1-3

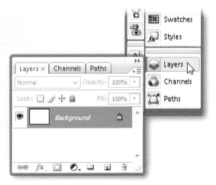

2. Click the folder icon in the bottom of the Layers palette to create a new group.

   A new Layer group appears titled Group 1 (Figure 1-4). You can easily rename your layer groups with more appropriate labels.

   FIGURE 1-4

3. Double-click the Group 1 name and rename it **Footer**.

4. Repeat steps 2 and 3 twice more to create group layers named **Content** and **Header**.

   You'll note that new layer groups are added above the currently selected one. Layers can be easily moved from one position to another.

5. Drag the Header layer group down below the Content layer group. Release your mouse button when you see a black line appear below Content.

   Layer groups can be stacked above or below another layer group or within it. Again, Photoshop gives you a visual indicator.

6. Drag the Footer layer group into the Content layer group. When you see a black border surrounding Content, release your mouse button (Figure 1-5).

   FIGURE 1-5

7. Press **Ctrl+Alt+Z** (Windows) or **Cmd+Opt+Z** (Mac) twice to undo the last two operations and restore the layer groups to their original order of Header, Content, and Footer.

> *The undo keyboard commands standard in many other programs Ctrl+Z (Windows) and Cmd+Z (Mac) are effective only for the last operation in Photoshop; pressing the keyboard shortcut a second time undoes your undo command, effectively redoing it. To undo the last series of operations, you'll need to bring in the Alt/Opt key: use Ctrl+Alt+Z (Windows) or Cmd+Opt+Z (Mac) for multiple undo commands.*

8. Select **Header** and insert a new layer by clicking **Create a new layer** at the bottom of the Layers palette (Figure 1-6).

FIGURE 1-6

9. Choose **File ▶ Save**.

With the basic structure of the Web comp done, you're ready to begin adding content.

MAKING SELECTIONS

The act of selection is at the heart of working in Photoshop. In order to effectively alter a portion of an image, you must select it first. In testament to selection's central place in the mechanics of Photoshop, there are easily more than a dozen ways you can make a selection. Moreover, whether you've drawn it out freehand with the Lasso tool, surrounded it with the Marquee tool, or automatically chosen it with the Magic Wand, your selection can be adjusted or fine-tuned in myriad of ways.

PART **01**   PART **02**   PART **03**   PART **04**   APPENDIX

Photoshop to Dreamweaver   Fireworks to Dreamweaver   Flash to Dreamweaver   Photoshop to Bridge to   Additional Workflows
                                                                                Fireworks to Dreamweaver

Selections aren't just for modifying bitmaps, however—you can also use them to create a graphic element. Often Web comps cry out for a splash of color to delineate or otherwise decorate a page. Whereas in other graphic tools, such as Fireworks, you would typically draw out a shape and then adjust its fill and the stroke, in Photoshop it's common practice to define the area you want to color with a selection. In the example comp, you'll create selections in both the header and footer areas that will, in short order, contain gradient fills.

1. From the Layers palette, select the **Header** layer inserted in the last exercise.

   When defining color areas, it's important to realize that you need to tell Photoshop where you want your selection to go.

2. From the Tools palette, select the **Rectangular Marquee** tool, the second item from the top (Figure 1-7).

FIGURE 1-7

If the Rectangular Marquee tool is not displayed in the second position, click the tool and hold your mouse down until the menu group opens; you can then choose the Rectangular Marquee from the pop-up list.

Ps CORE TECHNIQUES

WORKING WITH LAYERS AND LAYER GROUPS

Every graphic element created in Photoshop is placed on its own layer in the Layers palette (**Windows ▶ Layers**). Layers can be organized into layer groups; both layers and layer groups can be arranged and modified in a number of ways. Photoshop supports a variety of types of layers including object, fill, and adjustment layers.

- Click **Create a new layer** (second icon from the right at the bottom of the Layers palette) to insert a standard layer.

- Click **Create a new group** (the folder icon at the bottom of the Layers palette) to add an organizing folder to the Layers palette.

- To move a layer or layer group directly above or below another element in the Layers palette, drag it until a single black line appears in your intended destination.

- To place a layer into a layer group, drag the layer onto the group until a black rectangle surrounds the layer group. The same technique can be used to nest one layer group inside another.

(continued)

(continued)

- If you prefer not to use a mouse to move your layers or layer groups, select the element you want to move in the Layers palette and choose **Layer ▶ Arrange** from the main menu.

- Layers or layer groups can be hidden by toggling the eye icon in the adjacent column or locked by selecting the layer and clicking the padlock icon at the top of the Layers palette.

3. Make sure you can see the entire width of the image.

   If necessary, use the Zoom tool (the magnifying glass icon just above the foreground/background color swatches) to increase or decrease the magnification; press **Alt** (Windows) or **Opt** (Mac) while clicking to zoom out.

4. Choose View ▶ Rulers.

   The horizontal and vertical rulers are very helpful to any layout and are recommended throughout the process.

5. Drag out a rectangle that starts above the top-left portion of the page and spans the full width of the image, with a height of approximately 150 pixels (Figure 1-8).

FIGURE 1-8

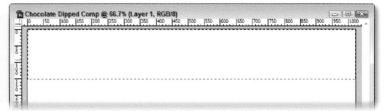

You don't have to be exact with your drawing—you'll adjust the height shortly. However, before you can, you need to fill the selection with pixels.

6. Choose the **Paint Bucket** tool from the middle of the Tools palette and click once in the selection.

   The selection fills with the current foreground color; if the color is white, you won't notice a change, but the selection is filled nonetheless.

7. With the marquee still active, choose **Edit ▶ Free Transform**.

   The Options bar, located at the top of the Photoshop document window, changes to display the transformation controls.

8. Change the **H** (Height) value to **160 px** and press **Tab** (Figure 1-9).

FIGURE 1-9

9. Double-click the filled marquee to apply the transformation

If you attempt to do anything else before applying the transformation, Photoshop gives you the option to do so or discard the change.

10. Choose Select ▶ Deselect.

11. Choose **File ▶ Save**.

Your first comp element—a simple, single color rectangle (Figure 1-10)—is now complete. Now you can add a gradient to spice it up.

FIGURE 1-10

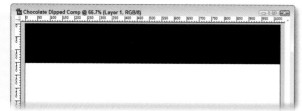

ADDING GRADIENTS

Gradients serve many purposes in design. While some are purely decorative, others provide a sense of dimension, as with drop shadows. In Photoshop, gradients are a special type of fill. Photoshop comes ready to roll with a full library—in fact, eight different libraries—of gradients. But, naturally, the real power comes from creating your own custom gradients.

In this next phase of building the comp, you're first going to add a bright green to dark gray gradient to the previously created page element in the header. Then, you'll create a mirrored, but shorter, element in the footer.

Ps CORE TECHNIQUES

MAKING A SELECTION

For many Photoshop operations, making a selection is the critical first step.

Here are the key tools and commands relating to Photoshop selections:

- **Marquee tool**—Draw out your selection with the Marquee tool. There are two primary varieties: Rectanglar and Elliptical. Press **Shift** while drawing out your marquee to create a square or circular selection, respectively.

- **Lasso tool**—For selections that are more organic, use the Lasso tool. Three variations are available: Freeform, for drawing freehand shapes; Polygonal, for creating multi-sided selections; and Magnetic, for drawing a freehand selection that adheres to the edge of an object.

- **Magic Wand**—Use the Magic Wand to select pixels of the same or similar color. Increase the Tolerance level in the Options bar to select a wider range of color; decrease it to select less.

(continued)

(continued)

- **Quick Select**—Found in the Magic Wand menu group, Quick Select allows you to "paint" your selection. As you move your cursor, the Quick Select tool expands the selection to include pixels of a similar color range.

- **Select Inverse**—Often it's easier to initially select the portion of an image surrounding your desired selection. Once you've accomplished that task, choose **Select ▶ Inverse** to reverse your selection.

- **Save Selection**—Once a selection has been made, you can save it in the alpha channel of your image. This is very useful when editing images in Photoshop from Dreamweaver; that workflow (Dreamweaver to Photoshop and back to Dreamweaver) relies on copying the selection before returning to Dreamweaver.

- **Deselect**—After your selection is complete, removing the selection is vital. Press Ctrl+D (Windows) or Cmd+D (Mac) to deselect any selection.

1. Choose the **Magic Wand** from the Tools palette and click once in the previously created header rectangle.

   Because the image is a solid color, the entire rectangle is selected.

   > It's important to select a specific area for the gradient; otherwise, the gradient is applied to the entire document.

2. Click the **Paint Bucket** tool to expose the pop-up menu and select the **Gradient tool** (Figure 1-11).

   FIGURE 1-11

3. In the **Options** bar, click the gradient color swatch to open the **Gradient Editor**.

   The Gradient Editor has two major sections: Presets and the properties area. After you define your gradient colors, you can establish a new preset for reuse.

4. Double-click the first color stop on the bottom-left side of the gradient (Figure 1-12) to open the color picker.

   The initial default gradient—and the one you'll create—has two color stops, one at either end of the gradient preview. You can add as many color stops as you'd like by simply clicking along the bottom of the preview.

FIGURE 1-12

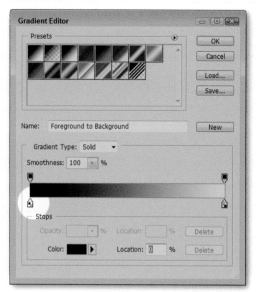

5. In the color picker, enter hexadecimal for solid green, **00ff00**, in the **#** field (Figure 1-13). Alternatively, you can enter **R:0 G:255 B:0**. Click **OK** when you're done to close the picker.

FIGURE 1-13

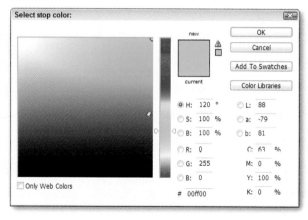

6. Double click the second color stop on the far right of the preview gradient to again open the color picker.

7. In the # field, enter **66666** and click **OK**.

   Your new gradient is ready (Figure 1-14); save it as a preset so it can be reused later in the comp.

FIGURE 1-14

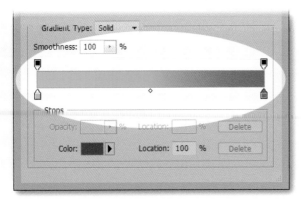

8. In the Name field, enter **Header Footer** and press **Tab**. Click **New**. Click **OK** when you're done.

    Now you can apply the gradient you constructed. The area needed to be filled with the gradient is already selected—all you need to do is provide the direction.

9. Press **Shift** and drag your cursor from the top of the selection to its bottom. Release your mouse button to complete the gradient (Figure 1-15).

FIGURE 1-15

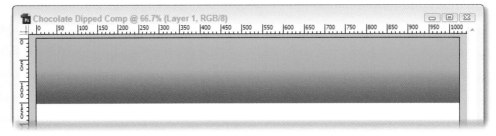

You can draw out gradients in any direction; pressing Shift constrains the line drawn to be straight.

The next series of steps pulls together everything covered up to this point in the chapter.

1. In the Layers palette, select **Footer**.

2. Insert a new layer by clicking **Create a new layer**.

3. Select the **Rectangular Marquee** tool and draw out a selection from the lower right of the document that spans the width of the page and is about **50 pixels** high (Figure 1-16).

FIGURE 1-16

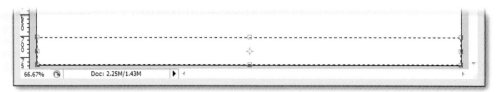

4. Select the **Paint Bucket** tool and fill the selected area with the foreground color.

5. Choose Edit ▶ Free Transform.

6. Change the **H** (Height) value to **50 px** (Figure 1-17) and press **Tab**. Double-click the filled area to apply the transformation.

FIGURE 1-17

7. Select the **Gradient** tool and, with the last gradient still selected, drag your cursor from the bottom of the selected area to its top, while pressing **Shift**. (See Figure 1-18.)

FIGURE 1-18

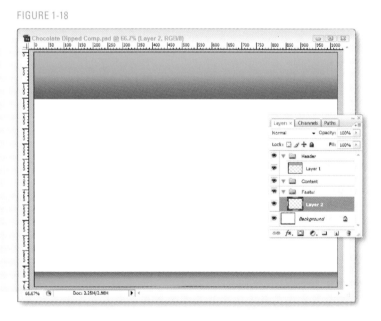

8. Choose **File ▶ Save**.

Now the basic header and footer graphics are good to go. As you can see, the creation process goes much quicker once you're familiar with the toolset.

INSERTING IMAGES

Photoshop positively excels when working with bitmapped images, whether they are digital photographs or previously created art. Once brought onto your canvas, they can be altered in almost immeasurable ways: rescaled, rotated, flipped, distorted, color corrected, blended—the list goes on and on.

This exercise focuses on a few central bitmap operations to build up sections of the Web page comp. These operations include:

- Placing an external image in your comp

- Duplicating images

- Rotating and moving images on the canvas

- Removing an image from its background

The first task is to bring in a bit of scrollwork to give the gradient a little more depth and subtlety.

1. If you haven't already downloaded the book exercise files, do so now. The files can be obtained from `www.wiley.com/go/adobecs3webworkflows`; download the zipped files and uncompress them to a folder on your system.

2. In the Layers palette, select the gradient layer inside the **Header** group folder.

   When images are brought into Photoshop, they automatically create a new layer; by preselecting a group folder, the new layer will be put just where you want it to go.

3. Choose **File ▶ Place**. When the Place dialog opens, navigate to the book exercise files and open the **Chapter 1** folder. Locate the **spiral.gif** file and click **Place**.

   The inserted image is initially placed in the center of the document and marked with an X-shaped line and border with sizing handles (Figure 1-19).

020

PART **01** Photoshop to Dreamweaver

PART **02** Fireworks to Dreamweaver

PART **03** Flash to Dreamweaver

PART **04** Photoshop to Bridge to Fireworks to Dreamweaver

APPENDIX Additional Workflows

FIGURE 1-19

4. Place your cursor inside the image and drag it over the top gradient, until it is about 150 pixels from the left and 50 pixels from the top (Figure 1-20). After you've placed it where you like, double-click the image to confirm the move.

FIGURE 1-20

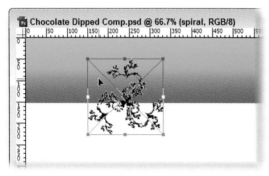

You'll notice some artifacting as the spiral overlays the gradient; you'll handle that in the next step by adjusting the opacity of the image.

5. With the spiral image still selected in the Layers palette, change the **Opacity** value, located in the top right of the Layers palette, to **10%** (Figure 1-21). You can either use the slider or manually alter the value.

FIGURE 1-21

The design goal here is to break up the gradient somewhat, but not so much that it overpowers the rest of the comp. Now that you have your basic filigree graphic, add a few more to heighten the effect.

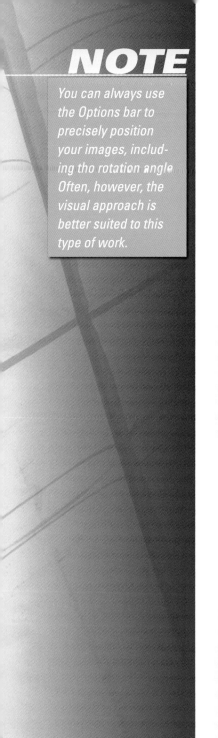
6. **Right-click** (Windows) or **Control-click** (Mac) on the spiral layer. From the pop-up menu, choose **Duplicate Layer**. When the Duplicate Layer dialog box appears, change the name to **spiral 2**.

   The layer is cloned and inserted on top of the original. Now you can try out a few of Photoshop's bitmap transformation tools.

7. Drag **spiral 2** to the right about **50 pixels** and position it close to the top of the document. Rotate the image about **15 degrees** counterclockwise by moving your cursor outside the bottom-left corner of the graphic until you see the curved two-headed arrow and dragging up (Figure 1-22). When you find a suitable position, double-click the image to complete the transformation.

FIGURE 1-22

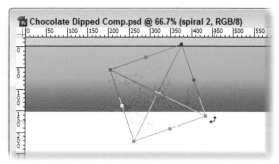

8. Repeat step 6 to duplicate another image layer; name this one **spiral 3**. Move the new image a bit further to the right of spiral 2 and down **75 pixels** or so. Rotate the new spiral clockwise about **20 degrees**. Double-click the image when you're done (Figure 1-23).

FIGURE 1-23

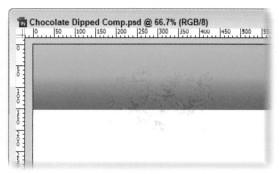

Now, you can apply the same techniques to the footer.

9. Repeat step 6 again to duplicate another layer and name it **spiral 4**. Drag the layer to the **Footer** group above Layer 2, which holds the bottom gradient.

10. Drag the selected image down to the footer region and place it on the left side of the document, positioned so that the top of the graphic does not go above the gradient. The lower portion of the spiral will spill out of the document (Figure 1-24).

FIGURE 1-24

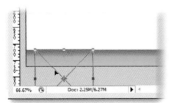

11. Continue to duplicate the spiral layer and place it along the bottom gradient until the full span is filled. Remember to vary the angle of the image to avoid a discernible pattern (Figure 1-25).

FIGURE 1-25

Not all the graphics you might want to incorporate in a Web page come ready to be placed. Who hasn't seen the perfect image for a design—if only it were flipped the other way or a slightly different size? Modifications like these are one-step operations in Photoshop (most of which can be found in the Edit ▶ Transform commands), but another common problem—isolating an image from its background—requires a bit more work.

Perhaps to better handle the full range of images, Photoshop provides a number of ways to pull out a section of a graphic. The following exercise walks you through

TIP

Here are a couple of tips to help speed up this detailed work. First, you can dupli-cate a layer by drag-ging it to the Create a new layer icon on the bottom of the Lay-ers palette. Your new layer will be called LayerName copy, which you can modify by double-clicking on it and entering a new name. To vary the look of the spiral, choose Edit ▶ Trans-form ▶ Flip Vertical or Edit ▶ Transform ▶ Flip Horizontal. Finally, cloned layers can be moved hori-zontally just by using the left and right ar-row keys, so that ev-ery spiral stays in the same plane.

one approach—using a Quick Mask—that has consistently worked well for me. A number of other methods are described in the Core Techniques sidebar "Extracting an Image from the Background" that appears near the end of this chapter.

1. In Photoshop, choose **File ▶ Open** and navigate to the **Chapter 1** folder. Select **strawberries_bg.jpg**. (See Figure 1-26.)

FIGURE 1-26

The goal here is to extract the two strawberries from their background without extracting the surrounding drop shadow. If you retained the shadow, it would be much harder for the image to blend into the comp. It's better to isolate just the desired figure and apply your own shadow, as needed.

2. From the Tools palette, select the **Magic Wand** and click into anywhere in the brown background.

The first step in this technique is to select the portion of the image you want to keep. You could use any of the available selection tools, such as lasso or polygon lasso, to do this but in this case the Magic Wand does an adequate job quickly. The selection does not have to be exact as it is refined in the following steps.

024   PART **01**   PART **02**   PART **03**   PART **04**   APPENDIX

Photoshop to Dreamweaver   Fireworks to Dreamweaver   Flash to Dreamweaver   Photoshop to Bridge to Fireworks to Dreamweaver   Additional Workflows

3. Choose Select ▶ Inverse Selection.

Because you want to select the strawberries rather than the background, the selection is reversed. Although it may appear to you that little has changed, note that the marquee previously surrounding the outer border is now gone and only the strawberries are selected (Figure 1-27).

FIGURE 1-27

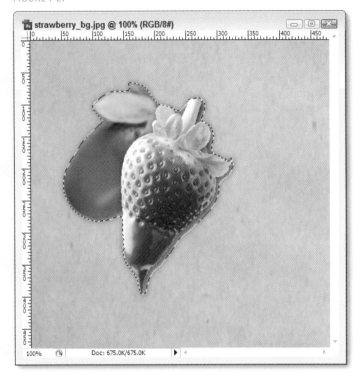

Another approach to create the selection is to use the Quick Select tool (found in the Magic Wand group) to paint over the strawberries, being careful not to move into the shadow. With this method, there's no need to invert the selection.

4   Press **Q** to create a Quick Mask.

The nonselected background is now tinted red to indicate the application of the Quick Mask (Figure 1-28).

FIGURE 1-28

Masking is a key concept in Photoshop. As the name implies, a mask is used to hide part of what lies beneath, which, in Photoshop, is an image. What is hidden in Photoshop can't be altered, so masks are also used to protect parts of a graphic. Entering into Quick Mask mode changes whatever is selected into a temporary mask. When you exit the Quick Mask mode, the temporary mask is reverted to the selection.

5.   From the Tools palette, select the **Brush** tool, located in the second tool grouping on the palette.

The real power in the Quick Mask technique comes from using the Brush tool to fine-tune the selection by drawing with either black or white. When abstracted, a mask is shown in black and white; the mask itself is black, while the unmasked portion is white. In Quick Mask mode, you use black to extend the mask and white to extend the unmasked, or selected, area.

PART **01**   PART **02**   PART **03**   PART **04**   APPENDIX

Photoshop to Dreamweaver   Fireworks to Dreamweaver   Flash to Dreamweaver   Photoshop to Bridge to   Additional Workflows
                                                                                 Fireworks to Dreamweaver

6. Make sure that the foreground color is black and begin painting over the shadow surrounding the strawberries. You might find it helpful to zoom in on the section you're working on by pressing **Ctrl++** (Windows) or **Cmd++** (Mac) (Figure 1-29).

FIGURE 1-29

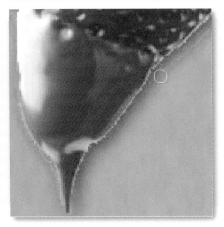

7. Continue to work your way around the strawberries. If you extend the mask into the desired figure, switch the foreground color to white by clicking the curved two-headed arrow above the foreground and background color swatches and apply your brush from within the strawberries.

Understanding the relationship between drawing with black to extend the mask and drawing with white to push back the mask was my "Oh, wow!" moment with this technique. By zooming in and changing the brush size (in the Options bar), I'm able to precisely control the boundaries of the mask and, thus, the selection.

8. To see the results of your progress, press **Q** to exit Quick Mask mode and review the current selection marquee. Press **Q** again to continue refining the mask.

9. When you're done, press **Q** a final time to leave Quick Mask mode. With your selection finalized, press **Ctrl+C** (Windows) or **Cmd+C** (Mac) to copy it to the clipboard.

Since it's a signature element in the design, you may want to reuse it at some later point, so it's a good idea to save the isolated image separately.

10. Choose **File ▶ New** to create a new PSD file. In the New dialog, keep the default dimensions Photoshop picked up from the clipboard and change the Background Contents to **Transparent**. Click **OK**.

11. When the new file opens, press **Ctrl+V** (Windows) or **Cmd+V** (Mac) to paste it to the clipboard (Figure 1-30).

FIGURE 1-30

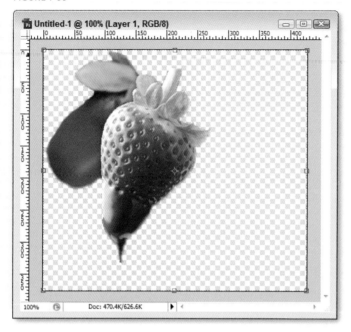

You'll notice the image appears, minus the background. Now, take one more step to clean it up before saving.

12. Choose the **Crop** tool, fourth from top of the Tools palette, and drag out a rectangle from the top-left corner that encloses the strawberries. Double-click inside the cropped area to confirm your choice.

13. Choose **File ▶ Save As** and store the file in your **Chapter 1** folder as **just_strawberries.psd**.

14. Select the **Chocolate Dipped Comp** document and, in the Layers palette, select the **Header** layer group. Drag the just_strawberries image onto the Chocolate Dipped Comp document (Figure 1-31).

Naturally, you could have used the copy/paste method, but in this circumstance dragging from one document to the other is just as effective and a bit faster.

The strawberries are a bit too big for the comp, so you'll want to scale the image down.

028   PART **01**   PART **02**   PART **03**   PART **04**   APPENDIX

Photoshop to Dreamweaver   Fireworks to Dreamweaver   Flash to Dreamweaver   Photoshop to Bridge to Fireworks to Dreamweaver   Additional Workflows

FIGURE 1-31

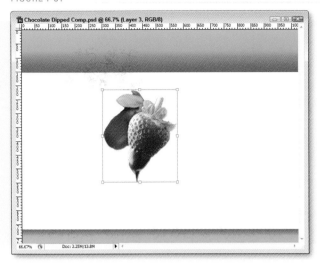

15. In the Options bar, make sure **Show Transform Controls** is selected. Click the lower right corner of the bounding box around the strawberries, press **Shift** to constrain the aspect ratio and drag toward the upper left corner, rescaling the image. Release your mouse when the **W** and **H** values are approximately **60%**.

16. Drag the rescaled strawberries into the header area, about **200** pixels from the left and **50** from the top. Double-click inside the strawberries to confirm the move.

17. Press **Ctrl+S** (Windows) or **Cmd+S** (Mac) to save your changes. Figure 1-32 shows the final result.

FIGURE 1-32

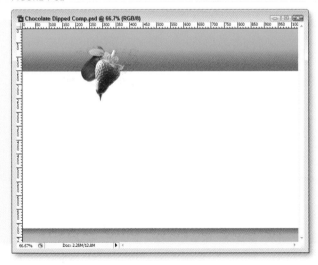

INITIALIZING THE COMP // SETTING PREFERENCES // CHAPTER
WORKING WITH LAYERS // MAKING SELECTIONS //
ADDING GRADIENTS // INSERTING IMAGES //

029

01

Ps CORE TECHNIQUES

In this chapter, you got a solid foundation for creating the basic graphic elements of a comp. In the next chapter, you'll complete the comp with other elements, including decorative and content-oriented text before moving on to construct the layout in Dreamweaver in the final chapter of this part.

EXTRACTING AN IMAGE FROM THE BACKGROUND

Figures isolated from their normal background provide powerful imagery and are often incorporated into Web designs. In addition to copying and pasting a selection, Photoshop offers three key methods for extracting an image from the background: the Extract filter, Background Eraser, and Quick Mask.

- The **Extract filter** is Photoshop's dedicated user interface for the task of isolating an image from its background. Choose your image and select **Filter ▶ Extract**. When the Extract filter appears, select the Edge Highlighter tool and draw around the portion of the image you want to keep. Then click the Fill tool and click within the desired section. Click Preview to see the results and fine-tune the background selection with the Cleanup tool and the foreground with the Edge Touchup tool.

- The **Background Eraser** tool changes any pixels it encounters to transparent. You simply draw over the unwanted portion of your image to remove the background.

- The **Quick Mask** technique (used in this section's exercise) converts a selection into a mask that can then be easily adjusted and returned to a selection. When in Quick Mask mode, draw with black using the brush tool to extend the mask (and consequently, the background) or white to extend the unmasked area (the foreground). You can easily go back and forth between the Quick Mask and selection by toggling the letter Q.

Page Title

Lorem ipsum dolor sit ame
rutrum ut, rhoncus laoree
pulvinar metus nec lacus.
malesuada pede, quis lao
purus. Pellentesque et ur

In the first chapter of this Photoshop-to-Dreamweaver workflow, you saw how Photoshop is used to create the basic structure of the layout. However, Web design is much more than just graphics. Text plays a big—some would argue the biggest—role in successful Web sites. In this chapter, you'll explore the use of text, both as decorative and informational elements. Incorporating text into a design, however, is more than just putting it on the page. Other sections in this chapter show you how to apply the important design principal of alignment—a key aspect to keep in mind when you later develop the page in Dreamweaver—and also take advantage of Photoshop's numerous effects as the comp is completed.

Core techniques in this chapter include:

- Aligning with guides
- Working with text
- Applying effects

CHAPTER

02

COMPLETING THE COMP

ALIGNING GRAPHIC ELEMENTS

Alignment is one of the key tenets of design, regardless of the medium. A layout where various page elements are aligned with one another is generally more pleasing to the eye and easier to comprehend quickly. Elements can be aligned vertically or horizontally or both.

Again, Photoshop has a plethora of tools to help you line up your design objects, but the primary ones are guides and the grid. I tend to use guides more than the grid because of their flexibility: You can drag as many horizontal or vertical guides into the layout as you need, position them precisely, and just as easily remove them from view or from the document.

NOTE

Don't forget, you can download the book's exercise files at www.wiley.com/go/adobecs3web-workflows.

1. Choose **File ▶ Open** and navigate to your folder of exercise files. Navigate to **Chapter 2** and select **Chocolate Dipped Comp.psd**.

    This file contains all the exercises completed through the end of Chapter 1.

2. If necessary, choose **View ▶ Rulers**.

    Photoshop requires that the rulers be displayed before any guides can be dragged onto the document.

3. From the vertical ruler, drag out a guide to line up with the right side of the near strawberry's stem at about 320 pixels from the left edge of the document (Figure 2-1).

    FIGURE 2-1

    Guides can also be precisely placed, without dragging them into place.

4. Choose **View ▶ New Guide**. When the New Guide dialog appears, select the **Horizontal** orientation and enter **180 px** in the Position field. Click **OK** when you're done (Figure 2-2).

FIGURE 2-2

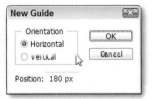

Because you want the navigation buttons to span a specifically sized column, you should set another vertical guide numerically.

5. Choose **View ▶ New Guide** again. Select **Vertical** orientation and enter **890 px** in the Position field; click **OK**.

The pixel placement, 890, was arrived at by adding 570 (the desired column width) to 320 (the position of the first vertical guide). Now you're ready to bring in the navigation graphics.

6. Choose **File ▶ Open** and, from the **Chapter 2** folder, select all four icon JPG files: **icon_contact**, **icon_home**, **icon_print**, and **icon_web**. Click **Open** when you're ready.

7. From the Chocolate Dipped Comp Layers palette, click **Create a new group**. When Group 1 is created, double-click the name and rename it **Nav**. Drag **Nav** into the **Header** group (Figure 2-3).

FIGURE 2-3

8. Drag the **icon_home** image onto the comp and place it at the intersection of the left and top guides (Figure 2-4).

You probably noticed a bit of a pull from the guides just as you placed the image. By default, Photoshop's snap is enabled; to turn it off, select **View ▶ Snap**.

034   PART **01**   PART **02**   PART **03**   PART **04**   APPENDIX

Photoshop to Dreamweaver   Fireworks to Dreamweaver   Flash to Dreamweaver   Photoshop to Bridge to Fireworks to Dreamweaver   Additional Workflows

FIGURE 2-4

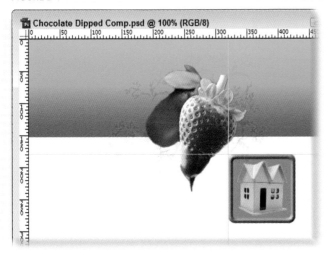

9. Drag the graphic from **icon_web** onto the comp and place it to the right of **icon_home**. Add **icon_print** and **icon_contact** to the comp as well, and align the right edge of **icon_contact** to the second vertical guide (Figure 2-5).

FIGURE 2-5

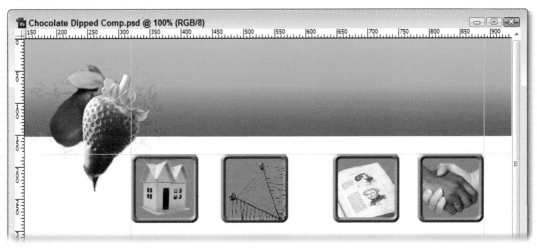

Don't worry about the spacing between the icons at this point. In the next step, you'll use a Photoshop command to space them out equally.

Ps CORE TECHNIQUES

ALIGNING GRAPHIC ELEMENTS

In Web site design, alignment serves to connect page elements to one another and provide an overall cohesiveness. Photoshop offers a wide array of alignment aids, many of which can be used together:

- **Ruler**—Both vertical and horizontal rulers appear when **View ▶ Ruler** is selected. The unit of measurement for the rules is set in **Preferences ▶ Units & Rulers**.

- **Grid**—By default, the grid is presented as a mesh of thin gray lines, in 1-inch increments, subdivided 4 times (every 1/4 inch). For Web work, it's better to modify this setting in **Preferences ▶ Guides, Grids, Slices and Count** to 50-pixel increments, subdivided 5 times, every 10th pixel.

- **Guides**—Photoshop offers three different types of guides:

  - **Standard guides**—Drag a guide from the horizontal or vertical ruler. The ruler must be displayed to use guides in this manner.

    (continued)

10. While pressing **Shift**, select each of the navigation images. From the Options bar, click **Distribute Horizontal Centers**, the third icon from the right (Figure 2-6).

FIGURE 2-6

Because the leftmost and rightmost icons are positioned according to the guides, the Distribute Horizontal Centers command adjusts the position of the other two icons so that all four are evenly distributed.

11. Choose **File ▶ Save** to store your work.

In the next exercise, you'll have an opportunity to add the final pure graphic elements to the comp—and to see how important layer arrangement is in the process.

POSITIONING WITH THE LAYERS PALETTE

The concept of stacked layers is essential to Photoshop. Every element is on its own layer, and all layers are above or below other layers; no two layers are on the same level. The Layers palette is a critical tool for both depicting and arranging your elements to get the desired effect.

In this exercise, you'll insert the remaining graphics and make sure they are placed properly in the Layers palette.

PART **01**
Photoshop to Dreamweaver

PART **02**
Fireworks to Dreamweaver

PART **03**
Flash to Dreamweaver

PART **04**
Photoshop to Bridge to Fireworks to Dreamweaver

APPENDIX
Additional Workflows

1. Make sure all the icons added in the last exercise are within the **Nav** layer group in the Layers palette. If necessary, drag any icons outside the group into it. Select the **Nav** layer group after you're done.

2. Choose **File ▶ Place** and, when the Place dialog opens, navigate to the **Chapter 2** folder and select **blue_white_gradient.jpg**. Click **Place**.

3. Move the imported image directly under the green header gradient; press the **down arrow** once to move the image one pixel down. Double-click the new gradient to confirm its position (Figure 2-7).

FIGURE 2-7

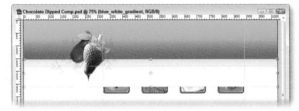

The gradient, although beneath the spirals and the strawberries, is obscuring the navigation icons. You can adjust the position in the Layers palette.

Moving the new gradient down one pixel reveals the white background and effectively creates a highlighted line.

4. In the **Layers** palette, drag the **blue_white_gradient** below, but not in, the **Nav** layer group and above the **Content** layer group (Figure 2-8).

(continued)

- **Numerically positioned guides**—Choose **View ▶ New Guide** to precisely place a horizontal or vertical guide.

- **Smart Guides**—Once enabled (**View ▶ Show ▶ Smart Guides**), Smart Guides display guidelines whenever you move a graphic object that relate to the edges and centers of other objects on the page.

- **Alt+click** (Windows) or **Opt+click** (Mac) on any guide to change its orientation.

- **Alignment tools**—A full collection of alignment and distribution commands is available from the Options bar when the Move tool is selected. The first group aligns two or more elements along the various edges and centers (horizontal and vertical) while the second group allows selected elements to be distributed evenly. The final group contains the Auto-Align Layers command, which is primarily used to align digital photographs for retouching or for stitching together in large landscape images.

FIGURE 2-8

Now, the gradient is displayed behind all header elements, while staying within the Header layer group.

5. Choose **View ▶ New Guide**. In the New Guide dialog, select **Horizontal** orientation and enter **340 px** in the Position field. Click **OK**.

Here the guide is used to quickly place another simple graphic included for your convenience.

6. Choose **File ▶ Place** and, in the Place dialog, select **gray_bar.gif**; click **Place**. Move the imported object until its top edge is aligned with the just added horizontal guide and double-click to set the placement (Figure 2-9).

FIGURE 2-9

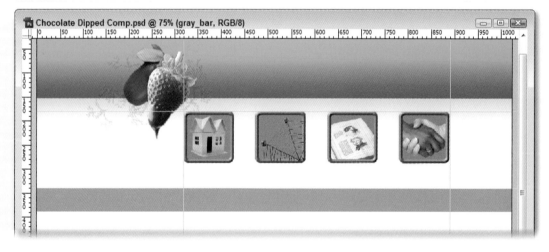

This gray bar marks the beginning of the content section; you can now move it into its proper place in the Layers palette.

038   PART **01**   PART **02**   PART **03**   PART **04**   APPENDIX

Photoshop to Dreamweaver   Fireworks to Dreamweaver   Flash to Dreamweaver   Photoshop to Bridge to Fireworks to Dreamweaver   Additional Workflows

7. In the Layers palette, drag the **gray_bar** layer into the **Content** layer group.

Reuse the **blue_white_gradient** image and drag a copy into position.

8. Make sure the **Move** tool, the first icon on the Tools palette, is selected. Press **Alt** (Windows) or **Option** (Mac) and drag the **blue_white_gradient** image directly below the **gray_bar** in the comp. Again, press the **down arrow** once to create a single white line between the two elements (Figure 2-10).

FIGURE 2-10

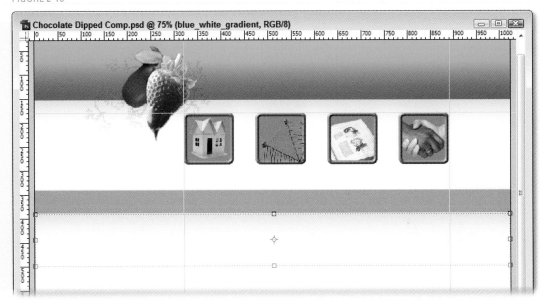

By pressing Alt/Option, you drag out a copy of the selected image. However, the copy remains in the same position as the original in the Layers palette. You can now move it to the correct group.

9. In the Layers palette, drag the **blue_white_gradient copy** layer below the **gray_bar** layer.

There's one last graphic element to add to the Content layer group: a white rectangle to hide the blue-white gradient.

10. Select the **Rectangle** tool and make sure that the white foreground color is selected. Drag out a rectangle starting just below the gray bar and inside the guides. The rectangle should snap to both guides and extend to the start of the footer gradient (Figure 2-11).

FIGURE 2-11

Notice that because new objects are inserted above the current selection in the Layers palette, the rectangle properly obscures a portion of the gradient.

All graphics are now in place and the comp is ready for some text, both decorative and content-oriented.

040   PART **01**   PART **02**   PART **03**   PART **04**   APPENDIX

Photoshop to Dreamweaver   Fireworks to Dreamweaver   Flash to Dreamweaver   Photoshop to Bridge to Fireworks to Dreamweaver   Additional Workflows

WORKING WITH TEXT

On the Web, content is king and virtually every comp contains some textual elements. Text on the Web is divided into two main types: decorative text and content text. Decorative text will be inserted in the Web design as an image. As image-based text cannot be searched or selected and copied to a text document, it's best to keep decorative text to a minimum.

Content text, on the other hand, is implemented with standard HTML tags such as `<h1>` through `<h6>` tags for headings or `<p>` tags for paragraphs. Modern Web design strives to be syntactically correct—a practice search engines reward heartily. When crafting a comp for the Web, it's best to follow the intended HTML structure of headings and paragraphs. For example, always use `<h1>` tags as the top-level heading; don't use an `<h2>` tag or lower because their default rendered size is closer to what you have in mind—the tags can always be styled appropriately with Dreamweaver's CSS features. It's also a good idea to indicate on the comp itself the desired tags. You'll see one method for accomplishing this goal later in this chapter.

APPLYING SIMPLE TEXT LABELS

In this exercise, you'll add labels to each of the navigation buttons. When converted to HTML, labels such as these could be inserted either as a graphic or as text. The general trend among Web designers is to use standard text wherever possible; this practice helps with search engine optimization, especially for text that also serves as links.

In addition to learning how to work with simple text in this exercise, you'll also have an opportunity to apply an advanced guide feature that is very helpful when positioning text: Smart Guides. Smart Guides are object-specific lines that are dynamically displayed in relation to the top, bottom, and middle of other elements on the page. As you'll see in the first part of this exercise, Smart Guides are especially useful when working with small bits of text like navigation button labels.

1. If necessary, open the working file, **Chocolate Dipped Comp.psd**.

2. From the Layers palette, select the **Nav** layer group inside the **Header** layer group.

   Every text object you create automatically creates its own layer; this action ensures that the layers are properly placed in the Layers palette. The first text elements here will be labels for each of the four navigation buttons in the Header area.

3. Choose the **Horizontal Type** tool from the Tools palette, the large T in the third group from the top.

4. In the Options bar, select **Verdana** from the **Font** list and make sure the **Font Style** is set to **Regular**. Select **12** from the **Font Size** list and set **Anti-Aliasing** to **Smooth** (Figure 2-12). Click the **color swatch** and, in the hexadecimal field (**#**), enter **5d3a2c** for a dark brown color.

FIGURE 2-12

These text objects are represented as straight text when the comp is translated to a page layout, so it's important to choose a Web-accessible font like Verdana. Web-accessible fonts are those generally available on both PC and Mac systems.

5. Click approximately 10 pixels below the first navigation icon and enter **Home**. Choose the Move tool to confirm your entry.

To more precisely align your text, you can try out Photoshop's Smart Guides.

6. Choose **View ▶ Show ▶ Smart Guides**. Drag the **Home** text object horizontally toward the middle of the icon above until you see the vertical purple center line (Figure 2-13).

FIGURE 2-13

The Smart Guides quickly identify the center of both objects: the Home icon and the Home text.

7. Choose the **Horizontal Type** tool again and enter **Web** below the second navigation icon. Choose the **Move** tool to center the text below the icon and align it horizontally with **Home** text.

042

PART  Photoshop to Dreamweaver

PART 02 Fireworks to Dreamweaver

PART 03 Flash to Dreamweaver

PART 04 Photoshop to Bridge to Fireworks to Dreamweaver

APPENDIX Additional Workflows

As you can see, the more you use Smart Guides, the more useful they become. The ability to quickly align objects on the page without standard guides dramatically hastens the design process.

8. Repeat step 7 to center a **Print** label below the third icon and a **Contact** label below the fourth (Figure 2-14).

FIGURE 2-14

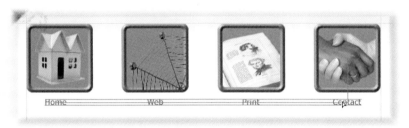

9. Choose **File ▶ Save** to store your page.

As you can see, adding simple text to a page is pretty straightforward in Photoshop and Smart Guides make aligning text labels a snap. Next, you'll learn how to insert blocks of properly formatted text into your comp.

ADDING HEADINGS AND BLOCKS OF TEXT

Because text-based content is pervasive on the Web, you need to represent both headings and blocks of text in your designs. When you're inserting such text, it's important to keep in mind the ultimate goal: to style the text in the Web page to resemble the comp as closely as possible. Following a few simple rules when creating your design will go a long way toward reaching this goal:

- **Use fonts common to both PC and Mac**. Browsers use whatever fonts are available on the local system to render text, so it's important you pick a font that is commonly available on most computers. Typical serif fonts are Georgia, Palatino Linotype (Palatino on the Mac), and Times New Roman (Times on the Mac). Sans-serif fonts include Arial, Tahoma (Geneva on the Mac), Trebuchet MS (Helvetica on the Mac), and Verdana.

- **Size in pixels**. Web designers use either pixels or ems—a percentage-based measurement—when specifying the size and line height of their text. Because Photoshop does not support ems, use pixels.

- **Set paragraph margins.** CSS gives Web designers control over both margins and padding surrounding text (and other block elements). Using Photoshop's margin options—left and right—makes it easier for designers to translate these values into the ones they need. You can also specify margins above and below the paragraphs or headings for further CSS styling.

- **Avoid hyphenation.** Photoshop has great hyphenation support, but it's useless on the Web.

In this exercise, you'll insert both the headings and initial paragraphs for your comp.

1. In the Layers palette, select the Content layer group.

   The heading will be placed in gray bar that begins the content section.

2. From the Tools palette, choose **Horizontal Type**. In the Options bar, change the **Font Size** list to **24**, the **Font Style** to **Bold**, and **color** to white (**#ffffff**) (Figure 2-15).

   FIGURE 2-15

   A quick way to pick a color already on the page is to use the **Eyedropper** tool. Select it from the Tools palette (second from the top of the fourth group) and sample any color on the page, such as the white rectangle in the content area.

3. Place your cursor in the gray bar about 20 pixels from the left guide and enter **Page Title – and subheading**.

   This design requires a somewhat unorthodox use of headings: two headings are on the same line. Here, both the <h1> and <h2> tags are side by side. As you'll see when you create the CSS in Dreamweaver, this is not difficult to do, but you do want to differentiate them somehow. You can do this by changing the color of the <h2> portion.

4. With the **Horizontal Type** tool still selected, select the phrase **– and subheading**. Click the color swatch in the Options bar once and, when the color picker opens, enter **cccccc** in the hexadecimal (**#**) field. Click **OK**. Choose the **Move** tool and adjust the placement so that the text is in the vertical center of the gray bar (Figure 2-16).

   FIGURE 2-16

044

PART **01** Photoshop to Dreamweaver   PART **02** Fireworks to Dreamweaver   PART **03** Flash to Dreamweaver   PART **04** Photoshop to Bridge to Fireworks to Dreamweaver   APPENDIX Additional Workflows

To convey your intention to use the `<h1>` and `<h2>` tags for this text element, you can rename it.

5. In the Layers palette, double-click on the name of the just entered text layer and replace it with **h1 and h2** (Figure 2-17). Press **Enter** (Windows) or **Return** (Mac).

FIGURE 2-17

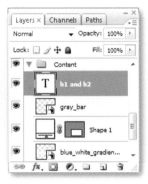

Now, you can add some body text. I've included a basic paragraph of placeholder text—commonly referred to as *lorem ipsum* for its first two pseudo-Latin words—in the files for this chapter for your convenience.

6. Open your favorite text editor and choose **File ▶ Open**. Navigate to the **Chapter 2** folder, select the **Lorem ipsum.txt** file and open it. Select all the text in the document and press **Ctrl+C** (Windows) or **Cmd+C** (Mac). Close your text editor.

7. In Photoshop, choose **Content** in the Layers palette and then select the **Horizontal Type** tool. In the Options bar, change **Font Size** to **12** and the **Font Style** to **Regular**. Click the font color swatch and, in the color picker, enter **666666** in the hexadecimal (**#**) field. Click **OK**.

   If you didn't choose a different layer or layer group in the Layers palette, the Options bar changes would have been applied to your just entered text.

8. Drag out a rectangle to contain your text from the first guide to the second, starting about 20 pixels below the bottom of the gray bar and extending all the way to the top of the footer gradient. Press **Ctrl+V** (Windows) or **Cmd+V** (Mac) to paste in your copied text (Figure 2-18).

   The text flows in to fill the drawn-out rectangle. Now, you can fine-tune the text block to add in a custom line height and margins.

FIGURE 2-18

9. Choose **Select ▶ Select All** to highlight the text block. From the **Panels** palette, choose **Character**, the A icon that is third from the bottom. In the **Leading** field, which by default is set to (Auto), enter **20 px** and press **Enter** (Windows) or **Return** (Mac).

    Leading in Photoshop is the same as line height in CSS. The text is now nicely spaced; now you can bring it in from the edges a bit.

10. Switch to the **Paragraph** palette. Change the **Left Margin** value to **20 px** and press **Tab** and do the same for the **Right Margin**. Press **Tab** again (Figure 2-19).

FIGURE 2-19

Why don't you just draw a smaller text box instead of setting margins? By drawing out your text box to the full width of the guides, you're emulating the way the Dreamweaver layout in CSS works. With the margins set, all it takes is a quick look at the PSD to tell how to set the equivalent CSS and get the same results.

11. Press **Ctrl+S** (Windows) or **Cmd+S** (Mac).

With your headings and text blocks properly styled in Photoshop, the layout will be easier and faster to reproduce in Dreamweaver. You'll start work on the final text element, the logo, in the next exercise.

INSERTING DECORATIVE TEXT

The defining difference between decorative text and content-based text is that the former is inserted into the Web as an image and the latter as text. Decorative text is often used for logos or eye-catching typographical design elements. In this exercise, you'll take the first step toward creating the title graphic for the comp.

1. In the Layers palette, select the **Header** layer group.

2. From the Tools palette, choose the **Horizontal Type** tool.

3. In the Options bar, select **Brush Script Std** from the **Font** list, set the **Font Size** to **48 px**, and change the **Font Color** to **white** (Figure 2-20).

Ps CORE TECHNIQUES

WORKING WITH TEXT

There are four variations of the Photoshop type tool: Horizontal Type, Vertical Type, Horizontal Mask Type, and Vertical Mask Type. Of these, the Horizontal Type tool is by far the most commonly used. Once selected, key attributes are presented in the Options bar including font, size, style, alignment, and color.

The complete range of Photoshop text options are divided into two key palettes: Character and Paragraph.

- **Character**—The Character palette repeats the same properties contained in the Options bar and adds control over leading (or line height), kerning, tracking, vertical and horizontal scaling, and baseline shift. You can also set the language to use for hyphenation and anti-aliasing.

- **Paragraph**— Open the Paragraph palette to adjust alignment and margins (left and right) as well as space above and below paragraphs. The toggle for Hyphenation is also found on the Paragraph palette.

(continued)

FIGURE 2-20

> If your system does not have Brush Script Std, feel free to use any other font decorative available.

One of the key benefits of working with text that you know will be reproduced as an image is that you can use any font you'd like; you're not restricted to Web-safe typefaces.

4. Click between the two guides about **50 pixels** above the bottom of the upper gradient and enter **Chocolate Dipped Design**.

5. From the Tools palette, choose the **Move** tool and center the text object between the two guides. Click anywhere when you're satisfied with the placement (Figure 2-21).

6. Press **Ctrl+S** (Windows) or **Cmd+S** (Mac).

FIGURE 2-21

Although you could just use the pure white text to simulate a dropped-out approach, this particular typographic element cries out for added color and enhancement—all of which will be applied with effects in the next exercise.

APPLYING EFFECTS

Effects in Photoshop are applied through the use of filters. There are three types of filters: standard, smart, and layer filters. The standard filters change the pixels of the target object directly and cannot be modified once the image is closed. However, by your adding

---

(continued)

Other text-related possibilities in Photoshop include warping text. To use, select any text object and choose **Warp Text** from the Text Options bar. Adjustments to the degree of contortions can be made within the Warp Text dialog box and easily previewed. To place text on a path, draw any path using the Pen or other vector-based tool and then select the Horizontal Type tool. Place the cursor on the path and begin entering text.

Additional type options can be found in the **Layer ▶ Type** submenu.

048   PART **01**   PART **02**   PART **03**   PART **04**   APPENDIX

Photoshop to Dreamweaver   Fireworks to Dreamweaver   Flash to Dreamweaver   Photoshop to Bridge to Fireworks to Dreamweaver   Additional Workflows

a smart or layer filter to an image, the resulting effect is achieved but the underlying image is not modified. This technique permits constant updating and encourages ongoing experimentation; this exercise demonstrates the use of layer filters.

Effects can be applied to any object through its layer. In this exercise, you'll apply a variety of effects to the decorative type entered in the previous series of steps and round out the comp by applying a drop shadow to the strawberries.

1. In the Layers palette, select **Chocolate Dipped Design**.

2. Click **Add a layer style**, the fx icon at the bottom of the Layers palette (Figure 2-22), and choose **Gradient Overlay**.

FIGURE 2-22

3. In the **Gradient Overlay** category of the **Layer Style** dialog box, click the gradient preview to open the Gradient Editor.

> *If you need a reminder on using the Gradient Editor, review the section "Adding Gradients" in Chapter 1.*

4. Establish three color stops:

   • Set the first color stop to **#694734**, a deep brown, and move it about 1/3 of the way from the left of the gradient range.

   • Set the second color stop to red (**#ff0000**) and position it approximately 2/3 of the way from the left.

   • Set the final color stop to white (**#ffffff**) and place it all the way to the right.

Click **OK** when you're done (Figure 2-23).

FIGURE 2-23

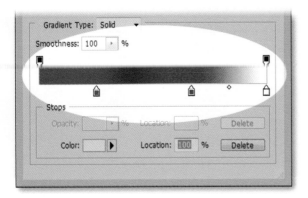

You can see the gradient applied to your text if you move the Layer Style dialog box out of the way.

5. Leave all the other settings at their default and switch to the **Bevel and Emboss** category.

    Now, you will apply another effect to the same text object.

6. In the **Structure** section, choose **Emboss** from the **Style** list. Leave **Depth** at **100%** and set **Size** to **3 px** and **Soften** to **2 px**. In the **Shading** section, change the **Angle** to **135°** (Figure 2-24). Click **OK** when you're done.

FIGURE 2-24

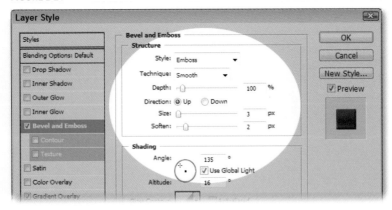

050   PART 01   PART 02   PART 03   PART 04   APPENDIX

Photoshop to Dreamweaver   Fireworks to Dreamweaver   Flash to Dreamweaver   Photoshop to Bridge to Fireworks to Dreamweaver   Additional Workflows

7. Click anywhere to confirm your modifications (Figure 2-25).

FIGURE 2-25

Now, finally you can add a drop shadow to the strawberries to give them a more realistic feel.

8. In the Layers palette, select **strawberries** and click **Add a layer style**. Choose **Drop Shadow** from the submenu.

9. Keep the **Blend** mode to **Multiply** and change the **Opacity** to **50%**. Set the **Distance** to **8** and leave the remaining values at their default (Figure 2-26). Click OK.

FIGURE 2-26

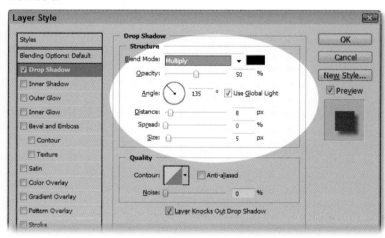

Lowering the opacity allows more of the delicate spiral graphics to come through the shadow, while altering the distance slightly emphasizes it a bit more (Figure 2-27).

Ps CORE TECHNIQUES

FIGURE 2 27

APPLYING EFFECTS

Photoshop uses filters to apply effects in two ways: directly, thus modifying the pixels, and via layer filters that change the layer appearance non-destructively. Wherever possible, it's best to use the layer filters to maintain editability. Filters may be applied to any layer object; multiple filters can be assigned and can be toggled on or off through the Layers palette. There are ten different layer filters, each of which can be configured separately.

- **Drop Shadow**—Places a shadow behind the selected object in a specified direction.

- **Inner Shadow**—Places a shadow inside the outer boundary of the selected object in a set direction, thus giving a recessed appearance.

- **Outer Glow**—Places a glow around the outside of a selected object.

- **Inner Glow**—Places a glow within the inside of a selected object.

- **Bevel and Emboss**—Gives a beveled or an embossed look to an object.

- **Satin**—Applies a satin-like finish to an image.

- **Color, Gradient, and Pattern Overlay**—Applies a solid color, gradient, or pattern over an object, respectively.

- **Stroke**—Outlines the outer edge of a selected object; the stroke filter works well with type to provide a contrasting color outline.

10. Press **Ctrl+S** (Windows) or **Cmd+S** (Mac) to save your page.

Congratulations! Your Photoshop comp is now complete (Figure 2-28) and you're ready to move your design into Dreamweaver for layout. Keep in mind that your completed comp not only provides a visual reference for recreating the design in HTML layout form, but actual components that will either be reused physically or through the properties, such as measurements. The flow from comp to Web is a strong one, solidly connected.

052

PART **01**
Photoshop to Dreamweaver

PART **02**
Fireworks to Dreamweaver

PART **03**
Flash to Dreamweaver

PART **04**
Photoshop to Bridge to Fireworks to Dreamweaver

APPENDIX
Additional Workflows

FIGURE 2 28

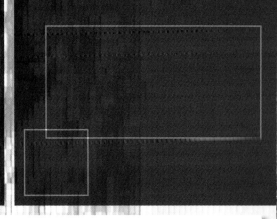

Now you come to a critical juncture: the transition from comp to layout. Moving work from one medium to another is always exacting and often stressful. Happily, Adobe has integrated Photoshop and Dreamweaver to smooth this work-flow through a variety of techniques, as you'll see in this chapter.

Just as Web designers trying out Photoshop for the first time, graphic artists new to Dreamweaver can also experience the "where do I start" phenomenon. Dreamweaver's feature-set runs the gamut from straightforward static Web pages to dynamic database-driven sites. This chapter takes a ground-up approach with Dreamweaver and demonstrates how to create both your first site and first layout.

The following core techniques in this chapter will help you get started down the right path for working in Dreamweaver and transitioning from Photoshop:

- Setting up a Dreamweaver site
- Declaring CSS styles
- Inserting `<div>` tags
- Adding background images
- Inserting foreground images from Photoshop

CHAPTER

03 FROM COMP TO LAYOUT

SETTING UP A DREAMWEAVER SITE

In Dreamweaver, the site is a key concept. Dreamweaver sites are developed on your own system and are referred to as your *local* site. When you're ready to publish your pages to the Web, a mirror image of your local site is set up on your Web host and becomes your the remote site.

When you're just starting development, however, you only need to create the local site. This is quickly handled in Dreamweaver's Site Definition dialog box.

1. In Dreamweaver, choose **Site ▶ New Site**.

2. When the Site Definition dialog box appears, select the **Advanced** tab, if necessary.

   Ironically, it's actually simpler—and far quicker—to create a simple site in Dreamweaver's Advanced Site Definition mode than in the Basic mode, a step-by-step wizard.

3. Make sure you're in the **Local Info** category and **Site name** field, enter **Adobe CS3 Web Workflows**.

   The site name is just for your internal reference and will not be made public, so always enter something meaningful to you. For your initial site, you only need to complete a couple of fields in the Local Info category.

4. Click the folder icon next to the **Local root folder** field (Figure 3-1). When the Choose local root folder dialog opens, navigate to the folder containing the exercise files for this book previously downloaded and un-compressed. When you locate the folder, click **Select**.

FIGURE 3-1

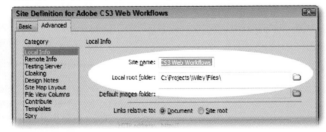

5. Click **OK**.

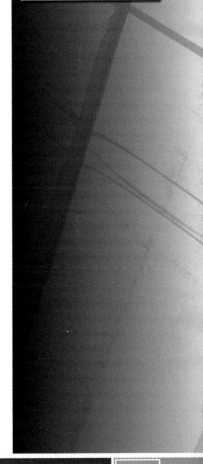

To complete this exercise, you must have already downloaded the exercise files from this book's Web site (www.wiley. com/go/adobe-cs3webworkflows), uncompressed them, and stored the folders and files on your own system.

DEFINING A DREAMWEAVER SITE

The concept of sites runs throughout the development process in Dreamweaver. A *site* is a series of interconnected Web pages stored within a single folder; the pages are often saved in subfolders for organizational purposes. Sites are defined in the Dreamweaver Site Definition dialog box (**Site ▶ New Site**); Dreamweaver supports three different types of site definitions:

- **Local**—Used during the design and development stage, the local site root is a folder maintained on the designer's computer.

- **Remote**—The remote site is for files published from the local site. The remote site may be on an Internet host or a networked server. Some organizations set up their remote sites on a staging server, which allows the pages to be reviewed before being pushed live.

- **Testing**—Testing servers are used when server-side code is involved. Dreamweaver supports a range of server models, including classic ASP, ColdFusion, and PHP. The testing server is often a local Web development environment; for such systems, the folder is maintained in the `C://Inetpub/wwwroot` (Windows) or `[Username]:Sites` (Mac) folder.

(continued)

As you can see there are a great number of options for establishing a site—but one of the great things about Dreamweaver is that you can learn about them when you need to and get right to work.

ESTABLISHING BASIC PREFERENCES

Like Photoshop, Dreamweaver has an extensive set of preferences options. Before you start to convert the comp, you can set a couple of options to hasten the workflow and standardize the output code.

1. Choose **Edit ▶ Preferences** (Windows) or **Dreamweaver ▶ Preferences** (Mac).

2. Select the **Accessibility** category in the left column and make sure all four checkboxes—**Form objects**, **Frames**, **Media**, and **Images**—are selected in the **Show attributes when inserting** area.

   When these options are selected, whenever you insert one of these types of objects, an initial dialog box appears so you can enter accessibility related attributes, such as alt text for images. Alt text is displayed when the user's mouse rolls over an image in a tooltip or read by screenreaders when given focus.

056   PART **01**   PART **02**   PART **03**   PART **04**   APPENDIX

Photoshop to Dreamweaver   Fireworks to Dreamweaver   Flash to Dreamweaver   Photoshop to Bridge to Fireworks to Dreamweaver   Additional Workflows

3. Switch to the **CSS Styles** category. Select all five options in the **Use shorthand for** area: **Font**; **Background**; **Margin and padding**; **Border and border width**; and **List-style** (Figure 3-2).

FIGURE 3-2

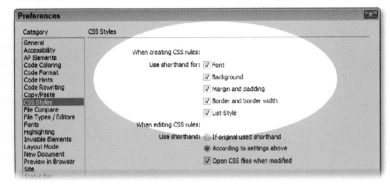

By opting to use shorthand for these CSS rules, you're significantly reducing the file size of your CSS external style sheet. For example, setting all margin sides (top, right, bottom, and left) would take four lines without the shorthand option enabled and one with.

4. Click **OK** to verify your preference choices.

Dreamweaver preferences take effect immediately; there's no need to close and reopen the program.

CREATING CSS LAYOUT STYLES

Modern Web design carefully separates presentation from content through the use of Cascading Style Sheets (CSS). CSS is employed from the ground up to create the basic page layout as well as style the text and other content. Dreamweaver is totally integrated with this design philosophy and provides a full range of CSS commands, tools, and other aids.

In this exercise, you'll develop the core CSS rules to structure your layout. As comped, the design can be divided into three primary areas: header, content, and footer (Figure 3-3). A separate CSS rule is required for each. Additionally, it's a good

(continued)

It is possible to work in Dreamweaver without defining a site; however, as this workflow involves modifying Web pages directly, it is recommended only for advanced Web professionals. Moreover, when you work without a site, you sacrifice numerous site-wide benefits such as link checking. To connect directly to a server via File Transfer Protocol (FTP) or Remote Development Service (RDS), choose **Site ▶ Manage Sites** and then click **New** in the **Manage Sites** dialog box. From the New list, choose **FTP & RDS Server**.

idea to establish a CSS rule to normalize key properties such as margins and padding for certain HTML tags; this rule is often called a *reset* statement. One final CSS rule is needed to restrain portions of the layout. This CSS style, here called *outerWrapper*, is a commonly used technique to help shape many CSS layouts.

FIGURE 3-3

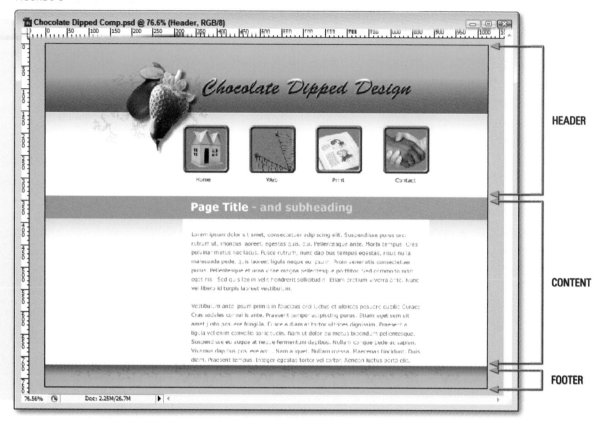

1. Choose **File ▶ New**. When the **New Document** dialog box opens, choose **Blank Page** (Figure 3-4). In the **Page Type** column, select **HTML** and, from the **Layout** column, select **<none>**. Click **Create** when you're done.

    As you can see in the New Document dialog, Dreamweaver can create a full spectrum of Web-related files, including a number of CSS-based layouts. These layouts make terrific starting points for general Web pages and can be easily customized in Dreamweaver.

058
PART 01 Photoshop to Dreamweaver
PART 02 Fireworks to Dreamweaver
PART 03 Flash to Dreamweaver
PART 04 Photoshop to Bridge to Fireworks to Dreamweaver
APPENDIX Additional Workflows

FIGURE 3-4

2. In the **Title** field of the new document, located in the **Document** toolbar, replace **Untitled Document** with **Chocolate Dipped Design** and press **Return** (Windows) or **Enter** (Mac). Choose **File ▶ Save**; when the Save As dialog box appears, navigate to the Chapter 3 folder and enter **choc_dip_design.htm** in the **File name** field. Click **Save**.

    I find it a good practice to title and save my Web page immediately after creation; as a result, the file is now clearly identified in Dreamweaver's title bar and tabbed interface. Moreover, there's no chance I'll publish the file untitled.

    Now that you've got a blank document to work with, it's time to create a few CSS styles.

3. Choose **Window ▶ CSS** Styles. When the **CSS Styles** panel appears, choose **New CSS Rule**, the second icon from the left in the rightmost group at the bottom of the CSS Styles panel (Figure 3-5).

FIGURE 3-5

The first style to define is the reset statement mentioned at the beginning of this exercise.

4. In the **New CSS Rule** dialog box, choose **Selector Type: Advanced**. In the Selector field, enter **body, h1, h2, p, ul, li**. Finally, select **Define in: This document only** and click **OK** (Figure 3-6).

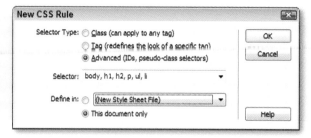

With the Advanced selector type chosen, you can group any tags or other selectors together in a comma-separated list. The style is stored in the current document to cut down on development time; Dreamweaver makes it easy to move these embedded styles to an external style sheet when you're ready.

5. In the **CSS Rule definition for body, h1, h2, p, ul, li** dialog box, switch to the Box category. Leave the **Same for all** checkboxes in both the Margin and Padding area selected and enter a **0** in the **Margin Top** field and **Padding Top** field. Click **OK** (Figure 3-7).

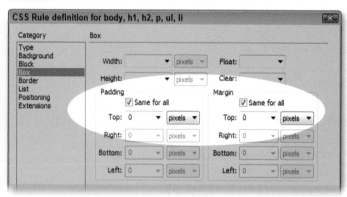

This reset rule makes sure that all browsers use the same initial value for the margin and padding properties of key HTML tags. Later, you'll specify values for these tags to get exactly the desired look and feel. After the dialog closes, you'll notice your first style in the CSS Styles panel. Now, you can follow a similar procedure to create a rule for the outerWrapper.

6. From the **CSS Styles** panel, click **New CSS Rule**. In the **New CSS Rule** dialog box, enter **#outerWrapper** in the **Selector** field, leave the other options at their current settings and click **OK**.

Because Dreamweaver remembers your settings from one rule to the next, you can quickly create a number of CSS rules.

> The number sign or hash mark (#) indicates an ID selector in CSS. Each ID on a page must be unique; IDs are typically used to create styles for <div> tags used in CSS-based layouts.

7. In the **CSS Rule Definition for #outerWrapper** dialog box, switch to the **Box** category and in the **Width** field enter **784 pixels**. Deselect the **Margin Same for all** checkbox and enter the following values: **Top: 0**; **Right: auto**; **Bottom: 0**; and **Left: auto**. Click **OK** when you're done (Figure 3-8).

FIGURE 3-8

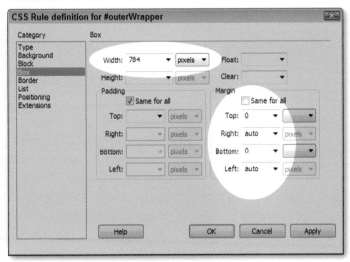

The width is calculated by measuring the distance from the left edge of the spiral figures in the header to the right edge of the content area in Photoshop.

TIP

Photoshop includes a very handy device called the Rule tool. Found in the Eyedropper group on Photoshop's Tool palette, you can use the Rule tool to measure distances from one point in a file to another; the results are displayed in the Options bar. I like to use the Rule tool in combination with guides and with Snap to Guides enabled to take the guesswork out of pixel measurement.

SETTING UP A DREAMWEAVER SITE // ESTABLISHING BASIC PREFERENCES // CHAPTER
CREATING CSS LAYOUT STYLES // INSERTING <DIV> TAGS // INCORPORATING BACKGROUND
IMAGES // ADDING A BACKGROUND IMAGE TO THE <BODY> // BRINGING IN FOREGROUND
IMAGES // INSERTING AND STYLING TEXT // INCLUDING NAVIGATION //

061

03

Now you're ready to create the layout rules for the three main divisions: header, content, and footer.

8. Click **New CSS Rule** and in the dialog box, enter **#header** in the **Selector** field; click **OK**. When the **CSS Rule definition for #header** dialog box opens, switch to the **Box** category and, in the **Height** field enter **340 pixels**. Click **OK**.

The header area extends from the top of the page to the top of the gray bar in the comp

9. Click **New CSS Rule** and in the dialog box, enter **#content** in the **Selector** field; click **OK**. When the **CSS Rule definition for #header** dialog box opens, switch to the **Box** category and, in the **Width** field enter **530 pixels**. Clear the **Padding Same for all** checkbox and enter these values: **Top: 10**; **Right: 20**; **Bottom: 20**; and **Left: 20**. Clear the **Margin Same for all** checkbox and enter **Left: 212**. Click **OK** (Figure 3-9).

FIGURE 3-9

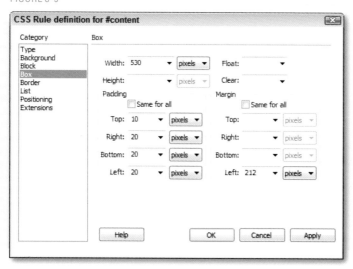

The active section of the content area is within the white rectangle below the gray bar. If you measure that in Photoshop, you'll come up with 570 pixels. So why do you enter a width of 530 pixels in Dreamweaver? Every block element in CSS, including all `<div>` tags, uses what is referred to as the *box model*. In the box model, the distance from one end of the element to the other is equal to the following:

```
Width + padding + border + margins
```

where width is the area on the screen that contains the actual content. So, to calculate the CSS width from a Photoshop comp, follow this formula:

062 PART **01** PART **02** PART **03** PART **04** APPENDIX

Photoshop to Dreamweaver   Fireworks to Dreamweaver   Flash to Dreamweaver   Photoshop to Bridge to Fireworks to Dreamweaver   Additional Workflows

```
Photoshop width = CSS width + padding + border + margins
```

In this example, you use these values:

```
570 = CSS width + (20+20) + 0 + 0
```

which, after you do the math, gives you 530 for the CSS width. Now, if you add the left margin of 212 pixels—which positions the active content section properly, the total is 784 pixels: the same value as the width of the outerWrapper rule.

Now there's one last layout rule to define: footer.

10. Click **New CSS Rule** and in the dialog box, enter **#footer** in the Selector field; click **OK**. When the **CSS Rule definition for #footer** dialog box opens, switch to the **Box** category and, in the **Height** field enter **50 pixels**. Click **OK**.

At this point, you'll have five CSS rules defined, all grouped under the `<style>` entry in the CSS Styles panel (Figure 3-10), which indicates embedded styles. Notice that as you select each defined style, the different associated attributes appear in the Properties pane of the CSS Styles panel. As you'll see later in this chapter, the properties can be modified directly through this interface.

FIGURE 3-10

11. Choose **File ▶ Save**.

In the next exercise, you'll start applying these rules to building up the page layout.

Dw CORE TECHNIQUES

DECLARING CSS STYLES

CSS has taken center stage in Web design, and Dreamweaver befittingly provides numerous tools for creating styles both for presentation and layout. Most CSS activity is centered on the multifaceted CSS Styles panel. Creating a new CSS rule is a two-stage process:

1. Declare the rule's selector type, name, and where you'd like to store it in the **New CSS Rule** dialog box. Dreamweaver allows you to define any type of selector from tags, classes, and IDs to advanced selectors; if Dreamweaver doesn't recognize the selector type, it alerts you and gives you the option to continue or not. Rules can be embedded in the head of the document or stored in an external file. If you don't have an existing external style sheet, you can create one on the fly.

2. Define the rules properties in the **CSS Rule Definition** dialog box. This dialog comprises seven different categories: Type, Background, Block, Box, Border, List, Positioning, and Extensions.

(continued)

INSERTING <DIV> TAGS

The primary building blocks of CSS layouts are `<div>` tags. You can stack `<div>` tags on top of one another or nest them to any level needed. Dreamweaver has a dedicated object for inserting `<div>` tags that works in any scenario to position the elements correctly. Once the tag is added to the page, Dreamweaver displays a `<div>` tag with a dotted border and a single line of placeholder content. As more `<div>` tags are inserted, you'll get a good sense of the page layout.

In this exercise, you'll add four `<div>` tags, each with a corresponding CSS style: outerWrapper, header, content, and footer.

1. From the **Common** category of the **Insert** bar, click **Insert Div Tag**, the fifth icon from the left (Figure 3-11).

   You can also find Insert Div Tag on the Layout category.

   FIGURE 3-11

2. In the **Insert Div Tag** dialog box, leave the **Insert** list set to **At insertion point** and from the **ID** list choose **outerWrapper** (Figure 3-12).

   FIGURE 3-12

064   PART **01**   PART **02**   PART **03**   PART **04**   APPENDIX

Photoshop to Dreamweaver   Fireworks to Dreamweaver   Flash to Dreamweaver   Photoshop to Bridge to Fireworks to Dreamweaver   Additional Workflows

Dreamweaver inserts the `<div>` tag (noted with a dotted border) with a placeholder phrase. Next, you'll insert the header `<div>` tag inside the outerWrapper.

3. Select the placeholder text **Content for id "outerWrapper" Goes Here** and delete it.

   Because the outerWrapper `<div>` tag acts as a container for other `<div>` tags, it's a good idea to remove the unneeded placeholder text.

4. Click **Insert Div Tag**. In the dialog box, select **After start of tag** from the **Insert** list and **<div id="outerWrapper">** from the adjacent list. From the **ID** list, choose **header** and click **OK** (Figure 3-13).

FIGURE 3-13

Placing the header `<div>` tag after the start of the outerWrapper `<div>` tag effectively nests the former inside the latter. As you'll remember, the #header style was created with a height of 340 pixels, which is readily apparent in Dreamweaver's Design view. Now, it's time to add the content `<div>` tag.

You may also have noticed that the ID list did not contain the previously inserted outerWrapper. Dreamweaver keeps track of which CSS styles with ID selectors have been already been applied and removes them from the list to keep IDs unique on the page.

(continued)

Once defined, a CSS rule is accessible through the **CSS Styles** panel, which has two modes: All and Current. The All mode displays a tree of every CSS style in the document while Current shows all the styles applicable to the current document selection. In either mode you can select any style to see its properties in the Properties pane and, if desired, modify the values or add new properties.

5. Click **Insert Div Tag** In the dialog box, select **After tag** from the **Insert** list and **<div id="header">** from the adjacent list. From the **ID** list, choose **content** and click **OK**.

   The final <div> tag, footer, needs to be placed outside of the outerWrapper so that it can expand the full width of the browser window.

6. Click **Insert Div Tag**. In the dialog box, select **After tag** from the **Insert** list and **<div id="outerWrappor">** from the adjacent list. From the **ID** list, choose **footer** and click **OK**.

The basic layout structure is now visible in Dreamweaver (Figure 3-14). The section within the outerWrapper—containing the header and content <div> tags—is centered in the page while the footer spans its width. The content <div> tag is positioned to the left as defined in the #content style.

FIGURE 3-14

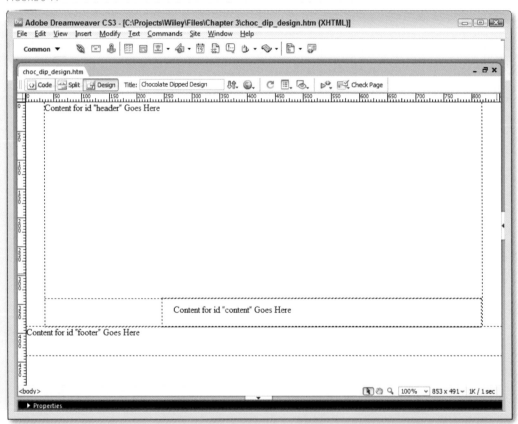

Next, you'll begin to add a splash of color to the page by adding background images to various tags and styles.

066

PART **01** Photoshop to Dreamweaver

PART **02** Fireworks to Dreamweaver

PART **03** Flash to Dreamweaver

PART **04** Photoshop to Bridge to Fireworks to Dreamweaver

APPENDIX Additional Workflows

INCORPORATING BACKGROUND IMAGES

So far, you've worked separately in both Photoshop and Dreamweaver; it's time to bring the two programs together. In this section, you'll take a small section of the Photoshop comp and insert it into the Dreamweaver page as a background image through CSS.

While foreground images may be dragged and dropped on the Web page or inserted through an object, background images are also applied via a CSS rule. In exchange for a small loss in terms of a WYSIWYG application, you gain a great deal of control. CSS background images can be made to *tile*, or fill, a containing element of any size, repeated in just a horizontal or vertical direction, or not repeated at all. In fact, background images are one of the most important tools in the Web designer's palette. To verify this claim, visit www .csszengarden.com, the home of cutting-edge Web design and examine any of the CSS source; the background-image property is used heavily throughout.

In the following exercises, you'll have an opportunity to apply background images in both basic and advanced scenarios.

ADDING A BACKGROUND IMAGE TO THE <BODY>

In a sense, the <body> tag is the Web designer's canvas. Every element that is put within the <body> is displayed, unless specifically hidden in one way or another. Applying a background image to the <body> can

Dw CORE TECHNIQUES

INSERTING <DIV> TAGS

In CSS, <div> tags are the foundation of any layout. Dreamweaver provides a flexible, easy-to-master interface for adding <div> tags anywhere on the page. The **Insert Div Tag** object, found on the Insert bar in both the Common and Layout categories, requires two bits of information: Where should the tag be placed and what CSS style should be assigned to it.

A <div> tag can be inserted at the current cursor location, after another tag, or in the middle of another tag. If any portion of the page is selected when Insert Div Tag is invoked, a fourth option—Wrap around Selection—appears. Once you've chosen where the tag should go, you select which CSS class or ID should be assigned to it. If you don't have a style already defined, you can create one from within the dialog box.

Once inserted, a dashed border surrounds the <div> tag and a line of placeholder text is inserted. The <div> tag border and other design-time tools can be disabled or turned on through the Visual Aids menu option on the Document toolbar.

SETTING UP A DREAMWEAVER SITE // ESTABLISHING BASIC PREFERENCES // CHAPTER
CREATING CSS LAYOUT STYLES // INSERTING <DIV> TAGS // INCORPORATING BACKGROUND
IMAGES // ADDING A BACKGROUND IMAGE TO THE <BODY> // BRINGING IN FOREGROUND
IMAGES // INSERTING AND STYLING TEXT // INCLUDING NAVIGATION //

067

03

effectively transform the entire design, whether a single large graphic is used like a watermark or, as in this example layout, a repeating portion is made to fill the canvas.

1. In Photoshop, choose **File ▶ Open** and navigate to **Chapter 3** in the folder of exercise files. Open **Chocolate Dipped Comp.psd**.

2. Select the **Rectangular Marquee** tool and drag out a rectangle from the top-left portion of the image down to the white section below the gray bar and adjacent gradient. Your selection should be approximately **10 pixels** wide by **600 pixels** tall (Figure 3-15).

FIGURE 3-15

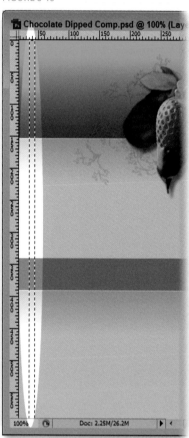

When making selections of gradients, I like to start my selection in a bit from the edge, where possible. This practice avoids capturing any outer borders that may be applied in the comp that are not desired in the final layout.

PART **01**   PART **02**   PART **03**   PART **04**   APPENDIX

Photoshop to Dreamweaver   Fireworks to Dreamweaver   Flash to Dreamweaver   Photoshop to Bridge to Fireworks to Dreamweaver   Additional Workflows

3. Choose **Edit ▶ Copy Merged**.

Photoshop has two primary copy functions: Copy and Copy Merged.

- The standard Copy command grabs the selected portion of the current layer; if you try to copy a selection that does not appear in the current layer, Copy is unavailable.

- Copy Merged, on the other hand, duplicates all the visible layers within the selection and merges them together. As this selection spans numerous layers, Copy Merged is the right way to go.

As you may recall from the Part I overview, there are a couple of methods for getting images from Photoshop to Dreamweaver. While either technique could be used when working with background images, it's a little cleaner to create PSD files to open in Dreamweaver and convert. Therefore, the next step is to create a new document for the copied selection.

4. Choose **File ▶ New**. In the **New** dialog box, click **OK**. When the document window opens, choose **Edit ▶ Paste**.

The key advantage of saving this image as a separate file is that it can easily be reused on other layouts, without reopening the initial comp.

5. Choose **File ▶ Save** and store the file in the **Chapter 3 ▶ images** folder as **body_bg.psd**.

With the image saved, you're ready to bring it in to Dreamweaver.

6. In Dreamweaver, open the **choc_dip_design.htm** file, if necessary.

7. From the CSS Styles panel, click **New CSS Rule**. When the dialog box appears, choose **Selector Type: Tag** and enter **body** in the **Tag** field; click **OK** (Figure 3-16).

FIGURE 3-16

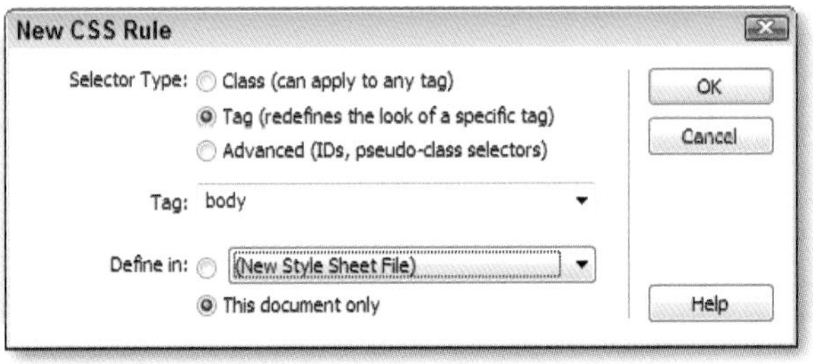

8. In the **CSS Rule Definition for body** dialog box, switch to the **Background** category. Click the **Background color** color swatch to open the color picker and select **white** (#FFFFFF). Click the **Background image Browse** button and, in the **Select Image Source** dialog box, navigate to the **Chapter 3 ▶ images** folder and select **body_bg.psd**. Click **OK** (Windows) or **Choose** (Mac).

   If you were to pick an image that was already in a Web-ready format—GIF, JPEG, or PNG—you would be returned to the CSS Rule Definition dialog with the path to the image in Background image field. However, because PSD files are not viewable on the Web, the Image Preview dialog opens to convert the graphic.

9. In the **Image Preview** dialog box, choose **JPEG** from the **Format** list. Set the **Quality** to **80** and click **OK**. When the **Save Web Image** dialog box appears, navigate to the **Chapter 3 ▶ images** folder and enter **body_bg.jpg** in the **File name** field; click **OK** (Figure 3-17).

FIGURE 3-17

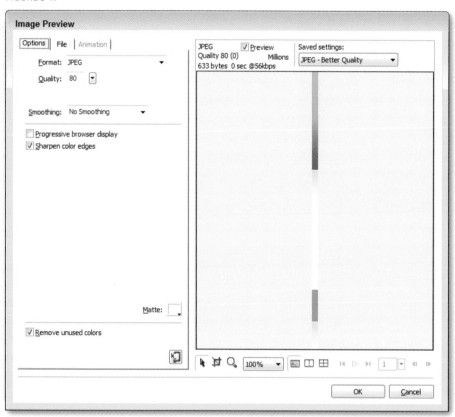

It's important that you remember to add the file extension (.jpg, .gif, or .png) to the filename. A bug in Dreamweaver CS3 occasionally omits the extension and prevents the image from being displayed.

10. In the CSS Rule definition for body dialog, choose **repeat-x** from the **Repeat** list and click **OK**.

You'll notice a drastic change to the page. The horizontally repeating image fills the canvas with the comp gradients (Figure 3-18). In combination with the CSS styled `<div>` tags, the layout is really taking shape.

FIGURE 3-18

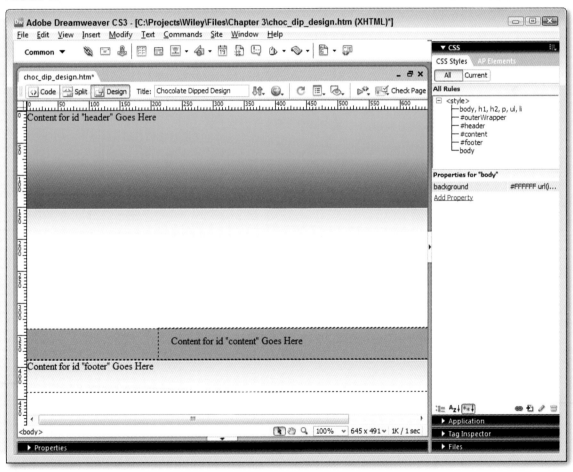

Dw CORE TECHNIQUES

INCORPORATING BACKGROUND IMAGES

The advent of background properties in CSS greatly expanded the Web designer's palette. In Dreamweaver, these attributes are assigned through the **Background** category of the **CSS Rule Definition** dialog box. The key attributes are:

- **Color**—Sets a solid color for the background.

- **Image**—Allows a Web-ready graphic to be displayed in the background.

- **Repeat**—Determines how the image is tiled. Possible values are: no-repeat, repeat-x, repeat-y, and repeat.

- **Attachment**—Defines the mobility of the background image. If attachment is set to scroll (the default), the image moves with the browser window; if attachment is set to fixed, the image stays in one place if the browser windows scrolls.

- **Horizontal position**—The placement of the image along the X-axis; in addition to pixel or percentage values, named values (left, center, and right) can also be applied.

- **Vertical position**—The placement of the image along the Y-axis; in addition to pixel or percentage values, named values (top, middle, or bottom) can also be applied.

LAYERING BACKGROUND IMAGES

Layered background images are one of the key secrets to sophisticated Web design. Because `<div>` tags can be nested and, through use of the z-index CSS property, stacked on top of one another, a multilayered layout is possible.

This exercise applies this technique to two different areas. In the header, the strawberries and adjacent spirals are added as a background image and sit atop the green gradient portion of the body background. The footer uses two `<div>` tags—one nested inside the other—each with its own background image to achieve a tiling effect appropriate for any size browser window. You can start by getting the image necessary for the header.

1. In Photoshop, select the **Home icon** in the navigation area. Open the **Layers palette** and toggle the **eye icon** next to the selected layer to hide it. Repeat this step to hide the **Chocolate Dipped Design** text logo.

   Sometimes, to get the desired image, you need to hide portions of the comp before making your selection. This method allows you to place certain imagery in the background and keep other graphics—such as the navigation icons—in the foreground.

072

PART **01**
Photoshop to Dreamweaver

PART **02**
Fireworks to Dreamweaver

PART **03**
Flash to Dreamweaver

PART **04**
Photoshop to Bridge to
Fireworks to Dreamweaver

APPENDIX
Additional Workflows

2. Select the **Rectangular Marquee** tool from the Tools palette and drag a selection that encompasses all the spirals and two strawberries in the header area. Your selection should be approximately **285 pixels** wide by **250 pixels** tall (Figure 3-19).

FIGURE 3-19

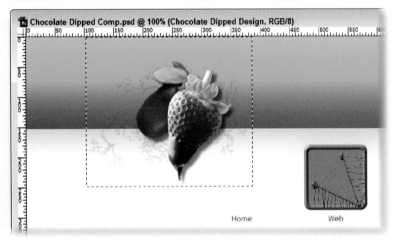

3. Choose **Edit ▶ Copy Merged** and create a new document (**File ▶ New**). When the new file opens, choose **Edit ▶ Paste** and save your image in the **Chapter 3 ▶ images** folder with the name **strawberries.psd**.

Now, it's time to bring the image into the existing #header CSS style.

4. In Dreamweaver's **CSS Style** panel, select **#header** and, from the **Properties** pane, click **Edit Style**, the pencil icon second from the right at the bottom of the panel (Figure 3-20).

FIGURE 3-20

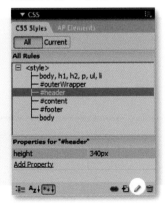

SETTING UP A DREAMWEAVER SITE // ESTABLISHING BASIC PREFERENCES // CHAPTER   073
CREATING CSS LAYOUT STYLES // INSERTING <DIV> TAGS // INCORPORATING BACKGROUND
IMAGES // ADDING A BACKGROUND IMAGE TO THE <BODY> // BRINGING IN FOREGROUND
IMAGES // INSERTING AND STYLING TEXT // INCLUDING NAVIGATION //

03

Once defined, CSS rules are easily modified. By default, clicking Edit Styles reopens the CSS Rule Definition dialog.

5. When the **CSS Rule Definition** dialog box appears, switch to the **Background** category. Click the **Background image Browse** button and in the **Select Image Source** dialog box navigate to the **Chapter 3 ▶ images** folder and select **strawberries.psd**. Click **OK** (Windows) or **Choose** (Mac).

    Again, you'll convert the Photoshop document to a Web-ready format.

6. In the Image Preview dialog box, choose **JPEG** from the **Format** list. Set the **Quality** to **80** and click **OK**. When the **Save Web Image** dialog box appears, navigate to the **Chapter 3 ▶ images** folder and enter **strawberries.jpg** in the **File name** field; click **OK**.

7. When the **CSS Rule Definition** dialog reappears, select **no-repeat** from the **Repeat** list and click **OK** (Figure 3-21).

FIGURE 3-21

The strawberries and swirls appear layered above the green gradient, perfectly aligned. Now there's just one last bit of cleanup to take care of.

8. Select the placeholder text **Content for id "header" Goes Here** and delete it (Figure 3-22). Choose **File ▶ Save**.

FIGURE 3-22

In the next series of steps, you'll layer two more background graphics atop one another to create the desired effect in the footer. As this method requires two separate images, you can get them both at the same time in Photoshop.

1. In Photoshop, choose **Select ▶ Deselect**, if necessary. With the **Rectangular Marquee** tool, drag out a selection the full height of the footer near its left edge. Your selection should be approximately **10 pixels** wide by **50 pixels** tall (Figure 3-23).

FIGURE 3-23

Make sure you do not include any of the spiral images in this selection.

2. Choose **Edit ▶ Copy Merged** and create a new document (**File ▶ New**). When the new file opens, choose **Edit ▶ Paste** and save your image in the **Chapter 3 ▶ images** folder with the name **bg_footer.psd**.

Now, while still in Photoshop, you can get the second footer image, the spirals.

3. Choose **Select ▶ Deselect**. With the **Rectangular Marquee** tool, drag a selection around the spiral portion of the footer. Your selection should be approximately **918 pixels** wide by **50 pixels** tall (Figure 3-24).

FIGURE 3-24

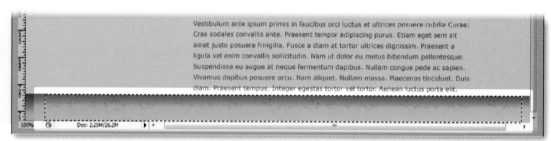

4. Repeat step 2 and save the new file as **spiral_footer.psd**.

Now, it's time to bring the first of those images into the Dreamweaver layout.

5. In the **Dreamweaver CSS Styles** panel, select **#footer** and click **Edit CSS Rule**. When the **CSS Styles Definition** dialog box opens, switch to the **Background** category. Click the **Background image Browse** button, and in the **Select Image Source** dialog box, navigate to the **Chapter 3 ▶ images** folder and select **bg_footer.psd**. Click **OK** (Windows) or **Choose** (Mac).

6. In the **Image Preview** dialog box, choose **JPEG** from the **Format** list. Set the **Quality** to **80** and click **OK**. When the **Save Web Image** dialog box appears, navigate to the **Chapter 3 ▶ images** folder and enter **bg_footer.jpg** in the **File name** field; click **OK**.

7. When the **CSS Rule Definition** dialog reappears, select **repeat-x** from the **Repeat** list and click **OK**. Delete the placeholder phrase **Content for id "footer" Goes Here** (Figure 3-25).

FIGURE 3-25

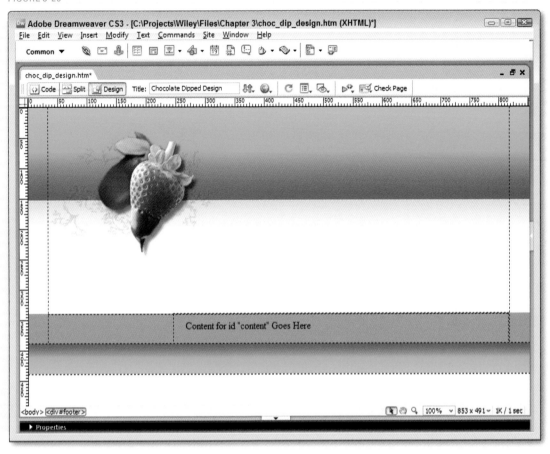

Once you're familiar with the steps for converting a PSD file to a background image and applying it to a `<div>` tag, you can adopt a more streamlined workflow, as demonstrated in this next series of steps.

1. From the **Common** category of the **Insert** bar, choose **Insert Div Tag**. When the **Insert Div Tag** dialog box appears, choose the **After start of** tag from the **Insert** list and **<div id="footer">** from the adjacent list. Click **New CSS Style**.

    Rather than applying an existing CSS rule to a new `<div>` tag, you have the option in Dreamweaver to create the rule on the fly.

SETTING UP A DREAMWEAVER SITE // ESTABLISHING BASIC PREFERENCES // CHAPTER 077

CREATING CSS LAYOUT STYLES // INSERTING <DIV> TAGS // INCORPORATING BACKGROUND
IMAGES // ADDING A BACKGROUND IMAGE TO THE <BODY> // BRINGING IN FOREGROUND
IMAGES // INSERTING AND STYLING TEXT // INCLUDING NAVIGATION //

03

2. When the **New CSS Rule** dialog box opens, choose **Selector Type: Advanced** and in the **Selector** field enter **#footerContent** (Figure 3-26). Click **OK**.

FIGURE 3-26

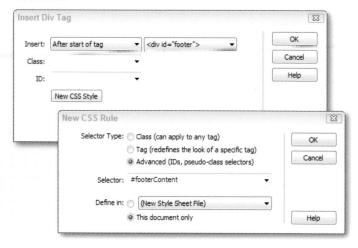

3. In the **CSS Rule definition for #footerContent** dialog, switch to the **Background** category. Click the **Background image Browse** button, and in the **Select Image Source** dialog box, navigate to the **Chapter 3 ▶ images** folder and select **spiral_footer.psd**. Click **OK** (Windows) or **Choose** (Mac).

4. In the Image Preview dialog box, choose **JPEG** from the **Format** list. Set the **Quality** to **80** and click **OK**. When the **Save Web Image** dialog box appears, navigate to the **Chapter 3 ▶ images** folder and enter **spiral_footer.jpg** in the **File name** field; click **OK**.

5. When the **CSS Rule Definition** dialog reappears, select **repeat-x** from the **Repeat** list.

   To make sure the spiral graphic is displayed properly, you'll need to add a couple of additional CSS properties.

6. Switch to the **Box** category and enter **50 pixels** in the **Height** field. Clear the **Margin Same for all** checkbox and set the following properties: **Top: 0**; **Right: auto**; **Bottom: 0**; and **Left: auto** (Figure 3-27). Click **OK**.

FIGURE 3-27

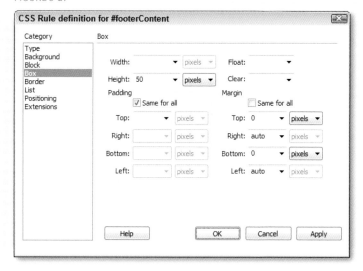

7. When you return to the **Insert Div Tag** dialog, click **OK**.

   Not bad, eh? You were able to insert a new `<div>` tag, create a new CSS rule, and convert a PSD file to a Web format, all in one operation. Now you can finish up the footer with a couple more details.

8. Delete the placeholder phrase Content for id "footerContent" Goes Here.

   Now the spiral design completely obscures the footer background—you can adjust that by changing the #footer padding properties.

9. In the CSS Styles panel, select **#footer** and then in the **Properties** pane click **Add Property**. In the first column, enter **padding** and press **Tab**. Enter **0 20px** and press **Enter** (Windows) or **Return** (Mac) (Figure 3-28).

FIGURE 3-28

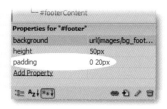

   The entered padding value is CSS shorthand that sets the top and bottom padding to zero while adding 20 pixels to the left and right.

10. Choose **File ▶ Save**.

Now, your footer displays the pure gradient on both ends and the spirals in the middle, regardless of the browser window width (Figure 3-29). If you'd like to test this, you can either change the width of the Dreamweaver document window or press F12 to preview the file in your browser and change its size.

FIGURE 3-29

Feel like you mastered background images? Next, it's time to move on to adding foreground images.

PART 01   PART 02   PART 03   PART 04   APPENDIX

Photoshop to Dreamweaver   Fireworks to Dreamweaver   Flash to Dreamweaver   Photoshop to Bridge to Fireworks to Dreamweaver   Additional Workflows

BRINGING IN FOREGROUND IMAGES

The two basic methods for inserting an image in Dreamweaver are to use the Image object or to drag it onto the page. If you like, you can choose a PSD file from Photoshop and convert it as you have with the background images. However, another approach is better suited to adding foreground graphics: copy and paste.

The integration of these Adobe CS3 tools enables you to copy a selection in Photoshop and paste it into Dreamweaver. When you paste your clipboard, Dreamweaver recognizes it as a Photoshop-generated image and opens the Image Preview dialog to convert it to a Web-based format. From this point, the process is the same as with PSD files.

In this exercise, you'll integrate the decorative text logo into your layout, and you'll also learn how you can return to Photoshop to modify a Dreamweaver-inserted image.

1. In the Photoshop **Layers palette**, locate the **Chocolate Dipped Design** layer and toggle its **eye icon** on.

2. Choose **Rectangular Marquee** from the Tools palette and drag a selection from the top of the comp, surrounding the text logo (Figure 3-30). Your selection should be approximately **486 pixels** wide by **125 pixels** tall.

FIGURE 3-30

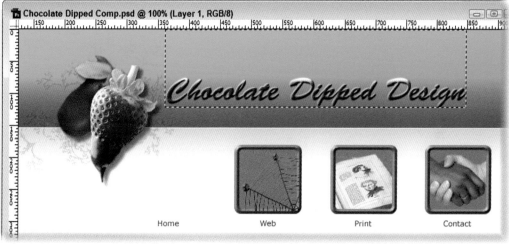

3. Choose **Edit ▶ Copy Merged**.

   Again, you've copied your Photoshop selection to the clipboard. However, before switching to Dreamweaver, you can take one additional step to make it easier to make modifications later.

4. Choose **Select ▶ Save Selection**. When the **Save Selection** dialog box appears, enter **logo** in the **Name** field and click **OK** (Figure 3-31). Choose **Select ▶ Deselect** to clear the marquee.

FIGURE 3-31

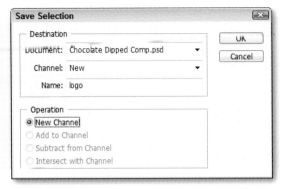

Photoshop allows you to save and load selections. This is a very valuable feature for integration with Dreamweaver as you'll see later in this exercise.

5. Switch to Dreamweaver. Place your cursor in the header area and press **Ctrl+V** (Windows) or **Cmd+V** (Mac).

As when you open a PSD in Dreamweaver, the Image Preview dialog box appears.

6. In the **Image Preview** dialog box, choose **JPEG** from the **Format** list. Set the **Quality** to **80** and click **OK**. When the **Save Web Image** dialog box appears, navigate to the **Chapter 3 ▶ images** folder and enter **straw_logo.jpg** in the **File name** field; click **OK**.

As you may remember, you set your Dreamweaver preferences to include the accessibility options for images. The just-opened dialog box is a result of that choice.

7. In the **Image Description (Alt Text)** dialog box, enter **Chocolate Dipped Design** in the **Image Description** field and click **OK**.

Your logo is added to the document, but in the wrong position (Figure 3-32). You can fix that with one additional CSS property.

082 PART **01** PART **02** PART **03** PART **04** APPENDIX

Photoshop to Dreamweaver   Fireworks to Dreamweaver   Flash to Dreamweaver   Photoshop to Bridge to Fireworks to Dreamweaver   Additional Workflows

FIGURE 3-32

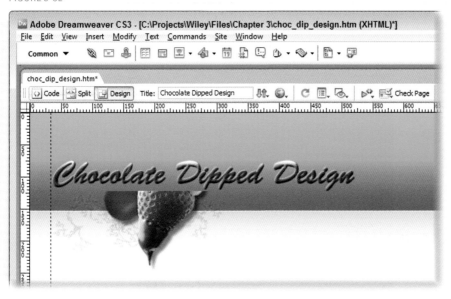

8. In the CSS Styles panel, select **#header** and click **Add Property**. In the first column, enter **padding-left** and press **Tab**; in the second column, enter **270** and press **Enter** (Windows) or **Return** (Mac).

Now, the logo is in its proper place and blends in with the background perfectly (Figure 3-33).

FIGURE 3-33

But what happens if you need to make a change to this logo or any other foreground image that started out as part of a Photoshop comp? The integration of Photoshop and Dreamweaver has you covered, as you learn in the next series of steps.

1. Select the just-inserted image and choose **Window ▶ Properties**.

2. In the Property inspector, click **Edit**, the Photoshop logo in the middle of the inspector (Figure 3-34).

FIGURE 3-34

Photoshop now opens, if necessary, and displays the source image. Now you need to select the portion of the comp you want to modify. This is where your saved selection comes in super handy!

3. Choose **Select ▶ Load Selection**. When the Load Selection dialog appears, choose **logo** from the **Channel** list; click **OK**.

The previously saved selection is restored, and you're ready to make your alterations. Add a hyphen to the logo text.

4. Choose the **Horizontal Type** tool from the Tools palette. Place your cursor between *Chocolate* and *Dipped* and replace the separating space with a **hyphen** (Figure 3-35). Move your cursor in front of the hyphen and expand the **Character** palette. From the **Kerning** list, change **Metric** to **75**.

FIGURE 3-35

Because Photoshop keeps the text editable, changes like these are very easy. Now, it's time to return to Dreamweaver.

084 PART **01** PART **02** PART **03** PART **04** APPENDIX

Photoshop to Dreamweaver   Fireworks to Dreamweaver   Flash to Dreamweaver   Photoshop to Bridge to   Additional Workflows
Fireworks to Dreamweaver

5. Choose **Edit ▶ Copy Merged** and switch back to Dreamweaver. Once in Dreamweaver, choose **Edit ▶ Paste** (Figure 3-36).

   Dreamweaver automatically resaves the clipboard contents with the previous image settings and the same filename.

FIGURE 3-36

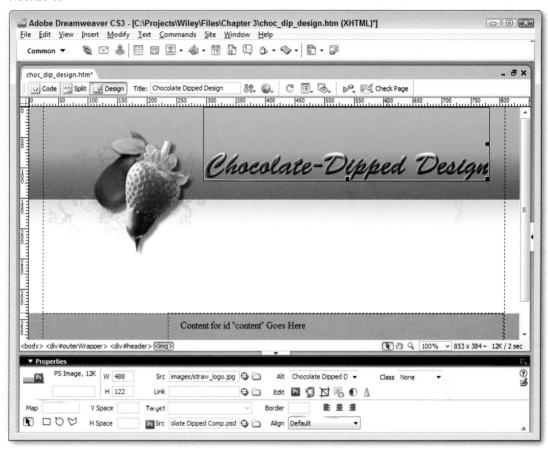

6. Choose **File ▶ Save**.

Next, you'll fill out the content section and stylize the text with CSS.

Dw CORE TECHNIQUES

INSERTING IMAGES FROM PHOTOSHOP

There are two ways to integrate native Photoshop images in Dreamweaver. Photoshop documents (PSD) can be opened directly in Dreamweaver. When opened, a dialog box—Image Preview— appears that allows you to optimize the image for the Web. The Image Preview dialog allows you to format the image as a GIF, JPEG, or PNG file, with appropriate options for each format. For example, you can limit the number of colors in a GIF file or modify the quality setting for a JPEG. You also have the ability to scale or crop the image in the Image Preview dialog before exporting it to the chosen format.

You can also copy any selection (or merged selection) in Photoshop and paste it into Dreamweaver. Once pasted, the Image Preview dialog box appears with all the same export capabilities.

Photoshop images brought into Dreamweaver in one of these methods can be modified in Photoshop and easily returned to Dreamweaver. The process requires that you select the image and click the Photoshop Edit icon in the Property inspector. The image will open in Photoshop for modification. When you're done, select the graphic and copy it. Paste the clipboard in Dreamweaver, and the file is updated with the previous Image Preview settings reapplied.

INSERTING AND STYLING TEXT

Out of all the CSS styles, text properties have been supported in Dreamweaver the longest. Consequently, defining, applying and modifying text styles are heavily integrated and accessible throughout the interface. This makes it quite easy to style text in Dreamweaver.

Typically, designers limit the number of font and font styles for a Web site to convey an over-all look and-feel. For example, it's not uncommon for a design to use one font-family—like Ver-dana, Arial, Helvetica, sans-serif—throughout the site or to make sure that all `<h1>` tags in the same context have matching properties such as color and size. In fact, text often brings out the cascade in Cascading Style Sheets and relies heavily on the CSS quality of inheritance. In this exercise, you see how inheritance is applied generally and handled when an exception is required.

1. In the **CSS Styles** panel, select **#content** and click **Edit CSS Rule**.

   Before you begin styling text directly, you'll need to add a solid white background color and an accompanying background image to the content area.

086   PART **01**   PART **02**   PART **03**   PART **04**   APPENDIX

Photoshop to Dreamweaver   Fireworks to Dreamweaver   Flash to Dreamweaver   Photoshop to Bridge to Fireworks to Dreamweaver   Additional Workflows

2. In the **CSS Rule definition for #content** dialog box, switch to the **Background** category. Click the **Background Color** color swatch and choose **white** (#FFFFFF) with the eyedropper cursor. Click the **Background Image Choose** button and, when the **Select Image Source** dialog box opens, navigate to the **Chapter 3 ▶ images** folder and choose **gray_bar.gif**; click **OK**. From the **Repeat** list, choose **no-repeat** and click **OK** (Figure 3-37).

FIGURE 3-37

The white background is necessary to prevent the gray-to-white gradient from displaying behind the content area while the background image keeps the illusion of a straight gray bar running across the page.

Now that the area is prepped, you can add some text styles.

3. In the **CSS Styles** panel, choose **body**. In the **Properties** pane, click **Add Property**. In the first column, enter **font-family** and press **Tab**. From the second column list, choose **Verdana, Arial, Helvetica, sans-serif**.

By declaring a specific font-family for the `<body>` tag, you're setting the general font for the entire page—and, eventually, site. Thanks to CSS inheritance, the same font declaration cascades down to all the other elements unless specifically redefined. This is immediately obvious in the remaining placeholder text on the page.

Now it's time to bring in and style the headings.

4. Select the placeholder text **Content for id "content" Goes Here** and delete it. In the Property inspector, choose **Heading 1** from the **Format** list. With your cursor in the same position, enter **Page Title** and press **Enter** (Windows) or **Return** (Mac). From the Property inspector's **Format** list choose **Heading 2** and enter **– and subheading** (Figure 3-38).

FIGURE 3-38

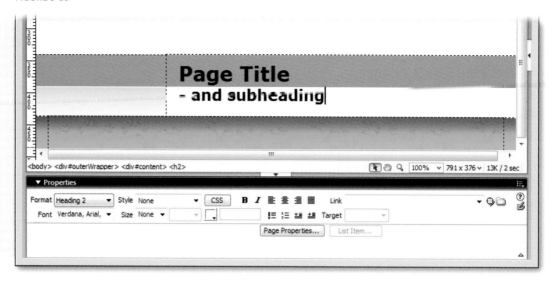

At this point, you're seeing the normal behavior of heading tags, with each on their own line. To massage this text into the design as specified in the comp requires two new CSS declarations.

5. From the **CSS Styles** panel, click **New CSS Rule**. In the New CSS Rule dialog box, choose **Selector Type: Advanced** and enter **#content h1** in the Selector field. Click **OK**.

   By establishing the selector as #content h1, only <h1> tags in the #content <div> tag are affected.

6. When the **CSS Rule definition for #content h1** dialog box appears, choose **24 pixels** from the **Size** list and **white** from the **Color** swatch. Switch to the **Block** category and from the **Display** list choose **inline** (Figure 3-39). Choose the **Box** category and clear the **Padding Same for all** checkbox; set the **Top** value to **10 pixels** and **Left** to **20 pixels**. Click **OK** when you're done.

FIGURE 3-39

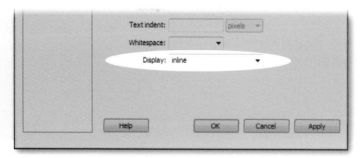

The Display: Inline declaration is key to getting both the two headings on the same line— but you also have to apply it to the #content h2 tag. In fact, these two styles are so similar, you can take advantage of a Dreamweaver shortcut: duplicating styles.

7. In the **CSS Styles** panel, **right-click** (Windows) or **Ctrl+click** (Mac) the **#content h1** entry and from the context menu choose **Duplicate**. In the **Duplicate CSS Rule** dialog box, change the **Selector** to **#content h2** and click **OK**.

When you duplicate a style, Dreamweaver doesn't open the CSS Rule Definition dialog box; the new style is just added to the CSS Styles panel, where you can easily make any necessary changes.

8. Select **#content h2** in the **CSS Styles** panel and in the **Properties** pane change the **color** value to **#CCCCCC**. Select the **padding-left** property and click the **Trashcan** icon in the bottom left of the panel to delete it.

The two headings now appear on the same line with different colors, as comped (Figure 3-40).

FIGURE 3-40

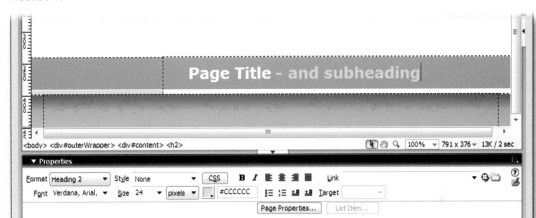

Now you can insert some placeholder paragraphs.

9. In Photoshop, select the **Horizontal Type** tool and place it anywhere in the two paragraphs of body copy below the heading. Choose **Select ▶ All** and press **Ctrl+C** (Windows) or **Cmd+C** (Mac).

It's good to know that paragraphs in Photoshop are recognized by Dreamweaver, so you can get your text directly from the comp.

10. In Dreamweaver, place your cursor after the phrase and subheading and press **Enter** (Windows) or **Return** (Mac). Press **Ctrl+V** (Windows) or **Cmd+V** (Mac).

With a big block of text inserted, it's obvious that some styling is needed (Figure 3-41). So, you need to create one more CSS rule.

FIGURE 3-41

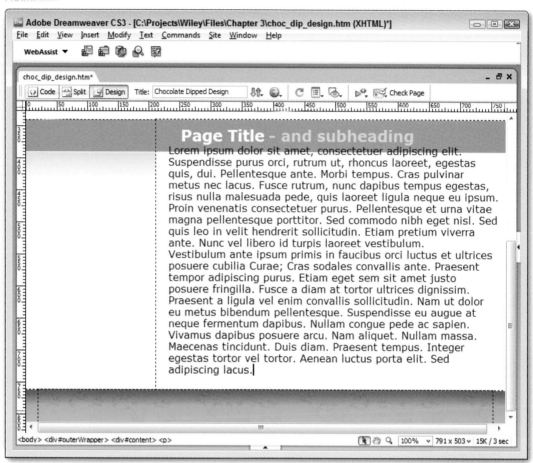

11. From the **CSS Styles** panel, click **New CSS Rule**. In the **New CSS Rule** dialog box, choose **Selector Type: Advanced** and enter **#content p** in the **Selector** field. Click **OK**.

Again, you make this style specific to the content area.

12. When the **CSS Rule definition for #content p** dialog box appears, choose **12 pixels** from the **Size** list and set the line-height to **20 pixels**. Switch to the **Box** category and clear the **Padding** and **Margin Same for all** checkboxes; set the **Margin Top** value to **30 pixels** and the **Padding Left** and **Right** both to **20 pixels**. Click **OK** when you're done.

13. Choose **File ▶ Save**.

The text now replicates the look-and-feel set in the comp (Figure 3-42). Where did I get the values for the margins? By careful measuring of the distance from the gray bar to the text for the top and the values entered in the Paragraph palette for the left and right. All the other properties came from Photoshop's Character palette.

FIGURE 3-42

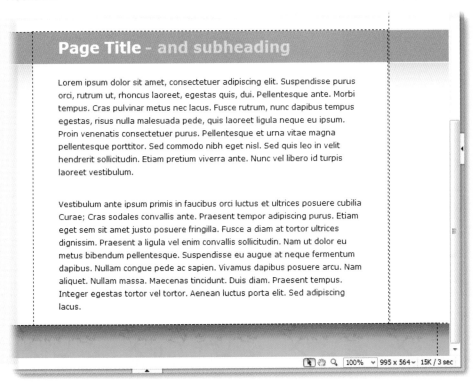

The final portion of the page, the navigation, is added in the next exercise.

SETTING UP A DREAMWEAVER SITE // ESTABLISHING BASIC PREFERENCES // CHAPTER 091

CREATING CSS LAYOUT STYLES // INSERTING <DIV> TAGS // INCORPORATING BACKGROUND IMAGES // ADDING A BACKGROUND IMAGE TO THE <BODY> // BRINGING IN FOREGROUND IMAGES // INSERTING AND STYLING TEXT // INCLUDING NAVIGATION //

03

INCLUDING NAVIGATION

Navigation, especially to the modern Web designer, often exemplifies another use of text. Although the designs of certain navigation bars still require the tried-and-true technique of graphic images with bitmapped text, the general trend is to use plain, searchable text as the label combined with background images.

In this exercise, you create the layout component you need to hold the navigation elements, insert the text labels, and apply the styles. To keep this goal obtainable, an external style sheet is provided for you—all you'll need to do is link it to your document. The in-depth nature of creating the styles for a navigation bar with CSS is beyond the scope of this chapter and is covered later in this book in Chapter 6.

1. From the **Common** category of the **Insert** bar, choose **Insert Div Tag**. When the **Insert Div Tag** dialog box appears, choose **After start of** tag from the **Insert** list and **<div id="header">** from the adjacent list. Click **New CSS Style**.

   The new <div> tag is nested in the header section.

2. When the **New CSS Rule** dialog box opens, choose **Selector Type: Advanced** and in the **Selector** field enter **#nav**. Click **OK**.

3. In the **CSS Rule definition for #nav** dialog, while in the **Type** category, enter **12 pixels** in the **Size** field and then switch to the **Positioning** category. Set the **Type** to **absolute** and **Width** to **610 pixels**. Enter **182 pixels** in the **Top** field and **203 pixels** in the **Left** field (Figure 3-43). Click **OK**. When the **Insert Div Tag** dialog appears, click **OK** again.

FIGURE 3-43

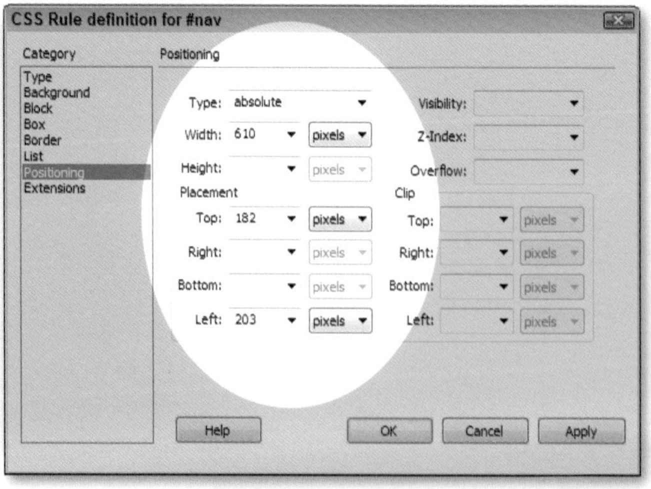

Absolute positioning is occasionally needed to place page elements properly. In order for absolute positioning to work properly, however, you need to make sure that the CSS for the enclosing element is set to position: relative. Here, the enclosing element is #header.

4. From the CSS Styles panel, select **#header**. In the **Properties** pane, click **Add Property**. In the first column, enter **position** and press **Tab**. In the second column, choose **relative** from the list.

Now that the `div` is properly placed, you're ready to enter your text for the navigation. Modern Web designers prefer to use unordered lists for CSS-based navigation. Unordered lists (also known as bulleted lists) are very flexible and easy to restyle.

5. Select the placeholder text **Content for id "nav" Goes Here** and delete it. From the Property inspector, click **Unordered List** and enter the following four items, each on their own line: **Home**, **Web**, **Print**, and **Contact**.

Your list is added to the page (Figure 3-44). Before you style it, you add in the links for each item.

FIGURE 3-44

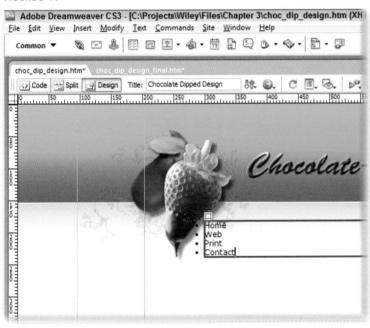

6. Select the first list item, **Home**, and in the **Property inspector Link** field enter **home.htm**. Repeat this operation for each of the remaining list items with the following links: **web.htm**, **print.htm**, and **contact.htm**.

SETTING UP A DREAMWEAVER SITE // ESTABLISHING BASIC PREFERENCES // CHAPTER   093
CREATING CSS LAYOUT STYLES // INSERTING <DIV> TAGS // INCORPORATING BACKGROUND
IMAGES // ADDING A BACKGROUND IMAGE TO THE <BODY> // BRINGING IN FOREGROUND
IMAGES // INSERTING AND STYLING TEXT // INCLUDING NAVIGATION //

03

To assign each of the list items a separate background image, you need to give them all unique IDs. Because there is no ID field on the list item Property inspector, you'll need to add them directly to the code. Luckily, Dreamweaver has a mechanism that keeps you in Design mode during this process: the Quick Tag Editor.

7. Place your cursor in the first list item, **Home** and select **<li>** from the **Tag Selector** at the bottom of the Document window. Press **Ctrl+T** (Windows) or **Cmd+T** (Mac). When the **Quick Tag Editor** opens, place your cursor before the closing angle bracket, press **Space** and then enter **id="homeNav"** (Figure 3-45). Press **Enter** (Windows) or **Return** (Mac) to confirm your change.

FIGURE 3-45

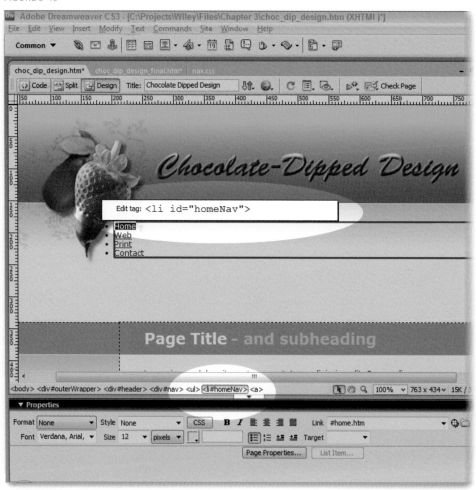

PART 01   PART 02   PART 03   PART 04   APPENDIX

Photoshop to Dreamweaver   Fireworks to Dreamweaver   Flash to Dreamweaver   Photoshop to Bridge to Fireworks to Dreamweaver   Additional Workflows

8. Repeat step 7 for each of the remaining list items with the following code:

- For Web, add **id="webNav"**.

- For Print, add **id="printNav"**.

- For Contact, add **id="contactNav"**.

Ready for some magic? It's time to attach the external style sheet that turns these bullet items into navigation buttons.

9. From the **CSS Styles** panel click **Attach Style Sheet**, the chain link icon at the bottom of the panel. When the **Attach External Style Sheet** dialog box appears, click **Browse**. Navigate to the **Chapter 3 ▶ styles** folder and select **nav.css**; click **OK**. Keep the default setting of **Add as Link** and click **OK** to incorporate the styles (Figure 3-46).

FIGURE 3-46

So how did this all happen? As noted earlier, converting a series of text items to a navigation bar requires a fairly sophisticated series of CSS styles, which are covered in depth later in this book in Chapter 6. Here are the highlights:

- The bullets are removed from the `<ul>` tag.

- Each list item is floated left (which makes the vertical list horizontal), the text is aligned to the center, and padding is added to separate the items.

- The anchor elements (the `<a>` tags) are set to display: block, which allows the background images to show, and the normal underline for links is removed with text-decoration:none.

- Each of the separate links is given a unique background image.

10. Choose **File ▶ Save** and press **F12** to preview the page in your primary browser. Move your mouse over any of the navigation buttons to see the rollover effect.

Congratulations! Your layout—comped in Photoshop and realized in Dreamweaver—is now complete (Figure 3-47)! From start to finish, it's been a long journey but hopefully the attention to detail gives you a better sense of how considering your goal—completing the page in Dreamweaver—from the very start of your design process in Photoshop has made the trek meaningful. In the next part, you see how you can follow a similar path to Dreamweaver, but from a different starting point: Fireworks.

FIGURE 3-47

PART **02**

W

HOME

Catch
it while you
Can

Major heading goes here

L orem ipsum dolor sit amet, consecte
tincidunt ut laoreet dolore magna al
nostrud exerci tation ullamcorper suscip
autem vel eum iriure dolor in hendrerit in
feugiat nulla facilisis at vero eros et accu
zzril delenit augue duis dolore te feugait

Subheading goes here

Lorem ipsum dolor sit amet, consectetue
laoreet dolore magna aliquam erat volutp
ullamcorper suscipit lobortis nisl ut aliqui
in hendrerit in vulputate velit esse molest
eros et accumsan et iusto odio dignissim

life adventure vacations

SOLO   GROUP   CONTACT

Special deal

Lorem ipsum dolor sit amet,
consectetuer adipiscing elit,
sed diam nonummy nibh
euismod tincidunt.

Special deal

Lorem ipsum dolor sit amet,
consectetuer adipiscing elit,
sed diam nonummy nibh
euismod tincidunt.

cing elit, sed diam nonummy nibh euismod
olutpat. Ut wisi enim ad minim veniam, quis
sl ut aliquip ex ea commodo consequat. Duis
elit esse molestie consequat, vel illum dolore eu
sto odio dignissim qui blandit praesent luptatum
.

Special deal

Lorem ipsum dolor sit amet,
consectetuer adipiscing elit,
sed diam nonummy nibh
euismod tincidunt.

elit, sed diam nonummy nibh euismod tincidunt ut
nim ad minim veniam, quis nostrud exerci tation
modo consequat. Duis autem vel eum iriure dolor
t, vel illum dolore eu feugiat nulla facilisis at vero

Special deal

Lorem ipsum dolor sit amet,
consectetuer adipiscing elit,
sed diam nonummy nibh
euismod tincidunt.

FIREWORKS TO DREAMWEAVER

Dreamweaver and Fireworks have a long history of working together. The initial version of Fireworks was released less than two years after Dreamweaver's debut, and from the start, they offered an enhanced workflow. Over the years, the partnership has deepened to the point that certain key Fireworks features are now incorporated into Dreamweaver—and are even integral to the Photoshop to Dreamweaver workflow.

Fireworks has evolved from an innovative Web-oriented graphics editor to a full-fledged Web comp engine. Through a combination of vector- and bitmap-based creation tools, Fireworks offers both backward compatibility with other graphics engines and future-facing ease of modification. With the release of Fireworks CS3, multiple page comps became a reality, thus catapulting Fireworks from a Web graphics editor to a Web site composition tool.

How you use Fireworks and Dreamweaver together depends on your desired output. If you're working on a legacy site that uses table-based layouts, the two products offer complete round-trip editing. You can design an entire page, designate the interactive slices—and even assign URLs to navigation elements—and export it as a Dreamweaver-compatible file. Import it through the custom Fireworks HTML command, and your page will open in Dreamweaver, ready for content. Any graphic portion of the page may be sent for extensive editing from Dreamweaver directly to Fireworks and, with the click of the Done button, returned modified.

For more modern Web–standards compliant, CSS-based layouts, a different workflow is advised. Individual foreground elements are sliced and then exported as optimized graphics where they are inserted into Dreamweaver as standard images. Portions of background graphics—if the background is to repeat in one direction or another—are also sliced and exported, but are brought into Dreamweaver through CSS style declarations. Further graphic changes can be made directly to the Fireworks document and re-exported or to the exported file itself. The workflow descriptions in this part will focus on this standards-oriented approach.

The following chapters will focus on introducing key graphic development techniques in Fireworks such as creating vector-based imagery, incorporating bitmapped graphics, and using symbols to cut down production time. You'll also learn how to build multiple page, interactive comps for persuasive client presentations—and how to bring those pages to life in Dreamweaver. Additionally, you'll learn how to bring navigation elements designed in Fireworks into Dreamweaver as search engine–friendly, HTML-valid, CSS structured code.

THE FLOW: FIREWORKS TO DREAMWEAVER

As noted earlier, the Fireworks to Dreamweaver workflow is dependent on the type of Web page developed. For table-based layouts, here are the general steps (Figure II-1):

1. In Fireworks, slice your images.

Designate areas intended to hold text and other non-graphic content with HTML slices.

2. Export the file with the HTML and Images setting. Make sure to choose the Include areas without slices option.
3. In Dreamweaver, choose Insert ▶ Image Objects ▶ Fireworks HTML and enter the filename of the Web page exported from Fireworks.

FIGURE II-1

To make any changes in the graphics, follow these steps (Figure II-2):

1. In Dreamweaver, select the image you want to modify.
2. From the Property inspector, choose Edit.
3. When Fireworks opens the original source file, make any desired changes.
4. Click Done to return to Dreamweaver.

FIGURE II-2

For Web standard, CSS-based layouts, follow this workflow (Figure II-3):

1. In Fireworks, slice your images.

Slice foreground images in their entirety and repeating background images according to the portion needed.

2. Export images only.
3. In Dreamweaver, insert foreground images onto the page directly and insert background images through CSS styles.

FIGURE II-3

To modify graphic images within this workflow, follow these steps:

1. Open the PNG file in Fireworks.
2. Make any necessary changes.
3. Re-export the images.

NOTE

The original design shown on the previous spread is the basis for the exercises in Part II; the image shown is just one of the pages created.

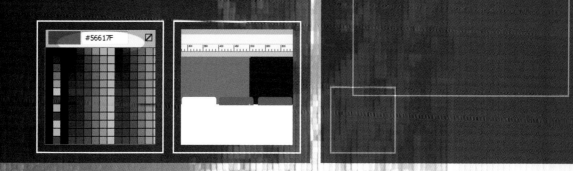

As a long-time partner to Dreamweaver, Adobe Fireworks is capable of outputting well-optimized graphics that are easily modified at any stage of development. Much of this flexibility comes from Fireworks's roots as an application that combines vector and bitmap graphic creation and editing. Firework's vector-based imagery is extremely malleable, yet exports to Web-ready formats such as GIF, JPEG and PNG in the smallest size possible, while retaining the original high-quality luster.

This chapter focuses on setting up your graphics in Fireworks to be properly implemented by Dreamweaver, later in Part II. Here, you'll begin to work with Fireworks powerful vector-based images as you lay down the foundation for the comp. The core techniques covered include:

- Creating with vectors
- Integrating gradients
- Inserting images

04
COMPOSING WITH VECTORS

GETTING STARTED IN FIREWORKS

Because Fireworks is Web-centric, there's no need to set the measurement units to pixels or define other preferences. There are, however, a number of tools you need to make sure are onscreen and available. In this first exercise, you familiarize yourself with the Fireworks user interface and create the initial page for the comp.

1. In Fireworks, choose **Window ▶ Toolbars ▶ Main** to display the Main toolbar; choose **Window ▶ Toolbars ▶ Modify** to show the Modify toolbar.

   The Main toolbar contains icons to support common document operations such as New, Open, Save, Import, Export, and Print, as well as basic Cut/Copy/Paste editing icons (Figure 4-1). Core object operations—such as Group, Ungroup, Join, Split—are found on the Modify toolbar, along with arrangement and alignment icons.

   FIGURE 4-1

2. Choose **Window ▶ Tools**.

   The Fireworks Tools panel is grouped into six sections: Select, Bitmap, Vector, Web, Color, and View. Click any Tool icon with a triangle in the lower-right corner to expose the related tools.

3. Choose **Window ▶ Layers** (Figure 4-2).

   FIGURE 4-2

   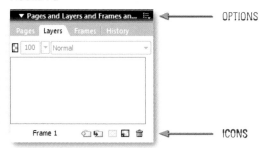

Make sure you've downloaded the book exercise files,
if you haven't already done
so. The files can be obtained
from www.wiley.com/go/
adobecs3webworkflows;
download the zipped files
and uncompress them to a
folder on your system.

NOTE

In general, Fireworks keyboard shortcuts correspond
to their counterparts in Photoshop, where available. For
example, press m once to
select Fireworks's Marquee
tool, which is the same as
Photoshop's Rectangular
Marquee tool; press it again
to choose the Oval Marquce
tool, known in Photoshop as
the Elliptical Marquee tool.
Modifiers are also generally
the same: Press Shift while
dragging out a rectangular
or oval selection to make the
marquee square or circular,
respectively.

NOTE

Fireworks uses a series of dockable panels that open when one, such as the Layers panel, is displayed. Many panels include a row of icons along the bottom for related operations; all panels have a set of options available from a menu button in the upper-right corner. You can expand any panel by clicking its name or maximize it with a double-click.

As you'll see throughout this part, the Layers panel is one of Fireworks's most frequently used.

Now it's time to create your first page so you can get started.

4. Choose **File ▶ New**. When the **New Document** dialog box opens, enter **1024** in the **Width** field and **768** in the **Height** field. Leave the resolution set to **72 pixels/inch** (Figure 4-3).

FIGURE 4-3

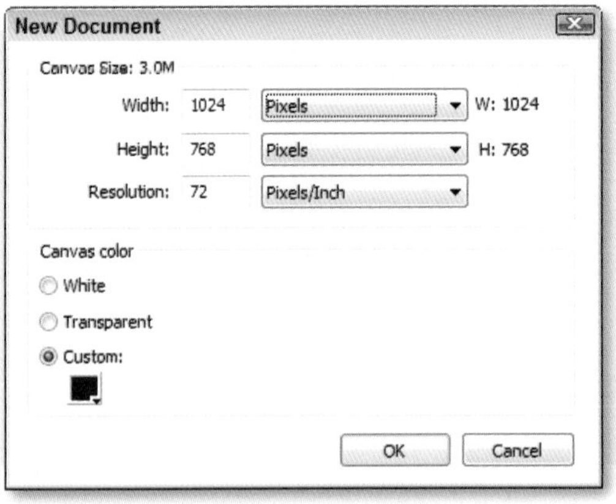

5. In the **Canvas** color area, choose **Custom** and click the color swatch. In the pop-up color picker, enter **#000064** in the field near the top. Press **Enter** (Windows) or **Return** (Mac) to confirm your choice. Click **OK** when you're done.

   Fireworks opens your new document in a reduced magnification so you can see the entire file at once (Figure 4-4).

6. Choose **File ▶ Save**. When the **Save As** dialog box appears, navigate to the **Chapter 4** folder of your exercise files. Enter **wildlife.png** in the **File name** field and click **OK**.

104 PART 01 PART 02 PART 03 PART 04 APPENDIX

Photoshop to Dreamweaver   Fireworks to Dreamweaver   Flash to Dreamweaver   Photoshop to Bridge to   Additional Workflows
                                                                                Fireworks to Dreamweaver

FIGURE 4-4

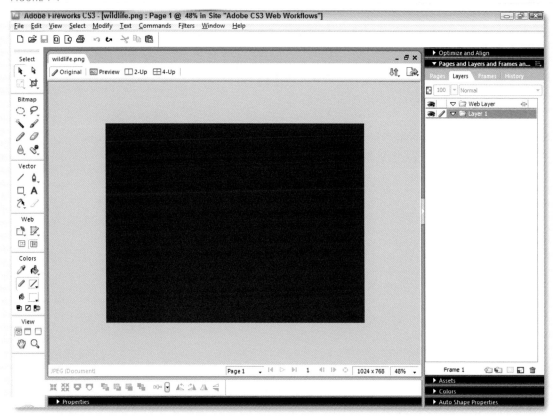

Fireworks's native format is PNG just as Photoshop's is PSD. It's important to realize that when you save a Fireworks PNG file, it includes all the metadata necessary to keep the various document elements (like text and vectors) editable. Fireworks is capable of exporting a Web-compliant PNG format that strips out all the metadata for a more optimized file. The typical workflow with Fireworks is to save your source files as a Fireworks PNG and export them for Web use as a GIF, JPEG, or standard PNG.

WORKING WITH VECTOR-BASED GRAPHICS

Unlike other graphic editors that output bitmapped graphics, Fireworks includes both bitmap and vector tools. As with vector-based programs such as Adobe Illustrator, Fireworks provides full control over a wide range of professional drawing tools. The key advantage vectors have over bitmaps is flexibility; anything drawn can be redrawn or reshaped. Every aspect of the illustration—from fills to effects—is always live and easy to update.

In this exercise, you use a few basic vector tools—Rectangle and Pen—to draw the basic building blocks of the Web page comp: the content container, the navigation buttons, and the sidebar highlight boxes.

ADDING ROUNDED RECTANGLES

In the almost exclusively straight-edged world of the Web—where images, <div> tags, and borders are all rectangular—it's great to include rounded corners in the designer's palette. Fireworks has two methods for inserting rounded rectangles. The older technique can be found in the Rectangle tool menu as Rounded Rectangle; the Rounded Rectangle is a Fireworks Smart Shape that can be modified by dragging control handles. The newer method—used in the following steps—allows more precise control.

1. From the **Tools** panel, choose the **Rectangle** tool, the middle icon on the left in the Vector section.

2. Drag out a medium-sized rectangle in the middle of the canvas.

    You don't need to be specific about the dimensions or placement; you can fine-tune all of those attributes in the Property inspector.

3. Choose **Window ▶ Properties** to open the Property inspector. Click the **Fill** color swatch and choose **white** from the pop-up color picker. Click the **Stroke** color swatch and choose **Transparent Button** to eliminate any color (Figure 4-5).

FIGURE 4-5

Fireworks's Property inspector is quite similar to the one found in Dreamweaver and changes according to the tool selected.

4. In the Property inspector, change the **Width (W)** value to **804** and press **Tab**. Change the **Height (H)** value to **586** and press **Tab**. Change the **X** value to **126** and **Y** to **152** and press Tab to confirm your entries.

    So far, the rectangle shape could have been drawn in any bitmap graphics program. So, now you can add a little vector magic with rounded corners.

5. Use the **Rectangle roundness** slider to change the value to **10**.

106   PART **01**   PART **02**   PART **03**   PART **04**   APPENDIX

Photoshop to Dreamweaver   Fireworks to Dreamweaver   Flash to Dreamweaver   Photoshop to Bridge to Fireworks to Dreamweaver   Additional Workflows

Because the rectangle is vector-based and not bitmapped, you can easily round straight corners (Figure 4-6).

FIGURE 4-6

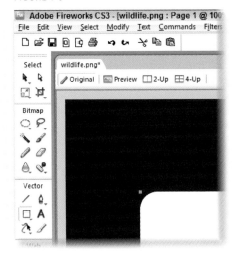

If you look at the Layers panel, you'll notice that the Rectangle object has been added to the Layers 1 folder. Every object or graphic element added to the document appears as a separate entry in the Layers panel. Objects can be renamed and easily reorganized in folders and subfolders.

6. In the **Layers** panel, double-click on the **Rectangle** entry; enter **Content** in the pop-up field and press **Enter** (Windows) or **Return** (Mac). Double-click the **Layer 1** entry and, in the Layer name field, enter **Background** and press **Enter** (Windows) or **Return** (Mac) (Figure 4-7).

FIGURE 4-7

7. Choose **File ▶ Save**.

You'll come back to the content rectangle later to add a bit more finesse with Fireworks effects, but now you can gain a little more experience with rounded rectangles as you create the navigation buttons.

INSERTING NAVIGATION TABS

To continue the rounded rectangle design theme, you now add a series of navigation buttons that, when realized in Dreamweaver, act as tabs. In Chapter 6 you'll learn how to create Fireworks symbols that can be easily exported. The focus in this exercise is to develop the two tabbed states—open and closed—for the comp.

1. In the Layers panel, select the **Background** folder and click **New / Duplicate Layer**, the far-left icon along the bottom of the panel. Double-click the new layer and enter **Header** in the Layer name field. Press **Enter** (Windows) or **Return** (Mac)

2. With the **Rectangle** tool selected, drag out a new small rectangle above the top of the content rectangle (Figure 4-8).

FIGURE 4-8

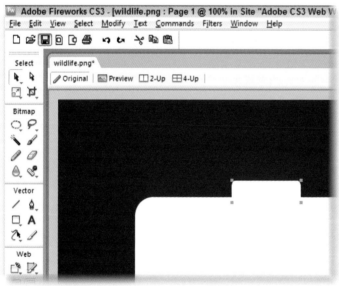

Again, the exact size and position will be defined in the Property inspector.

108
PART **01**
PART **02**
PART **03**
PART **04**
APPENDIX

Photoshop to Dreamweaver
Fireworks to Dreamweaver
Flash to Dreamweaver
Photoshop to Bridge to Fireworks to Dreamweaver
Additional Workflows

3. In the Property inspector, enter the following values:

   - **Width: 111**
   - **Height: 35**
   - **X: 282**
   - **Y: 126**
   - **Rectangle roundness: 50**

   While you could drag out another rectangle for the next tab, you can instead use one of Fireworks's most common shortcuts to duplicate the existing box.

4. From the Tools panel, click the **Pointer** tool, the top icon on the left.

   The Pointer tool is used to select or move objects around the document.

5. Drag the smaller rectangle to the right while pressing **Alt** (Windows) or **Option** (Mac). Release your mouse first to drop the copied rectangle and then release the key.

   Alt/Option dragging creates an exact duplicate of any object very quickly. In this case, you need to make a quick color change to convert the open state tab to a closed state.

6. With the second small rectangle selected, click the **Fill** color swatch in the Property inspector and enter **#56617F** in the **Hexadecimal** field of the pop-up color picker (Figure 4-9). Press **Enter** (Windows) or **Return** (Mac). In the Property inspector, change **X** to **402** and **Y** to **126**.

FIGURE 4-9

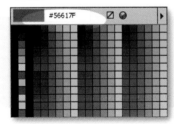

With the darker color added, it's obvious that the rounded rectangle is sitting on top of the content rectangle. To achieve the appearance of a closed tab, you need to bisect the rectangle.

7. From the Tools panel, choose the Knife tool, the third icon on right in the Vector group. Press **Ctrl+=** (Windows) or **Cmd+=** (Mac) twice to magnify the view. Click on the left side of the dark button just under the blue top, press Shift, and drag the Knife tool to the other side of the button (Figure 4-10).

FIGURE 4-10

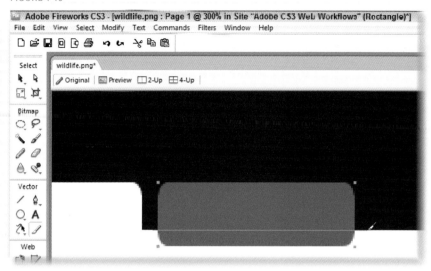

One of the advantages of working with vectors in Fireworks is that you can remove any section of an object and the rest retains the drawn shape—which allows the rectangle to have rounded corners on the top and square corners on the bottom.

8. Choose the **Pointer** tool and click anywhere outside of the rectangle to deselect the two sections. Select the bottom portion and press **Delete**.

Now that you have the exact shape needed, you can quickly add two more navigation rectangles.

9. Press **Ctrl+1** (Windows) or **Cmd+1** (Mac) to return to 100 percent magnification. Drag the second rectangle to the right while pressing **Alt** (Windows) or **Option** (Mac). Repeat the operation one more time to create a fourth small rectangle (Figure 4-11).

FIGURE 4-11

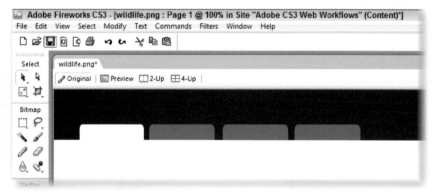

Now that all of your elements are on the page, it's time to use Fireworks alignment tools to get them into shape.

10. Press Shift and select each of the four small rectangles. Choose **Window ▶ Align**. In the **Align** panel, click **Align top edge** and then **Distribute horizontal center** (Figure 4-12).

FIGURE 4-12

11. Choose **File ▶ Save**.

With your tabs now in shape, you can add another series of graphic elements that combines the use of the Rectangle and Pen tools.

DRAWING WITH THE PEN TOOL

Fireworks includes a wide variety of vector drawing tools: Rectangle, Oval, Polygon, Line, Freeform Path, and the Pen. While the appropriately named Freeform Path tool gives you the most flexibility in drawing, it's not as precise as the Pen tool. With the Pen tool, you can draw bezier curves or—as you'll see in the next series of steps—just the straight lines you need.

In the following steps, you create a small box intended to highlight special text items in the sidebar. Once you've constructed the box, you duplicate it a number of times to fill out the page.

1. In the **Layers** panel, select the **Background** layer and click **New/Duplicate Layer**. Double-click the newly created folder and rename it **Content**; press **Enter** (Windows) or **Return** (Mac).

   Because the highlight boxes are eventually maintained in the content `<div>` tag, it's a good idea to structure your comp layout in the same format (Figure 4-13).

FIGURE 4-13

2. From the Tools palette, select the **Pen** tool, the first icon on the right in the Vector group.

   When used normally, the Pen tool draws bezier curves, which allow you to control the size and shape of each curved segment with a pair of control handles. You can also use the Pen to draw straight, connected lines—with the aid of a modifier key.

3. In the right side of the white content rectangle, press **Shift** and click to set the first point. Move the cursor down approximately **175 pixels** and click to set the second point; move the cursor to the left approximately **100 pixels** and double-click to close the line (Figure 4-14).

FIGURE 4-14

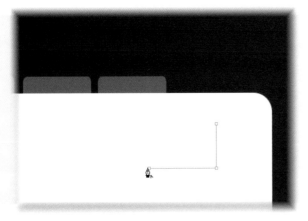

Now that you have the basic shape, let's fine-tune it with the Property inspector.

112 PART **01** PART **02** PART **03** PART **04** APPENDIX

Photoshop to Dreamweaver   Fireworks to Dreamweaver   Flash to Dreamweaver   Photoshop to Bridge to   Additional Workflows
                                                                              Fireworks to Dreamweaver

4. In the Property inspector, enter the following values:

- **Width: 172**
- **Height: 89**
- **X: 728**
- **Y: 180**
- **Fill color: None**
- **Stroke color: #56617F** (same as off-state tabs)
- **Stroke style: Pencil ▶ 1-Pixel Hard**

Fireworks provides a wide range of stroke styles. The 1-Pixel Hard style (Figure 4-15) most closely resembles a CSS defined 1-pixel solid border. Now you can use the Rectangle tool to add a thicker top border.

FIGURE 4-15

5. From the **Tools** palette, select the **Rectangle** tool. Drag out a rectangle the same width as the just-drawn horizontal line and approximately **25 pixels** high. In the Property inspector, enter these values:

- **Width: 171**
- **Height: 25**
- **X: 729**
- **Y: 179**
- **Fill color: #5476CC**
- **Stroke color: None**

With the parts of this graphic element now on the page, you can make it easy to rapidly duplicate the combined items.

6. Press **Shift** and select both the rectangle and the drawn lines. Choose **Modify ▶ Group**.

   Notice that in the Layers panel, the separate objects are now grouped (Figure 4-16). Now, quickly make three duplicates.

FIGURE 4-16

7. Press **Alt** (Windows) or **Option** (Mac) and drag out a duplicate of the grouped item. Repeat this operation twice more until there are a total of four rectangle and line groups.

8. Select the last of the groups and set the **X** value to **728** and **Y** to **629**.

9. Press **Shift** and select the other three groups. From the **Align** panel, click **Align Right Edge** and **Distribute Vertical Centers**.

10. Choose **File ▶ Save** to store your page.

At this point, you have most of the major graphic elements on the page (Figure 4-17). In the next series of steps, you begin to add design flourishes to make the comp stand out.

114 PART 01 PART 02 PART 03 PART 04 APPENDIX

Photoshop to Dreamweaver   Fireworks to Dreamweaver   Flash to Dreamweaver   Photoshop to Bridge to Fireworks to Dreamweaver   Additional Workflows

FIGURE 4-17

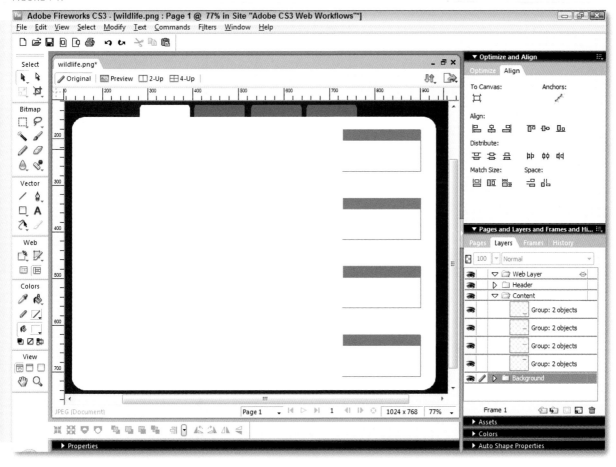

INTEGRATING GRADIENTS

Gradients are wonderful for adding depth to a graphic or breaking up a flat expanse of color. Fireworks's rich gradient implementation offers a wide range of preset options with complete flexibility for easy customization. In this exercise, you add a gradient to the top header area to serve as a highlight, which with the help of Fireworks's Fade Image command blends seamlessly into the background.

1. In the **Layers** panel, select **Background**. Select the **Rectangle** tool from the Tools palette.

    Although you could add a gradient fill to a selection as you do in Photoshop, I find working with vector objects to be much easier and more manageable.

CREATING WITH VECTORS

Fireworks's vector tools make it possible to draw illustrations that scale up or down without degradation, can be easily modified, and always remain editable. The vector creation tools include the following:

- **Pen**—For drawing precise lines or bezier curves. Drawn paths can be open or closed.

- **Rectangle**—For drawing rectangular or square paths. Press Shift while drawing to create square shapes.

- **Oval**—For drawing oval or circular paths. Press Shift while drawing to create circular shapes.

- **Freeform path**—For drawing freehand paths with the mouse or tablet pen.

- **Line**—For drawing straight lines; press **Shift** to constrain your paths to 45-degree increments.

Once the vector is on the page, Fireworks provides a slew of tools for modifying the path.

- **Subselection**—A partner to the Pointer tool, the Subselection tool allows you to alter paths on a point-by-point basis.

- **Redraw path**—Changes the selected path to include any paths drawn by the mouse or tablet pen.

- **Knife**—Cuts a path into separate sections.

- **Reshape area**—Pushes the existing path into new directions.

- **Path scrubber**—Alters the appearance of a path's stroke properties, such as stroke size, ink amount, hue, lightness, and saturation.

Finally, Fireworks also includes a variety of commands for working with one or more paths such as Join, Crop, or Simplify. The vector commands are found in the **Modify ▶ Combine Paths** and **Modify ▶ Alter Path** submenus.

116 | PART **01** | PART **02**  | PART **03** | PART **04** | APPENDIX

Photoshop to Dreamweaver | Fireworks to Dreamweaver | Flash to Dreamweaver | Photoshop to Bridge to Fireworks to Dreamweaver | Additional Workflows

2. Drag out a rectangle at the top of the page approximately **400** pixels wide by **150** pixels tall. The bottom of the rectangle should not overlap the wide content rectangle.

3. In the Property inspector, set the following values:

   - **Width: 400**

   - **Height: 149**

   - **X: 100**

   - **Y: 0**

   - **Fill color: #5476CC**

   - **Stroke color: None**

   The new rectangle appears behind the tabs because it was placed in the Background layer (Figure 4-18).

   Now, you can change the fill to a gradient.

FIGURE 4-18

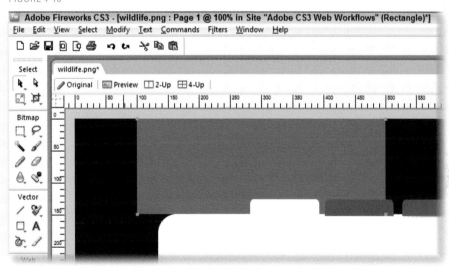

4. From the **Fill** style list in the Property inspector, select **Gradient ▶ Linear**.

   A default gradient color scheme is applied; take note of the gradient handle that appears in the rectangle—you use that later for positioning the gradient.

   Now, it's time to set up the proper colors and transparencies.

5. Click the **Solid color** swatch When the **Edit Gradient** pop-up window appears, leave the far left color swatch black and click the far right one: change its hexadecimal value to **#000064**. At approximately one-third from the left, click below the gradient ramp to add a third color swatch; click it and enter **#464FF** as its value. Add a fourth color swatch at the two-thirds position and in its hexadecimal field enter **#464FF** (Figure 4-19).

FIGURE 4-19

This gives a nice splash of color to the header area, but you have to use transparencies to integrate it better.

6. If necessary, click the **Fill** color swatch again to display the **Edit Gradient** pop-up window. Click the **opacity swatch** on the far left, above the gradient ramp, and change the value to **0**. Repeat the operation with the opacity swatch on the far right. Add a third opacity swatch to the middle and set its value to **75**. Click anywhere outside of the Edit Gradient pop-up window to confirm the change.

Now the color gradient fades in nicely, but is still too obvious. To deal with this you can change the direction.

7. Drag the top of the fill handle (with the white circle) to the top left of the rectangle. Drag the bottom of the fill handle to the top of the first tab in the middle (Figure 4-20).

FIGURE 4-20

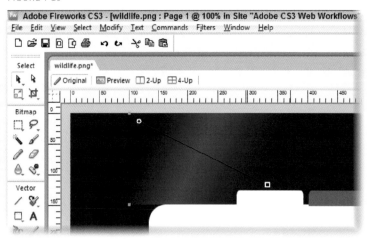

PART **01**
PART **02**
PART **03**
PART **04**
APPENDIX

Photoshop to Dreamweaver   Fireworks to Dreamweaver   Flash to Dreamweaver   Photoshop to Bridge to Fireworks to Dreamweaver   Additional Workflows

With the fill handle, you can modify the direction and length of the gradient range however you like.

Next, you can remove the hard edges of the gradient rectangle by adding a mask to fade it in.

To rotate the handle without changing its length, place your cursor to one side of the handle until you see the rotation symbol and drag in the desired direction.

8. Choose **Commands ▶ Creative ▶ Fade Image**. When the **Fade Image** dialog opens, select the top-to-bottom fade on the top row, all the way to the right (Figure 4-21). Click **OK**.

FIGURE 4-21

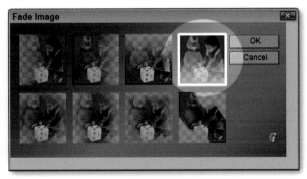

With one command, Fireworks creates another rectangle in the same size and shape of the selected image, fills it with a black-to-white gradient in the chosen direction, and then groups the two images as a mask.

Finally, one more bit of fine-tuning is needed to complete the gradient integration.

9. Drag the top of the fill handle until it is near the top of the document and centered over the first tab. Drag the bottom of the fill handle just above the top-left corner of the white content rectangle (Figure 4-22).

APPLYING GRADIENTS

Gradients are a special type of fill in Fireworks that can be applied to any selection or closed path. There are two methods for applying a gradient fill:

- **Gradient tool**—The Gradient tool is grouped with the Paint Bucket on the Tools panel. The Gradient tool Property inspector includes options for varying the edge (Hard, Anti-Alias, or Feather) or adding texture.

- **Fill style**—From the Fill style list on the Property inspector, choose Gradient to display any of the 12 gradient presets.

A gradient's color progression can incorporate both a range of colors and opacities. Set these options by clicking the Fill color swatch to reveal the Edit Gradient pop-up window.

Once a gradient has been applied to a vector (bitmap gradients must be redrawn), the direction and length of it can be adjusted by moving the fill handle; some gradient fill presets (such as Rectangle, Ellipse, and Starburst) have multiple handles.

Once created, gradients can be stored by creating a new style from the Styles panel.

FIGURE 4-22

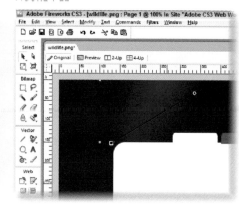

The gradient should now appear like a ray of bright blue light slicing through the dark blue background.

10. Choose **File ▶ Save**.

In next series of steps, you learn how to add bitmapped images to your Fireworks design.

INTEGRATING BITMAPPED IMAGES

Many sites incorporate bitmapped images, whether from stock or custom photography. Fireworks is well equipped to handle bitmapped images, whether they need to be cropped, rescaled, flipped, or color-adjusted. You can also remove images from their background through a variety of methods, as you see in this exercise.

1. In Fireworks, choose **File ▶ Open**. Navigate to the **Chapter 4** exercise folder and choose **source ▶ polar_bear.jpg** (Figure 4-23).

PART 01
Photoshop to Dreamweaver

PART 02
Fireworks to Dreamweaver

PART 03
Flash to Dreamweaver

PART 04
Photoshop to Bridge to Fireworks to Dreamweaver

APPENDIX
Additional Workflows

FIGURE 4-23

You need to extract the polar bear from its background, crop it, and rescale it before incorporating it in the comp.

2. Choose the **Magic Wand** tool, the second icon on the left in the Bitmap group, from the **Tools** panel. In the Property inspector, keep the default settings of **Tolerance: 32** and **Edge: Anti-Alias**.

   Because the large expanse of water surrounding the polar bear is a similar color range, the Magic Wand is a good first choice for removing the background.

3. Click the **Magic Wand** in the water above the bear. Press **Shift** and click the Magic Wand in the color area between the bear's legs twice more. Press **Delete** to remove the selection. Choose **Select ▶ Deselect**.

   While the water is quickly removed (Figure 4-24), the ground takes a little more effort. For this scenario, the Eraser tool serves to eliminate the background and smooth out the bear's silhouette.

FIGURE 4-24

4. From the **Tools** panel, choose the **Eraser** tool, the third tool on the right in the Bitmap group. Carefully begin to erase the visible ground by dragging the Eraser tool over the area. Press **Ctrl+=** (Windows) or **Cmd+=** (Mac) to zoom in as needed. When you've removed the ground, use the Eraser tool to remove any stray pixels around the polar bear (Figure 4-25).

FIGURE 4-25

I've found that it's best to use short strokes with the Eraser tool. You can control your efforts better, and—best of all—if you make a mistake and have to undo it, you don't lose a lot of work.

Now, you need to rescale the image to fit on the page.

5. Choose **Modify ▶ Transform ▶ Numeric Transform**. When the **Numeric Transform** dialog box opens, choose **Resize** from the list and set the Width value to **143** pixels. Click **OK**.

Fireworks automatically maintains the width to height ratio.

So, all that's left to do with this image is to trim the canvas.

6. Click anywhere outside of the canvas to display the Document Property inspector. Click **Fit Canvas** (Figure 4-26).

FIGURE 4-26

PART **01**   PART **02**   PART **03**   PART **04**   APPENDIX

Photoshop to Dreamweaver   Fireworks to Dreamweaver   Flash to Dreamweaver   Photoshop to Bridge to Fireworks to Dreamweaver   Additional Workflows

The Fit Canvas command reduces the size of the document to the current visible objects, or, if necessary, expands it.

You can bring your image over now.

7. Choose **File ▶ Save** to store the image for future use. Select the polar bear graphic and choose **Edit ▶ Copy**.

8. Switch to **wildlife.png** and, in the Layers panel, select **Header**. Choose **Edit ▶ Paste**; when Fireworks asks if you'd like to resample the image, click **Don't Resample**. Drag the polar bear into position above the white content rectangle and to the left of the first tab (Figure 4-27).

FIGURE 4-27

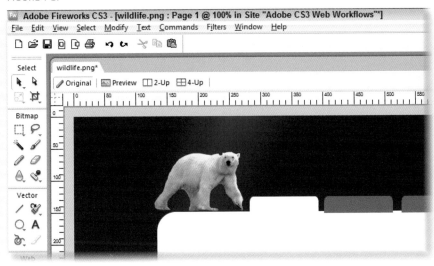

9. Choose **File ▶ Save**.

Fireworks offers a number of other methods for incorporating bitmapped images. The following series of steps uses another technique to bring an image into the content area.

1. From the **Layers** panel, choose **Content**. Choose **File ▶ Import**. When the **Import** dialog box appears, navigate to the **Chapter 4 ▶ source** folder and select **hand_fish.jpg**. Click **Open**.

    Fireworks is capable of importing graphics in a wide spectrum of image formats including JPEG, GIF, PNG, PICT, TIF, and PSD.

2. Position the import cursor in the middle of the white tab and the top of the first sidebar highlight box; click once to place the image (Figure 4-28)

FIGURE 2-28

Once imported, you can easily reposition the graphic by dragging it or through the Property inspector.

3. In the Property inspector, change the **X** value to **338** and press **Enter** (Windows) or **Return** (Mac). Change the **Y** value to **180**.

Next you can add a fade to the image to integrate it better into the page.

4. Choose **Commands ▶ Creative ▶ Fade Image**. When the **Fade Image** dialog box appears, choose the **right to left** fade, the first icon in the top row. Click **OK**.

The final step is to adjust the fill handle to limit the fade to the left edge.

PART 01   PART 02   PART 03   PART 04   APPENDIX

Photoshop to Dreamweaver   Fireworks to Dreamweaver   Flash to Dreamweaver   Photoshop to Bridge to Fireworks to Dreamweaver   Additional Workflows

5. Drag the square corner of the fill handle until it is about 50 pixels from the left edge of the image (Figure 4-29).

FIGURE 4-29

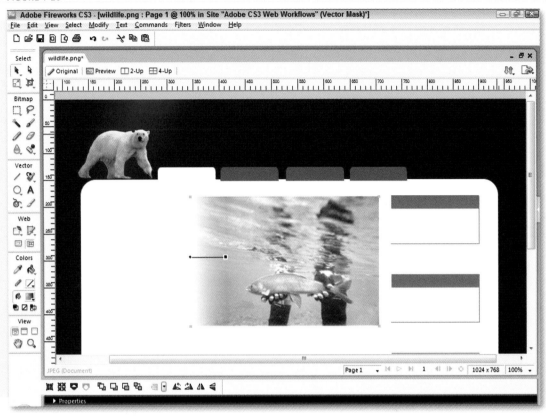

NOTE

To reveal the fill handle for adjusting gradients with a faded image, click the mask element in the Layers panel object.

6. Choose **File ▶ Save**.

With the practical experience of inserting images in the two techniques covered in this chapter—and additional methods noted in the Core Techniques sidebar entitled "Inserting Images"—you will be able to bring images into your compositions through a variety of workflows.

Fw CORE TECHNIQUES

INSERTING IMAGES

Bitmapped images are easily brought into Fireworks documents in a number of ways. They can be imported (**File ▶ Import**), pasted in from the clipboard, dragged into the document from the desktop, or inserted from Adobe Bridge (**File ▶ Browse**).

Once the images are inserted, Fireworks has a full slate of tools and commands with which they can be modified. The Bitmap group of the Tools panel includes the following:

- **Selection tools**—Marquee, Oval Marquee, Lasso, Polygon Lasso, and Magic Wand

- **Creation tools**—Brush and Pencil

- **Modification tools**—Eraser, Blur, Sharpen, Dodge, Burn, Smudge, Rubber Stamp, Replace Color, and Red Eye Removal

A specialized panel, Image Editing, contains all the Fireworks bitmap commands in a single location:

- **Transform tools**—Scale, Skew, Distort, and Free Rotate

- **Transform commands**—Numeric Transform, Rotate, Flip, and Remove Transformations

- **Adjust colors**—Auto Levels, Brightness/Contrast, Curves, Hue/Saturation, Invert, Levels, Convert to Grayscale, and Convert to Sepia

- **Filters**—Blur, Sharpen, Unsharpen Mask, Add Noise, Convert to Alpha, and Find Edges

- **View options**—Rulers, Grid, and Guide controls

Access the Image Editing panel by choosing **Window ▶ Others ▶ Image Editing**. One note of caution: The tools on the Image Editing panel permanently modify the bitmaps, and the effect cannot be undone once the file is saved and closed. For continued editability, use the Live Filters available from the Property inspector.

126 PART **01** PART **02** PART **03** PART **04** APPENDIX

Photoshop to Dreamweaver   Fireworks to Dreamweaver   Flash to Dreamweaver   Photoshop to Bridge to   Additional Workflows
                                                                                 Fireworks to Dreamweaver

Hopefully, this chapter has given you a good grounding in the powerful and flexible design functionality of vectors in Fireworks. Vectors offer a high degree of precision that you can always modify—a not uncommon occurrence, even after you've exported your work to Dreamweaver. It's comforting to know that you can always come back to your Fireworks source file and change shapes, gradients, and more without redoing everything from the ground up.

In the next chapter, you'll complete the initial comp in Fireworks and add text and effects to the page. You'll also learn how to expand the comp to multiple pages and make it interactive for client approval.

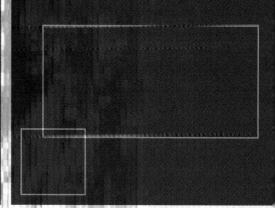

One Web page does not a site make—something Adobe Fireworks CS3 understands very well. When a designer comps a site, that designer needs to consider the paths taken by typical visitors and the interactivity needed to get there. Fireworks is a sophisticated graphics engine, finely tuned to create both Web-ready graphics and fully interactive Web-oriented comps that allow the client to experience the feel of the site—as well as the look—before any code is written.

This chapter focuses on setting up your graphics in Fireworks to be properly implemented by Dreamweaver (covered in Chapter 6). Here, you'll run the gamut from working with Fireworks text all the way to outputting a client-viewable comp. The core techniques covered include:

- Incorporating text
- Applying live filters
- Setting up interactive comps

CHAPTER

05

COMPING MULTIPAGE SITES

WORKING WITH TEXT

Fireworks is right at home when inserting and manipulating text, whether it is for building a logo or adding labels to navigation buttons or content to a page. When entered manually, Fireworks text can be inserted in a line-by-line free-form fashion or into a drawn-out text box. The full range of text controls is available, from font stylings to path attachment.

In the following sections, you have an opportunity to work with text in a number of ways, starting with a logo.

CREATING LOGOS AND DISPLAY TEXT

Logos don't have to be elaborate. Sometimes a simple line of type with a few variations can be quite effective.

1. From the **Layers** panel, select **Header**.

2. Choose the **Text** tool, the second icon on the right in the Vector group of the **Tools** panel.

   When inserting text, you can either predetermine font properties or apply them to entered text. For single lines of text, I like to start with the basic attributes such as font, size, and color already defined.

3. In the Property inspector, choose **Arial Narrow** or an equivalent typeface from the **Font** list and enter **38** in the **Size** field. From the **Color swatch**, choose **white** (Figure 5-1).

FIGURE 5-1

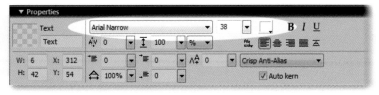

With a simple line of text, you can just click on the document and start typing.

4. Place your cursor to the right of the polar bear near the vertical middle of the header area and enter **wild life vacation adventures**.

Now you can make the text stand out a bit more.

5. Select the phrase **wild life** and, in the Property inspector, click **Bold**. Choose **Select ▶ Select All** and set the **Kerning** value to **18**. Choose the **Pointer** tool.

6. In the Property inspector, set the **X** value to **330** and the **Y** value to **45** (Figure 5-2).

FIGURE 5-2

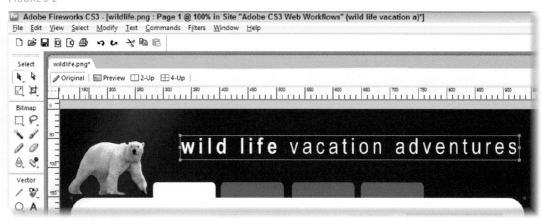

Next, you can add a bit of display text next to the primary image in the content area.

7. In the **Layers** panel, select **Content**. From the **Tools** panel, select the **Text** tool and drag out a rectangle to the left of the fish_hand image about **200 pixels** wide (Figure 5-3).

Create the rectangle so there is a margin on both its left and right side. Any text added to this rectangle constrains to this drawn out text area.

130

PART **01**
Photoshop to Dreamweaver

PART **02**
Fireworks to Dreamweaver

PART **03**
Flash to Dreamweaver

PART **04**
Photoshop to Bridge to Fireworks to Dreamweaver

APPENDIX
Additional Workflows

FIGURE 5-3

8. In the Property inspector, change the font **Size** value to **36**. Click the color swatch and then sample the dark blue canvas color. Choose **Right Alignment** and, in the drawn out text area, enter **Catch it while you Can**. If necessary, use line breaks (**Shift+Enter** on Windows or **Shift+Return** on Mac) to make sure the first and last words are on their own lines (Figure 5-4).

FIGURE 5-4

Now you can add a finishing touch and emphasize the first and last words even more.

9. Select **Catch** and, in the Property inspector, change the fonts **Size** to **48**; select **Can** and repeat. Choose **File ▶ Save**.

Display text is a clean and easy way to add varied, magazine-like touches to your comp (Figure 5-5). In the next section, you can see how to quickly add labels to each of the tabs.

FIGURE 5-5

ADDING NAVIGATION LABELS

Navigation button labels are typically one or two words, either centered or left justified in the button itself. In this comp, you need to add them in two colors: one for the white tab and another for the gray tabs.

1. From the **Layers** panel, select **Header**. Choose **New Sub Layer**, the second icon from the left on the bottom of the panel. When the new layer appears, double-click it and rename the layer **Nav**.

Because you're adding another series of objects to the comp, it's a good time to take advantage of Fireworks's hierarchical layer structure and group all of the navigation elements together.

2. Shift-select the **bottom 4 elements** in the **Header** layer group (the navigation buttons) and drag them into the **Nav** layer until the folder symbol changes to a darker color (Figure 5-6).

FIGURE 5-6

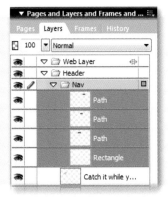

You can easily drag Fireworks objects to rearrange them in the Layers panel. A solid line indicates the position below an object, while the darker folder indicates the group to contain the object.

3. From the **Tools** panel, choose the **Text** tool.

4. Click in the middle of the white tab and, from the Property inspector, choose **Verdana** from the **Font** list and set the **Size** to **12**. Click the **Center alignment** and **Bold** options. Enter **HOME** (Figure 5-7).

FIGURE 5-7

5. In the Property inspector, change the **Color** to **#AFC6FF** and, in the middle of the first gray tab, enter **SOLO**. Click in the middle of the second gray tab and enter **GROUPS**. Click in the middle of the final tab and enter **CONTACT**.

Now, it's time to do a little cleanup to make sure everything is aligned correctly.

6. Choose the **Pointer** tool. Click the **first gray tab**, press **Shift**, and select the text **SOLO**. From the **Align** panel, choose **Align horizontal center** and **Align vertical center**. Repeat with each of the two remaining gray tabs. Select the **white tab** and the text **HOME** and, from the Align panel, choose **Align horizontal center** (Figure 5-8).

FIGURE 5-8

Because the white tab is taller than the gray tabs, you can't align the center vertically. However, you can use the other text objects to make sure all are lined up properly.

7. Shift-select **HOME** and **SOLO**. If SOLO is higher than HOME, choose **Align top edges** from the Align panel; otherwise, choose **Align bottom edges** (Figure 5-9).

8. Choose **File ▶ Save**.

FIGURE 5-9

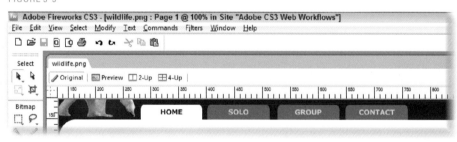

134 PART **01** PART **02** PART **03** PART **04** APPENDIX

Photoshop to Dreamweaver   Fireworks to Dreamweaver   Flash to Dreamweaver   Photoshop to Bridge to   Additional Workflows
                                                                                   Fireworks to Dreamweaver

It's a good idea to make your comp as complete as possible, and real-world navigation terms go a long way toward achieving that goal. The alternate color choice that indicates the current page adds to the completeness of the comp, as does the cleanliness brought by selective use of the Align panel.

In the next exercise, you add placeholder text to fill out the comp.

INCLUDING SIDEBAR PLACEHOLDER CONTENT

This particular comp includes placeholder content in two places: along the sidebar in each of the individual pods and in the main content area. Both areas are restricted in both height and width—just perfect to use of Fireworks's text area feature.

Tackle the sidebar text first, which comprises both a heading and a bit of body text. You may recall that the last time you worked on the sidebar in Chapter 4, you grouped each of the four elements to align them properly. Because you're going to be aligning text with a portion of each pod during these series of steps, your first action is to ungroup the elements.

1. Shift-select each of the four sidebar elements. Choose **Modify ▶ Ungroup**.

   Many Fireworks commands, such as ungrouping, can be applied to multiple selected objects, which results in faster comp development.

2. From the **Tools** panel, select the **Text** tool.

3. In the Property inspector, choose **Arial** from the **Font** list, **12** from the **Size** list, **white** from the **Color swatch**, and toggle **Bold** on (Figure 5-10).

   FIGURE 5-10

4. Place your cursor approximately 10 pixels in the blue rectangle of the first sidebar element and enter **Special deal**.

5. From the **Tools** panel, select the **Pointer** tool.

6. Shift select the text object and the associated blue rectangle. From the Align panel, choose **Align vertical center** (Figure 5-11).

FIGURE 5-11

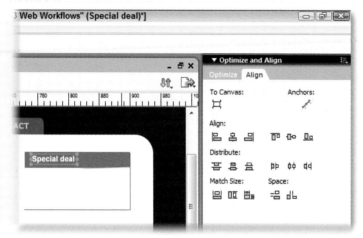

Now you can duplicate the same text for each of the remaining sidebar elements.

7. Click anywhere to clear the selection and then select the **Special deal** text object. Choose **Edit ▶ Duplicate** and drag the new copy into position in the second sidebar element. Repeat this step twice more to create text headings for the last two elements.

8. Repeat step 6 for each of the text and blue rectangle pairs to align them correctly.

   Your headings are all in place—now it's time to add the body text for each element.

9. From the **Tools** panel, select the **Text** tool. In the Property inspector, set the **Size** value to **11** and toggle **Bold** off. Click the **Color swatch** and sample the dark blue canvas color.

10. With the Text tool, drag a rectangle inside the top sidebar element approximately **150 pixels** wide by **50 pixels** tall. Enter the following placeholder text: **Lorem ipsum dolor sit amet, consectetuer adipiscing elit, sed diam nonummy nibh euismod tincidunt** (Figure 5-12).

136   PART **01**   PART **02**   PART **03**   PART **04**   APPENDIX

Photoshop to Dreamweaver   Fireworks to Dreamweaver   Flash to Dreamweaver   Photoshop to Bridge to Fireworks to Dreamweaver   Additional Workflows

FIGURE 5-12

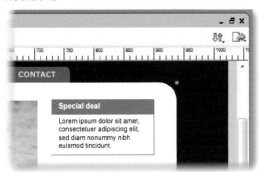

NOTE

Another rapid development technique for duplicating elements is to choose Edit ▶ Clone. This creates a duplicate object in the exact same position as the original. To then move that duplicate object into position, you can use the arrow keys to move it horizontally or vertically; press Shift to move the cloned object in 10-pixel increments.

11. Duplicate the just-entered text block for each of the remaining three sidebar elements.

12. Choose **File ▶ Save**.

Your sidebar text is now complete. However, before moving on to the main content area text, you can add a little flair to the sidebar elements. And, as part of the process, I'll show you another Fireworks technique for quickly replicating effects.

1. Select the solid blue rectangle in the first sidebar element.

In this series of steps, you add a gradient to the sidebar elements that echoes the one applied to the header.

2. From the Property inspector **Fill** list, choose **Gradient ▶ Satin**.

3. Click the Color swatch to display the **Edit Gradient** pop-up window. Click the left color swatch and change the hexadecimal field to **#4646FF**; press **Enter** (Windows) or **Return** (Mac) to confirm. Click the right color swatch and sample the dark blue canvas color (#**000064**); again, press **Enter** (Windows) or **Return** (Mac) (Figure 5-13).

FIGURE 5-13

Now it's time to adjust the fill handle so that the satin effect is seen only in one portion of the blue rectangle.

4. Drag the left fill handle so that it is in front of the left edge of the blue rectangle. Extend the right fill handle to below the bottom edge almost to the end (Figure 5-14).

FIGURE 5-14

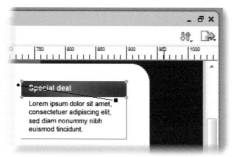

Now that you've got the gradient just the way you want it, you can apply it to the other sidebar elements through a specialized Fireworks copy-and-paste procedure.

5. With the top sidebar rectangle selected, choose **Edit ▶ Copy**. Shift-select the three other sidebar rectangles and choose **Edit ▶ Paste Attributes**.

The Paste Attributes command paints the selection (or selections) with whatever attributes—including fill and stroke color, effects, and opacity—found in the copied object.

6. Choose **File ▶ Save**.

The complete sidebar gives the client a much clearer picture of how the page can be used without getting bogged down in details. The use of specific Web-safe fonts, in this case Arial, for the header and sidebar elements make it easy to get the exact appearance in Dreamweaver when the comp is converted to a Web page.

In the next exercise, you flesh out the main content text area.

COMPING MAIN CONTENT TEXT

The primary text content in a Web page is a combination of one or more heading tags and series of paragraphs. The Fireworks text tool makes it easy to implement both and offers fine control over attributes like line height and kerning.

138
PART 01 PART 02 PART 03 PART 04 APPENDIX

Photoshop to Dreamweaver   Fireworks to Dreamweaver   Flash to Dreamweaver   Photoshop to Bridge to   Additional Workflows
                                                                                 Fireworks to Dreamweaver

1. From the **Tools** panel, select the **Text** tool. In the Property inspector, set the Font to Arial, the Size to **18** and color to **#425DA1**. Make sure **Bold** is toggled off.

   You can start with the h1 text.

2. Click in the content area underneath the fish_hand picture, about 20 pixels from the left edge of the white content area and enter **Major heading goes here** (Figure 5-15).

FIGURE 5-15

To replicate the effect of a bottom border, you need to use the line tool.

3. From the **Tools** panel, choose the **Line** tool. From the Property inspector, click the **Stroke color swatch** and enter **#425DA1** as the hexadecimal value. In the **Size** field, enter **2** and, from the **Stroke category** list, choose **Pencil ▶ 1-Pixel Hard**.

4. Press **Shift** to constrain the line and draw a line underneath heading text across the width of the content area, approximately **550 pixels** (Figure 5-16).

FIGURE 5-16

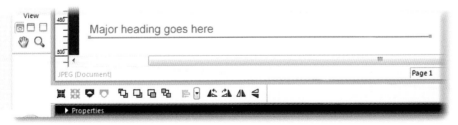

Now you can bring in the first paragraph of text. A text file has been included in the exercise files for you to import.

5. Select **File ▶ Import**. When the **Import** dialog box appears, navigate to the Chapter 5 exercise folder and select **Lorem ipsum.txt**; click **OK**.

6. Position your cursor underneath the heading text on the left and click once (Figure 5-17).

FIGURE 5-17

7. With the imported text object selected, drag the center sizing handle on the right to the right edge of the line.

   You don't need to switch to the Pointer tool to make adjustments to the text bounding box. When you hover over any of the nine sizing handles, your cursor changes to a white pointer, and you can drag the handles however you'd like.

8. In the Property inspector, set the **Font** list to **Arial** and **Size** to **12**, with a **Color** of **#000064** (the canvas color). Change the **Leading** to **150%** to achieve a less condensed paragraph (Figure 5-18).

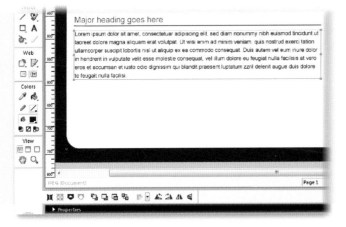

FIGURE 5-18

You can easily mix text with different properties in the same text area. So you can see that in action, you can use that facility to insert a subheading and more body copy.

9. Place your cursor at the end of the imported text and press **Enter** (Windows) or **Return** (Mac) twice. In the Property inspector, change **Size** to **14**, the **Color** value to **#425DA1** and toggle **Bold** on. Enter **Subheading goes here** and press **Enter** (Windows) or **Return** (Mac).

10. Select the first three lines of the body text and press **Ctrl+C** (Windows) or **Cmd+C** (Mac). Position your cursor in the line beneath the subheading and set the **Size** to **12**, with a **Color** of **#000064** and the **Bold** toggled off. Press **Ctrl+V** (Windows) or **Cmd+V** (Mac).

The final text element is now in place (Figure 5-19).

FIGURE 5-19

Fw CORE TECHNIQUES

INCORPORATING TEXT

Text is easily inserted into any Fireworks document and always remains modifiable. Text properties are set through the Property inspector, which can be preset before the content is entered or applied to a selected text object.

Fireworks has two methods for inserting text:

- **Free-form entry**—With the Text tool selected, click anywhere on the document to enter your content. The text area continues to expand horizontally until the edge of the document is reached and then wraps.

- **Text box entry**—When the Text tool is used to drag out a rectangle, text entered content is constrained to the width of the shape and expands vertically as needed.

Once on the page, text can be manipulated like any other object. Any effect can be applied to a text object, and text objects can be used as masks to display imagery within the lettering. Moreover, text may also be attached to a path, such as a wavy line or a circle by selecting both the text object and the path object and choosing **Text ▶ Attach to Path**. Once attached, choose any of the options under **Text ▶ Orientation** to further adjust the text; the text remains editable throughout the process.

11. Choose **File ▶ Save** to store your changes.

Although you could stop work on the comp right now, Fireworks has a few more tricks up its software sleeve, as you'll learn when you begin to apply filters in the next exercise.

APPLYING LIVE FILTERS

Filters can add a realistic dimensionality to an object, such as a beveled edge or a drop shadow, or can highlight a shape with an unnatural but eye-catching enhancement, such as a glow. One of the key advantages of Fireworks *live filters* is that they are always editable after they are applied. A live filter can be temporarily disabled with the click of a checkbox, modified through a variety of parameters, or totally removed at any point, even after the Fireworks document has been saved, closed, and reopened.

Filters can also be applied directly from the menu; however, it's better to use the Property inspector. Live filters defined through the Property inspector are easily adjusted, disabled, or removed. Filters applied through the menu can only be undone shortly after they have been put into place.

142   PART **01**   PART **02**   PART **03**   PART **04**   APPENDIX

Photoshop to Dreamweaver   Fireworks to Dreamweaver   Flash to Dreamweaver   Photoshop to Bridge to Fireworks to Dreamweaver   Additional Workflows

In the following exercise, you apply two different types of glow filters to round out the look and feel of your comp.

1. If necessary, open the **wildlife.png** file and, from the Tools panel, select the **Pointer** tool.

2. In the **Layers** panel, expand the **Background** layer folder and select **Content**.

   Although it's possible to select the rounded rectangle directly in the Fireworks document, selecting through the Layers panel is more exact.

3. From the Property inspector, in the **Filters** section click **Add (+)** and choose **Shadow and Glow ▶ Inner Glow**. After the settings pop-up window appears, change the **Softness** value (the editable list on the middle right) to **6** (Figure 5-20) and click anywhere in the workspace to confirm your choice.

FIGURE 5-20

The Inner Glow filter, when you are using a dark color, provides a shadow-like effect that adds depth to the interior of any shape but works particularly well with rounded rectangles.

Now, you can add a different type of glow filter to highlight the logo text a bit more.

4. Select the logo text **wild life adventure vacations**. From the **Filters** section of the Property inspector, click **Add (+)** and choose **Shadow and Glow ▶ Glow**. After the settings pop-up appears, click anywhere to accept the default options.

   While some might like the bright red glowing letters, it's a bit blatant for my taste, so I want to tone it down a bit. As easy as live filters are to apply, it's important to know how to modify them—and that's the purpose of this particular exercise.

5. Select the logo text and, in the Filters area, click **Info** in **Glow** entry. When the settings pop-up window reappears, change the **Width** to **3**, the **Softness** to **20** and the **Color** to **#4646FF**. Click anywhere in the workspace to confirm your modifications (Figure 5-21).

Fw CORE TECHNIQUES

APPLYING LIVE FILTERS

Live filters provide a robust method of modifying any image in Fireworks. Any filter in Fireworks can be applied to any vector or bitmapped object. Once applied, the filter can be changed, disabled, or removed at any time. Multiple filters can be applied to the same object, and the order in which the filters are executed can also be adjusted.

To apply a filter, select the object and, in the Property inspector, click Add in the Filters area. The primary filters menu groups include:

- **Adjust Color**—Set brightness/contrast, hue/saturation, fill color, levels, curves, and more color-related values.

- **Bevel and Emboss**—Add inner and outer bevels or insert raised embossing. Embossed objects can also be knocked out for a silhouette effect.

- **Blur**—Includes a variety of blur effects: standard (blur and blur more), Gaussian, radial, motion, and zoom blurs.

- **Noise**—Allows you to add a set degree of noise—colored or not—to any object.

- **Other**—Two miscellaneous filters, Convert to Alpha and Find Edges; neither of these filters offer any user-definable settings.

- **Shadow and Glow**—Adds dimensionality or emphasis to an object: drop shadow, inner shadow, solid shadow, glow, inner glow.

- **Sharpen**—Filters primarily used with bitmapped images: Sharpen, Sharpen More, and Unsharp Mask.

- **Photoshop Live Effects**—These filters replicate effects created in Photoshop and are automatically applied when needed with PSD imported files. The full range of Photoshop Layer Effects are available and are also supported by Photoshop if the file is brought back to Photoshop.

Filters can be disabled individually by toggling the check mark next to an entry in the Filters area or all at once through the Options menu. Additional third-party filters (either Fireworks-specific or compatible with Photoshop 5 and below) can be integrated with Fireworks by installing them in the Photoshop Plug-in directory specified in Preferences.

144

PART **01**
Photoshop to Dreamweaver

PART **02**

Fireworks to Dreamweaver

PART **03**
Flash to Dreamweaver

PART **04**

Photoshop to Bridge to
Fireworks to Dreamweaver

APPENDIX
Additional Workflows

FIGURE 5-21

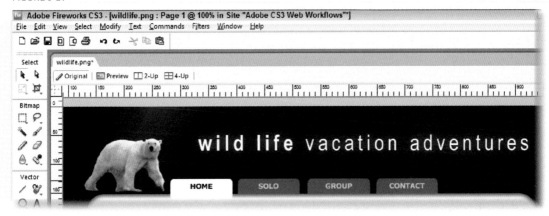

6. Save your page.

Congratulations! You've completed your first page comp in Fireworks. Next, you'll learn how to leverage your work to depict a more complete vision of the entire Web site.

ADDING PAGES

Fireworks offers a number of ways for you to include multiple views in a single document. To make it possible to design and edit animated GIFs, Fireworks supports frames; frames, however, share the same Web layer and are not truly appropriate for editing unique sections in a site. Fireworks's Pages feature, on the other hand, allows for completely different size canvases—so your homepage comp can be different from the designs for the rest of the site—as well individual image slicing.

CREATING A MASTER PAGE

Fireworks makes it possible to share common elements across all pages through its master page implementation; any changes made to the master page are instantly applied to all other pages in the document. In this exercise, you set up a master page and create two more pages based on the previous comp.

1. If necessary, open the **wildlife.png** file and, from the Tools panel, select the **Pointer** tool.

   You need to set up the master page first.

2. Choose **Window ▶ Pages**. In the **Pages** panel, click **New/Duplicate Page**, the first icon at the bottom of the panel (Figure 5-22).

FIGURE 5-22

The new blank page is added with the current canvas color. Next, you can rename it and set it as the master page.

3. Double-click the **Page 2** entry and, when the **Page Name** dialog box appears, change the name to **Main**. From the **Options** menu, choose **Set as Master Page**.

The new page is moved to the top of the Pages panel and designated as a master page.

Now it's time to add some content.

4. Click **Page 1** and switch to the **Layers** panel. Select the Background layer folder and choose **Edit ▶ Cut**.

The Background layer contains the rounded rectangle as well as the gradient highlight in the top of the comp. At the moment, your comp appears broken with missing elements—a situation you remedy in the next step.

5. From the Page list located in the bottom of the document window, choose **Main**. In the Layers panel, double-click **Layer 1** and rename it to **Background 1**. Press **Ctrl+V** (Windows) or **Cmd+V** (Mac) to paste the copied objects. From the **Page** list, choose **Page 1**.

Note that your page is back to normal by all appearances, however, there is a new item in the Layers panel: the Master Page layer. If you try to alter any of the items contained in this layer, you'll notice immediately that they are locked and unchangeable on any page but the master.

Now you can move one more common element over: the logo text.

6. Select the text **wild life vacation adventures** and choose **Edit ▶ Cut**. From the **Page** list, choose **Main**; in the **Layers** panel, click **New/Duplicate Layer** and rename it to **Header 1**. Press **Ctrl+V** (Windows) or **Cmd+V** (Mac).

The master page now has all the elements to a range of pages (Figure 5-23). If the name of the company or, more likely, the treatment of the logo ever change, you can make your modifications on the master page and instantly all the page comps are updated.

FIGURE 5-23

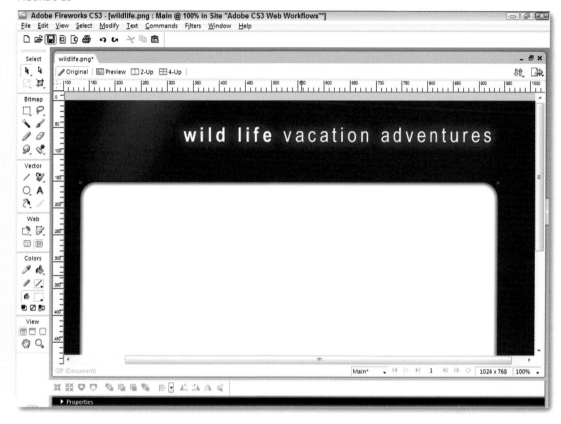

7. Save your page.

Now you're ready to create some new pages to fill out the site comp.

BUILDING NEW PAGES

In this exercise, you create the Solo and Group pages noted in the navigation. Because many of the elements remain the same from the initial page, the quickest technique is to copy the page. Once the page has been copied, you can implement any necessary changes to make each new page unique.

1. Make sure you have the **Pointer** tool selected. In the **Pages** panel, drag **Page 1** to the **New/Duplicate Page** icon. When Page 2 is created, select it.

   This technique creates an exact duplicate of a page, including the Master Page layer. There are four elements you can easily change for this new page: the navigation tabs, the two images, and the display text. For this example, you can adjust the tabs first.

2. Select the gray tab behind the text Solo. Note the **X** value in the Property inspector (in my design, it's 402) and choose **Edit ▶ Cut**. Select the white tab, note its X value (in mine, 282) and change the current X value to that of the Solo tab. Next choose **Edit ▶ Paste** and change the X value of gray tab to that of the white tab (Figure 5-24).

FIGURE 5-24

   Basically, you're just swapping one tab for another. Now, you just have to swap the text colors as well.

3. Select the **Home** text object and, in the Property inspector change the **Color** to **#AFC6FF**. Select the **Solo** text object and sample the dark canvas color, **#000064**.

   Now, it's time to change the primary images on the page.

148   PART **01**   PART **02**   PART **03**   PART **04**   APPENDIX

Photoshop to Dreamweaver   Fireworks to Dreamweaver   Flash to Dreamweaver   Photoshop to Bridge to   Additional Workflows
                                                                                     Fireworks to Dreamweaver

4. Select the polar bear image and delete it. Choose **File ▶ Import** and navigate to the **Chapter 5** exercise folder and select **seahorse.png**. Place the imported image above the tabs to the left of the logo text (Figure 5-25).

FIGURE 5-25

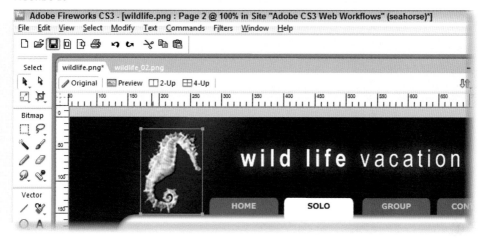

Now you have one last image to swap—and you'll want to make sure it's in the same place.

5. Select the **fish_hand** image and note its X and Y values; when you're ready, delete it. Choose **File ▶ Import** and, from the **Chapter 5** folder, select **solo.jpg**. Place the image in the same approximate position and then change the X and Y values to match the original graphic.

   Here's a neat trick you can use if you forget the exact position of the previous image: Just switch to Page 1, select the graphic, and review. This technique is especially useful when you're trying to line up elements across pages.

   Unfortunately, there's no way to replace the image and maintain the fade effect, so you have to recreate it.

6. With the new image selected, choose **Commands ▶ Creative ▶ Fade Image**. When the **Fade Image** dialog box appears, choose the **right to left** fade, the first icon in the top row. Click **OK**. After the dialog box closes, drag the square corner of the fill handle until it is about 50 pixels from the left edge of the image panel (Figure 5-26).

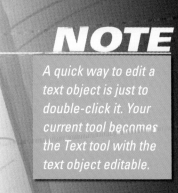
FIGURE 5-26

Now you have just one last task to complete the transformation of this page: modifying the display text.

7. From the Tools panel, select the **Text** tool. Click into the display text object and change the existing text to **Home Alone**, all in the larger font size.

Page 2 is now complete (Figure 5-27).

FIGURE 5-27

8. Save your page.

PART **01**   PART **02**   PART **03**   PART **04**   APPENDIX

Photoshop to Dreamweaver   Fireworks to Dreamweaver   Flash to Dreamweaver   Photoshop to Bridge to Fireworks to Dreamweaver   Additional Workflows

Ready for a challenge? You can apply the same basic steps in this exercise to create a third page. Here are the primary actions you need to accomplish:

- Duplicate Page 2 to create **Page 3**.

- Swap the gray tab behind Group with the white tab.

- Change the text colors of both Solo and Group, so that Group has the darker canvas color and Solo's color matches that of the other tabs.

- Replace the seahorse image with **penguin.png**.

- Delete the solo image and import **group.jpg**; apply and adjust the Fade Image command.

- Change the display text to **All aboard that's going Aboard**, with the larger text emphasis on the first and last words.

When you're done, you'll have a third completed page (Figure 5-28); an example of how the three pages should look is included in your exercise files as wildlife_3_pages.png. In the next exercise, you'll learn how to connect all the pages for an interactive, client-ready comp.

FIGURE 2-28

LINKING PAGES

Clients for Web sites are becoming increasingly sophisticated in their understanding of how the Web works and how, in particular, they want their Web site to function. Providing static, individual comps is often not enough these days; you need to give the client a sense of how the site flows and replicate to some degree the user experience. Fireworks makes it possible to quickly create just such an interactive comp.

The first step in creating an interactive comp is to establish hotspots for each of the navigation buttons.

1. From the **Pages** panel, switch to **Page 1**. Select the white tab and choose **Edit ▶ Insert ▶ Hotspot**. With the hotspot selected, from the Property inspector, choose **Page 1** from the **Link** list.

   All the pages in the document are displayed in the Link list below a dashed line separator.

2. Repeat step 1 with the second gray tab behind Solo and link to **Page 2** and again with the third gray tab behind Group and link to **Page 3** (Figure 5-29).

FIGURE 5-29

At the moment, the hotspots are applied only to Page 1. You need to take a few extra steps to share them across all pages, starting with creating a sub layer in the Web layer.

3. In the Web layer, click **New Sub Layer**, the second icon from the left at the bottom of the panel. Double-click the new sub layer and rename it **Navigation**.

   Now, it's time to place the hotspots into the sub layer.

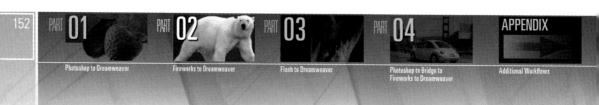

4. Shift-select the three hotspots in the Web layer and drag them into the **Navigation** sub layer (Figure 5-30)

This action can be a little tricky in Fireworks; I found it works reliably if you drag the hotspots onto the actual folder symbol in the sub layer entry.

With all of the hotspots grouped into a sub layer, you can now share them across various pages.

5. From the **Layers** panel **Options** menu, choose **Share Layers to Pages**. When the **Share Layers to Pages** dialog box opens, Shift-select **Page 2** and **Page 3** in the **Exclude layer from page(s)** column and click **Add >** to move them to the **Include layer to pages(s)** column panel (Figure 5-31). Click **OK**.

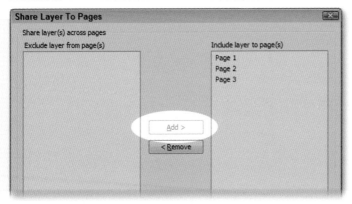

6. Choose **File ▶ Save**.

Your pages are now linked. Try it out by taking it for a test spin.

7. Choose **File ▶ Preview in Browser ▶ Preview All Pages in [your primary browser]**, where [your primary browser] is the executable for your main browser as defined in Fireworks preferences. When the first page opens in your browser, click **Solo** (Figure 5-32). After the Solo page appears, click **Group**. Finally, click **Home** to return to the first page. When you're finished previewing, close the browser and return to Fireworks.

FIGURE 5-32

Creating interactive comps goes a long way toward ensuring that you and your client are on the same page—no pun intended—regarding site navigation. As you can see from this exercise, Fireworks's capabilities in this regard are quite robust and flexible.

In the next exercise, you see how you can export your interactive comp to Dreamweaver for upload to your client's benefit.

154

PART **01**
Photoshop to Dreamweaver

PART **02**
Fireworks to Dreamweaver

PART **03**
Flash to Dreamweaver

PART **04**
Photoshop to Bridge to
Fireworks to Dreamweaver

APPENDIX
Additional Workflows

EXPORTING COMP PAGES

As satisfying as it is to preview your interactive comp on your own system, not all designers have the luxury (or the pressure) of having their clients at hand. Fireworks gives you the power to export your comped pages—complete with working links—so that you can publish them online from within Dreamweaver.

1. If necessary, open **wildlife.png**.

   At this stage, your Fireworks document has all the necessary pre-requisites for an interactive comp: a range of pages, hotspots (or slices) that link to the pages, and an established sub layer in the Web Layer folder that contains all the hotspots/slices and to which the Share Layer to Pages command has been applied.

2. Choose **File ▶ Export**. When the **Export** dialog box opens, navigate to the Dreamweaver local site root and leave the default entry in the Name field.

   It's recommended that you export your files directly to the associated Dreamweaver site; you may or may not want to create a new folder to store the files. Why do you leave the default name? Fireworks exports each page as a separate HTML file with the page name; for example Page 1 in Fireworks is exported as Page 1.htm or Page 1.html, depending on your Fireworks preferences.

3. From the **Export** list, choose **HTML and Images**. From the **HTML** list, choose **Export HTML**. Select **Export Slices** from the **Slices** list. Make sure that the **Include areas without slices** option is selected and that **Current page only** is unselected. Select the **Put images in subfolder** option and click **Save** (Figure 5-33).

FIGURE 5-33

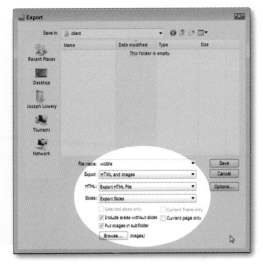

Fireworks exports each of the pages as HTML pages with a single image and the necessary code for each hotspot (also known as an image map). Each HTML page is named according to its Fireworks page name, so you end up with Page 1.htm, Page 2.htm, and Page 3.htm, as well as the master page, Main.htm. All images are stored in the images subfolder.

The next step is to publish the pages in Dreamweaver. This step assumes you have defined a remote site root in the Site Definition dialog box. A remote site may be available through FTP (File Transfer Protocol) or a networked site.

4. From Dreamweaver, choose **Window ▶ Files**. In the **Files** panel, expand the folder containing the exported pages and select all pages except Main.htm. Click **Put**, the up arrow icon at the top of the panel (Figure 5-34). When the **Dependent Files** dialog box appears and asks if you'd like to publish all dependent files, click **Yes**.

FIGURE 3 34

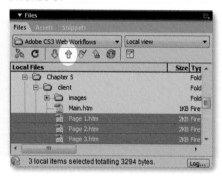

The Dependent Files feature is one of Dreamweaver's most useful. Instead of having to remember and locate every image, JavaScript file, or other file that is part of a Web page, all you need to do is select the HTML file and let Dreamweaver do all the work. If you'd prefer to do it yourself, you can disable this option in the Sites category of Dreamweaver preferences.

After Dreamweaver's Background File Activity dialog box, which represents your uploading progress, vanishes, your interactive comp is now online. After a quick test to verify everything is working correctly, you're free to contact your client and pass along the Web address to the first page.

Text, live filters, pages: Designing sites is often a balancing act. While it's important to make your comps as realistic as possible to get client sign-off, it's just as important to keep the design flexible enough to easily implement client changes. The text properties, live filters, and multiple linking page features of Fireworks help keep the balance even.

In the next chapter, you'll learn how to take your Fireworks comp to a full-fledged Web page—and take advantage of the tight Fireworks/Dreamweaver integration.

156   PART 01   PART 02   PART 03   PART 04   APPENDIX

Photoshop to Dreamweaver   Fireworks to Dreamweaver   Flash to Dreamweaver   Photoshop to Bridge to   Additional Workflows
                                                                                Fireworks to Dreamweaver

SETTING UP INTERACTIVE COMPS

Pages in Fireworks can be linked to one another to simulate the user's browser experience. To create an interactive comp, the following steps are required:

- Create the needed pages.
- Add hotspots or slices to navigation elements; either technique can be applied by selecting the object and choosing **Edit ▶ Insert ▶ Hotspot or Rectangular/Polygon Slice**. These options are also available from the context menu.
- Link each hotspot/slice to the appropriate page through the Link list in the Property inspector.
- Add a sub layer in the Web Layer folder and drag all linked hotspots/slices into the new sub layer.
- Select the sub layer and apply the Share Layer to Pages command (from the Layers panel Options menu); share the selected layer on all linked pages.

Once established within the Fireworks document, the interactive comp can be previewed by choosing **File ▶ Preview in Browser ▶ Preview All Pages in [your primary browser]**.

To make the interactive comp pages available for the client, choose **File ▶ Export** and, when the **Export** dialog box appears, choose **HTML and Images** with the following options:

- Export: HTML and Images
- HTML: Export HTML
- Slices: Export Slices
- Include areas without slices: selected
- Current page only: unselected
- Put images in subfolder: optional

Export the files to your Dreamweaver site and, from within Dreamweaver, put the pages online with all the dependent files.

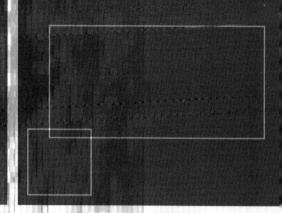

After your client has approved the interactive comp developed in Fireworks, you need to bring it to the Web for real. The process of realizing a Fireworks design in Dreamweaver is essentially one of artfully combining graphics and CSS. Graphic elements in the comp become either foreground or background images and are exported from Fireworks through its Web layer. The exported graphics are then incorporated into various style sheet rules or placed directly on the page and manipulated by CSS.

An essential aspect of the translation from comp to Web is the navigation. Before Web standards became a primary focus for designers, navigation bars with table-based graphic image rollovers was the norm. Today, Web designers prefer to use a combination of unordered (a.k.a. bullet) lists and background graphics for better accessibility and search engine readability. As you'll learn in this chapter, Fireworks and Dreamweaver are perfectly suited to this workflow.

In the following exercises, you'll learn these core Fireworks techniques:

- Exporting background and foreground graphics
- Building navigation symbols

And this Dreamweaver technique:

- Optimizing foreground graphics

CHAPTER

06 COMBINING NAVIGATION
AND LAYOUTS

INCORPORATING BACKGROUND IMAGES

In many modern Web pages, background images form the foundation of the design. This is particularly true of layouts that incorporate rounded rectangles like the Part II example. A two-part technique is required to make the comp: First, they are sliced from the overall image and then the individual slices are exported from Fireworks.

Once the proper graphic elements have been extracted from the comp, they are applied to specific structural `<div>` tags via related CSS rules in Dreamweaver. The CSS is designed to keep the layout flexible and displaying properly regardless of the amount or composition of interior content. Ideally, your rounded rectangle should look just as good with a single paragraph of text or multiple columns of imagery and content.

CREATING BACKGROUND SLICES

Whereas with Photoshop, the natural way to pull out portions of a comp is through selections, with Fireworks, slices offer the most natural route. A *slice* is a portion of the page that is cut out and exported as an individual graphic.

In this exercise, you work with a total of four background slices: one that contains the header gradient and logo text and three that recreate the rounded, shaded rectangle content area. If you remember how the Fireworks comp evolved in the last chapter, these elements are all contained in the master page.

1. In Fireworks, choose **File ▶ Open** and navigate to the **Chapter 6** exercises folder. Select **wildfire.png** and click **OK**.

   Because precision is critical when slicing background images—especially those that are intended to mesh together in HTML—guides become a very useful tool.

2. If necessary, choose **View ▶ Rulers**. Drag out a guide from the horizontal guide and place it at **149** pixels, between the gradient and the content rectangle; double-click the guide to display the **Move Guide** dialog box and precisely determine your placement. When you're done, drag two guides from the vertical ruler and place at **108** and **964** pixels, on either side of the content rectangle (Figure 6-1).

   Fireworks provides a variety of ways to create slices; one of the best choices for rectangular slices that overlap several objects is the Slice tool.

FIGURE 6-1

3. From the **Tools** panel, select the **Slice** tool, the first icon on the right in the Web group. Drag out a slice from the top of the first vertical guide to the right corner intersection of the second vertical and the horizontal. Your slice should form a rectangle encompassing the gradient and the logo text above the content rectangle.

    You'll probably notice a slight pull as your cursor gets close to the guides. Fireworks, by default, automatically snaps slices and other objects to guides; you can control this action through the View ▶ Guides ▶ Snap to Guides command.

4. With the Slice selected, change the name in the Property inspector to **logo_header**. From the Slice export settings list (designated by the clamp icon), choose **JPEG – Better Quality** (Figure 6-2).

FIGURE 6-2

It's a good idea for you to give your slices meaningful names. When slices are exported, their given names become the image filenames.

Now you can move on to slicing the content rectangle, starting with the top curved portion.

5. From the horizontal ruler, drag a guide to just above the display text, primary image, and first highlight element; the guide should be **181** pixels from the top. With the **Slice** tool, drag out a slice that starts directly underneath the previous slice and extends to the lower-right guide corner (Figure 6-3). In the Property inspector, name this slice **top_row**.

FIGURE 6-3

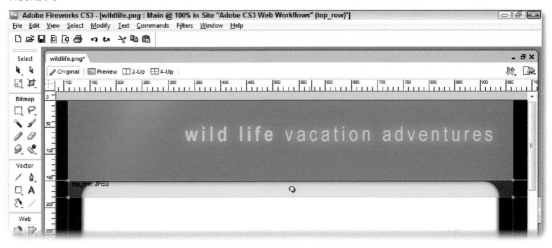

Once you've created a slice that spans the top content area, you can quickly use duplicate slices for the center and bottom.

6. With the **top_row slice** selected, choose **Edit ▶ Clone**. Drag the new slice into the center of the content rectangle, along the same vertical guides and rename it **mid_row** in the Property inspector. Repeat this step to create another slice; move it to the cover the bottom part of the rectangle and name it **bottom_row** (Figure 6-4).

FIGURE 6-4

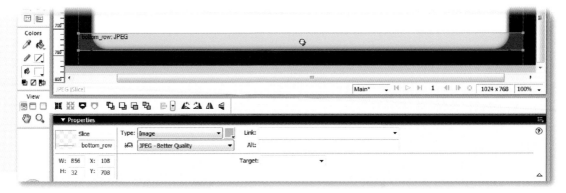

With those four slices defined, you're ready to export them for use in Dreamweaver.

7. Choose **File ▶ Export**. In the **Export** dialog box, navigate to the **images** folder. Leave the default entry in the **File name** field and, from the **Export** list, choose **Images Only**. From the **Slices** list, choose **Export Slices**. Make sure both the **Selected slices only** and **Include areas without slices** options are not selected. Select the **Current page only** option and click **Save**.

   These settings export all the slices on the page in a single operation and use the slice names in the Property inspector as the filenames.

8. Save your Fireworks document.

Now it's time to switch over to Dreamweaver and bring these exported images into a layout.

CRAFTING CSS BACKGROUNDS

When you are re-creating a rounded rectangle, the three images sliced from the comp are each set as background graphics for three different `divs`. In most cases, the top and bottom `<div>` tags hold only the graphic elements themselves; these are the top and bottom caps that contain the rounded portions of the image. The middle section is applied to a flexible content area that can grow or shrink as needed.

1. In Dreamweaver, choose **File ▶ Open**. When the **Open** dialog box appears, navigate to the **Chapter 6** folder and select **home.htm**.

   Rather than make you go through the steps of building up the page from scratch, I've included the core layout structure for home.htm:

   - A `<body>` tag set to the canvas color
   - An outerWrapper `<div>` tag
   - A header `<div>` tag
   - A contentWrapper `<div>` tag that contains `<div>` tags for the left and right content areas
   - A `<br>` tag that clears the float used in the content wrapper

   You start by placing the header image.

162
PART **01**
PART **02**
PART **03**
PART **04**
APPENDIX

Photoshop to Dreamweaver
Fireworks to Dreamweaver
Flash to Dreamweaver
Photoshop to Bridge to Fireworks to Dreamweaver
Additional Workflows

2. In the **CSS Styles** panel, make sure you're in **All** mode and double-click **#header**. When the **CSS Rule Definition for #header** dialog box opens, switch to the **Background** category. Click the Background image **Browse** button and navigate to the **Chapter 6 ▶ images** folder; select **logo_header.jpg** and click **OK**. From the **Repeat** list, choose **no-repeat**. Switch to the **Box** category and in the **Height** value field, enter **149 pixels** and click **OK**.

The image is now added to the page and the #header section resized to the proper dimensions (Figure 6-5). To start on the content area, your first action is to define the CSS rule for the top section of the content area and insert the associated `<div>` tag.

FIGURE 6-5

3. From the Common category of the Insert bar, choose **Insert Div Tag**. When the **Insert Div Tag** dialog box opens, set the **Insert** lists to **After start of tag <div id="contentWrapper">**. Enter **top_content** in the ID field and click **New CSS Style**.

This action nests the soon-to-be-created top_content `<div>` tag just inside the contentWrapper.

4. In the **New CSS Rule** dialog, make sure **Define in** is set to **This document only** and click **OK**. When the **CSS Rule Definition for #top_content** dialog box opens, switch to the **Background** category. Click the Background image **Browse** button and navigate to the **Chapter 6 ▶ images** folder; select **top_row.jpg** and click **OK**. From the **Repeat** list, choose **no-repeat** (Figure 6-6). Switch to the **Box** category and in the **Height** value field, enter **32 pixels**. Clear the **Margin Same for all** checkbox and, in the **Bottom** field, enter **0**; click **OK**. Click **OK** once more in the **Insert Div Tag** dialog box.

FIGURE 6-6

Dreamweaver inserts the new `div`, complete with the background element and placeholder text. After getting rid of that text, you can bring in the bottom row. The process is almost identical to the just-completed step, but requires a very precise placement.

5. Press **Delete** to remove the selected placeholder text. Switch to code view and place your cursor after the code **<br class="clearDiv" /></div>**. From the **Common** category of the Insert bar, choose **Insert Div Tag**. When the **Insert Div Tag** dialog box opens, set the **Insert** lists to **At Insertion Point**. Enter **bottom_content** in the ID field and click **New CSS Style**.

   The top and bottom corner graphics need to be inserted in `<div>` tags just inside the contentWrapper in their respective positions. It's important to place the bottom `<div>` tag after the closing `<.div>` tag following the `<br />` tag or else the corner imagery would get intertwined with the floated content.

6. Repeat step 4, but select **bottom_row.jpg** for the Background image and set **margin-top** to **0** instead of margin-bottom. Switch to **Design** view and press **Delete** to remove the placeholder content (Figure 6-7).

FIGURE 6-7

Although the layout closely resembles a flattened hamburger at this stage, after you add the middle background graphic, a more familiar shape emerges.

7. In the **CSS Styles** panel, make sure you're in **All** mode and select **#content**. When the **CSS Rule Definition for #header** dialog box opens, switch to the **Background** category. Click the Background image **Browse** button and navigate to the **Chapter 6 ▶ images** folder; select **mid_row.jpg** and click **OK**. From the **Repeat** list, choose **repeat-y**; click **OK**.

Now, page elements added to the content section expand the central area and leave the two rounded end caps in place (Figure 6-8).

FIGURE 6-8

8. Save your page.

If you begin experimenting with adding content to the middle area, you may find a gap emerge between either the top or bottom <div> tags and the content. As you'll learn later, you need to add first and last classes to set the top and bottom margin to zero, respectively, to avoid the gap.

INTEGRATING FOREGROUND IMAGES

Foreground images are exported from Fireworks and inserted into Dreamweaver as `<img>` tags. As with background images, the best way to select the graphic for export is often by defining a slice. Once the images are added to the Web page, they can be spaced precisely through CSS properties.

SLICING FOREGROUND GRAPHICS

When images are inserted into the Fireworks comp as separate objects, they can be sliced with one step. Once defined as a slice, they can be easily exported individually or collectively.

1. In Fireworks, open **wildlife.png** if necessary. Make sure you're on the **Main** page and, in the Layers panel, choose the **Web Layer** folder and press **Delete**.

    Because some of the foreground images overlap the slices previously defined on the master page, the relevant foreground images must be removed before continuing. Overlapping slices leads to unpredictable results and often no image is exported at all.

2. Select the bear image in the header area and choose **Edit ▶ Insert ▶ Rectangular Slice** (Figure 6-9). In the Property inspector, name the slice **bear** and press **Enter** (Windows) or **Return** (Mac). Make sure the Slice export settings list is set to **JPEG – Better Quality**.

    FIGURE 6-9

166 | PART **01** | PART **02** | PART **03** | PART **04** | APPENDIX

Photoshop to Dreamweaver   Fireworks to Dreamweaver   Flash to Dreamweaver   Photoshop to Bridge to Fireworks to Dreamweaver   Additional Workflows

Notice that Fireworks surrounds the slice with red lines; these lines indicate how Fireworks would slice the page if table-based layouts were being used and can be ignored.

Next, you set slices for two more foreground images.

3. Select the display text, **Catch it while you Can**, and repeat step 2; name the slice **catch_text** and set the Slice export settings list to **GIF Web 216** in the Property inspector. Repeat this procedure one more time with the fish image and name the slice **fish_hand**, with a Slice export setting of **JPEG – Better Quality**.

As with the background images, you can export all these slices (Figure 6-10) in a single operation.

FIGURE 6-10

4. Choose **File ▶ Export**. In the **Export** dialog box, navigate to the **Chapter 6 ▶ images** folder. Leave the default entry in the **File name** field and, from the **Export** list, choose **Images Only**. From the **Slices** list, choose **Export Slices**. Make sure both the **Selected slices only** and **Include areas without slices** options are not selected. Select the **Current page only** option and click **Save**.

The images are now ready and waiting for you in your Dreamweaver site.

5. Save your Fireworks document.

Fw CORE TECHNIQUES

EXPORTING GRAPHICS

Fireworks native file format, an enhanced PNG, is not suitable for the Web. Any images intended for the Internet must be exported from Fireworks in a viable format, such as GIF, JPEG, or standard PNG. You can export either an entire document or a portion of a document.

To export an entire document, select the desired format from the Optimization panel and select your settings. You can preview the original and another format or the original and three other formats to help you achieve the best balance of image representation and file size. Once you've completed your optimization fine-tuning, choose **File ▶ Export**; in the Export dialog box, choose **Images only** from the Export list.

To export a portion of a document, use Fireworks's slicing capabilities. Slices are displayed on the Web Layer in the Layers panel. A selected object—vector or bitmap—can be easily sliced by choosing **Edit ▶ Insert ▶ Rectangular Slice or Polygon Slice**. If multiple objects are selected, Fireworks gives you the option of creating one slice or one for each selected object. Slices can also be defined manually through use of the Slice tool.

Once the slices have been defined, you can either export all of the slices in one operation or individually. To export all the slices simultaneously, open the **Export** dialog box and choose **HTML and Images** from the **Export** list as well as **Export Slices** from the **Slices** list.

PLACING FIREWORKS IMAGES IN DREAMWEAVER

The following series of steps uses CSS defined classes to position the foreground graphics previously sliced and exported in Fireworks. Although this technique is very precise, it does not rely on absolute positioning; rather, the margin property can be used because the images are within the flow of the document. While not all foreground images can take advantage of this method, it's a handy one to have available and results in clean, Web standards–compliant code.

1. In Dreamweaver, from the **Files** panel, double-click the **Chapter 6 ▶ home.htm** file.

   You can start by bringing in the polar bear image.

2. Place your cursor in the **header** area. From the **Common** category of the Insert bar, select **Image**. Navigate to the **Chapter 6 ▶ images** and select **bear.jpg**. If the **Image Tag Accessibility Attributes** dialog box appears, enter **Polar Bear** in the **Alternate Text** field and click **OK**.

   The image is placed in the upper-left corner of the header `<div>` tag (Figure 6-11).

168 PART **01** PART **02** PART **03** PART **04** APPENDIX

Photoshop to Dreamweaver   Fireworks to Dreamweaver   Flash to Dreamweaver   Photoshop to Bridge to   Additional Workflows
                                                                                Fireworks to Dreamweaver

FIGURE 6-11

To position it correctly, you need to define and apply a CSS rule.

3. From the **CSS Styles** panel, click the **New CSS Rule**. When the **New CSS Rule** dialog box opens, choose **Selector Type: Class** and in the **Name** field, enter **.bear**. Make sure the **Define in** option is set to **This document only** and click **OK**.

4. In the **CSS Rule definition for .bear** dialog box, switch to the **Box** category and clear the **Margin Same for all** checkbox. Set **Top** to **54 pixels**, **Right** to **0**, **Bottom** to **0** and **Left** to **19 pixels**; click **OK** when you're done.

The final phase of this operation is to apply the just-defined rule.

5. With the bear image selected, from the **Class** list in the Property inspector, choose **bear**.

The margin property moves the graphic into the proper position (Figure 6-12).

FIGURE 6-12

Next, you insert the two other images exported from Fireworks.

6. Place your cursor in the **contentLeft** `<div>` tag. From the Insert bar, click **Image**. Select **catch_text. gif** and click **OK**; if necessary enter **Catch it while you can** as the **Alternative text**. After the image is inserted, press **right arrow** to move adjacent to the just inserted graphic. Click **Image** again and select **fish_hand.jpg** with **Man holding a large fish underwater** as the **Alternative text**.

At this stage, your images appear to be bursting out of the rounded rectangle; a minor CSS adjustment and a new CSS class brings them into place.

7. In the **CSS Styles** panel All mode, select **#content** and, in the Properties pane, click **Add Property**. In the first column, enter **padding-left** and press **Tab**. Enter **50** and press **Enter** (Windows) or **Return** (Mac).

The increased left padding (Figure 6-13) moves the images into the content rectangle.

FIGURE 6-13

Now, to get them to separate properly, you create another CSS class.

8. From the **CSS Styles** panel, click the **New CSS Rule**. When the **New CSS Rule** dialog box opens, choose **Selector Type: Class** and in the **Name** field, enter **.mainImage**. Click **OK**. In the **CSS Rule definition for .mainImage** dialog box, switch to the **Box** category and clear the **Margin Same for all** checkbox. Set **Bottom** to **20 pixels** and **Left** to **20 pixels**; click **OK** when you're done.

You can now apply the same class to both images.

170 PART **01**   PART **02**   PART **03**   PART **04**   APPENDIX

Photoshop to Dreamweaver   Fireworks to Dreamweaver   Flash to Dreamweaver   Photoshop to Bridge to Fireworks to Dreamweaver   Additional Workflows

9. Select the **catch_text** image and, from the Property inspector **Class** list, choose **mainImage**. Select the **fish_hand** image and apply the same class. While the **fish_hand** image is still selected, choose **Top** from the **Align** list.

    Now the page is really beginning to shape up, with all of your background and foreground images in place (Figure 6-14).

FIGURE 6-14

10. Save your page.

Next, you'll learn how to extract the necessary graphic elements from Fireworks for the navigation tabs and bring them to Web standards life in Dreamweaver.

OPTIMIZING FOREGROUND GRAPHICS

Once your images are inserted in Dreamweaver, you can quickly further optimize them without returning to Fireworks. The Optimize Image feature allows you to alter the graphic settings for any Web image. Furthermore, images can be cropped or rescaled.

To achieve the best balance of file size and image fidelity, select your image and choose **Commands ▶ Optimize Image** or select the Optimize icon (the C-clamp) on the Property inspector. When the Image Preview dialog opens, you find three categories:

- **Options**—Use the Options category to fine-tune settings for any Web-related format (such as changing a JPEG quality setting or restricting colors in a GIF) or to switch from one format to another. You can preview the optimizations in a two-up or four-up view.

- **File**—The File category rescales or resizes the image. Images can also be cropped through the Export Area interface in the File category.

- **Animation**—The Animation category, active when optimizing animated GIFs, allows you to set the number of repetitions as well as the duration of each frame.

The Image Preview dialog—along with the Export Area dialog—is also the same dialog used in the Fireworks Export Wizard.

IMPLEMENTING CSS NAVIGATION

There are almost as many different types of site navigation as there are sites. Many modern Web designers prefer to develop CSS-based navigation, which integrates HTML unordered lists with background images rather than relying on table-based rollover graphics. CSS-based navigation is more transparent to search engines as well as more accessible. To create such navigation elements, you need to export the various states of the navigation buttons from Fireworks and then create the necessary CSS rules and HTML code in Dreamweaver.

EXPORTING THE NAVIGATION STATES

In the previous chapter, you added hotspots to the navigation tabs to set up an interactive comp. To make this interactivity real, you need to replace the hotspots with slices—but only for the selected and non-selected states. The hover state can be added in Dreamweaver.

1. In Fireworks, choose **File ▶ Open**. When the **Open** dialog box appears, navigate to the **Chapter 6** folder and choose **wildlife.jpg**; click **Open**.

172
PART **01**
Photoshop to Dreamweaver

PART **02**
Fireworks to Dreamweaver

PART **03**
Flash to Dreamweaver

PART **04**
Photoshop to Bridge to Fireworks to Dreamweaver

APPENDIX
Additional Workflows

The first step is to remove the hotspots previously inserted to provide interactive links within the comp. Hotspots are known in HTML as image maps and are effective for providing links within a graphic; when exporting a portion of a comp as a separate image, you need to use slices rather than hotspots.

2. From the Pages list, choose **Page 1**. In the **Layers** panel, select **Web Layer ▶ Navigation** and press **Delete** to remove the existing hotspots.

    Next, because you are going to be adding the navigation button labels in Dreamweaver as unordered list items, you need to temporarily hide the labels.

3. Select the **Home** label and, in the **Layers** panel, locate the corresponding object in the Header layer and toggle its **eye icon** (Figure 6-15).

FIGURE 6-15

Now you're ready to slice and export the first navigation button state.

4. Select the white tab and choose **Edit ▶ Insert ▶ Rectangular Slice**. In the Property inspector, change the name to **nav_btn_selected** and press **Tab**. Set the Export slice settings to **GIF Web 216**.

    Because there are slices that have been already exported on the current page, it's best to just export this single slice.

NOTE

Fireworks provides another technique for exporting navigation buttons through symbols. Steps for working with symbols are outlined in the "Core Techniques: Fireworks—Building Navigation Symbols" sidebar later in this chapter.

5. **Right-click** (Windows) or **Control-click** (Mac) the just created slice and choose **Export Selected Slice**. When the **Export** dialog box appears, navigate to the **Chapter 6 ▶ images** folder and keep the default filename. Make sure the **Export** list is set to **Images Only** and the **Slices** list is set to **Export Slices**. Enable the **Selected slices only**, **Current frame only**, and **Current page only** options and make sure **Include area without slices** is not enabled (Figure 6-16). Click **Save**

FIGURE 6-16

6. In the Layers panel, toggle the **eye icon** next to the **HOME** text object to re-display the object.

   The image for the selected tab state is now ready for integration in Dreamweaver. You need to repeat the process for the unselected state.

7. Select the **SOLO** text object and, in the **Layers** panel, toggle its **eye icon** off. Select the gray tab behind the now hidden text object and repeat steps 4 and 5, naming the **slice nav_btn_unselected** (Figure 6-17). After you've exported the selected slice, restore the text object visibility and save your page.

FIGURE 6-17

Images for both tabbed states have now been exported and are ready to be applied in Dreamweaver.

174 PART **01** PART **02** PART **03** PART **04** APPENDIX

Photoshop to Dreamweaver   Fireworks to Dreamweaver   Flash to Dreamweaver   Photoshop to Bridge to   Additional Workflows
                                                                                 Fireworks to Dreamweaver

BUILDING NAVIGATION SYMBOLS

If you're working with navigation buttons that integrate labels and graphics, Fireworks symbols are an efficient method. Multiple instances of Fireworks symbols can be placed on a page as different navigation buttons, each with its own label and link attribute. Any changes made to the symbol—such as color or effects—are propagated to all instances. When the symbols are exported, a different graphic for each state is produced.

To set up a symbol, follow these steps:

1. Select all the elements for the up state of the navigation button, including the label.

2. Choose **Modify ▶ Symbol ▶ Convert** to Symbol.

3. When the **Convert to Symbol** dialog box appears, give it a unique name and choose **Type: Button**. If you want the button instances to be different heights or widths, choose the **Enable 9-slice scaling guides** option.

   A slice is automatically added to the button.

4. Double-click the slice to edit the button states.

5. Set the desired states in order: Up, Over, Down, and Over While Down. Typically, the Over state copies the elements of the Up state and is modified (with a different text color or effect) and then the Down state, if desired, copies the Over state and is modified.

   Rollover buttons include a minimum of Up and Over states and may include Down and Over While Down states.

6. Verify that the Active Area covers the desired slice section for all states and click **Done**.

7. Drag out a copy of the symbol instance and in the Property inspector change the label and link.

8. When exporting, choose **Export: HTML and Images and Slices: Export Slices** at a minimum.

   If you want to insert a table-based navigation bar, choose **HTML: Export HTML File** as well.

(continued)

(continued)

9. In Dreamweaver, place the base images on the page and then attach Swap Image behaviors. The Up state image will have the base name of the slice; the Over state will have the base name plus "_f2" appended; the Down state will have "_f3" appended; and so on.

If you want a table-based navigation bar, place your cursor where you'd like the table to appear and choose **Insert ▶ Image Objects ▶ Fireworks HTML** and locate the HTML file exported from Fireworks. All of the required images and associated behaviors will be imported.

The two files exported from Fireworks are incorporated as background images for CSS rules defined in Dreamweaver. While those two graphics are essential to replicating the look-and-feel of the compod navigation, they are just a part of what's required. In all, this technique requires a minimum of six different CSS rules to convert an unordered list to a Web standards–compliant tab-based navigation.

To save time and keep the focus on the navigation-building aspects of this section, all the necessary styles have been created and include the nonrelevant properties in the file used in the following exercise. In addition, the following elements have been added to round out the comp:

- **Headings and text**—Additional classes have been added to control the spacing: .no_top_margin was applied to the `<h1>` tag and .lastItem to the final paragraph. The .lastItem class sets the margin-bottom property to zero to prevent any separation between the content and bottom_content `<div>` tags, which would break the illusion of the rounded rectangle.

- **Sidebar highlight areas**—Each sidebar highlight consists of a `<div>`, an `<h1>`, and a `<p>` tag. The .special_deal class assigned to the `<div>` tag sets the right and bottom borders as well as the width and bottom margin, which keeps the deals spaced equally. The rule for the `<h1>` tag provides the background image gradient. A separate class (.special_deal_last) redefines the bottom margin for the final highlight element to zero, again to prevent a separation from the bottom_content `<div>` tag.

In the following exercise, you concentrate on building the navigation tabs to complete the conversion from Fireworks comp to Dreamweaver Web page.

1. In Dreamweaver, choose **File ▶ Open**, navigate to the **Chapter 6** folder, and select **home_nav.htm**; click **OK**.

   In addition to the added text and highlight elements, you might also notice a new `<div>` tag, with a #nav ID, that appears to span the header and top of the rounded rectangle (Figure 6-18). This absolutely positioned `<div>` tag will contain the unordered list.

FIGURE 6-18

2. Place your cursor in the **#nav <div>** tag and from the Property inspector choose **Unordered List**. Enter the four navigation labels, each—except the last—followed by a line return: HOME, SOLO, GROUP, and CONTACT.

Although the color, size, and line height have been predefined in the various CSS rules, the list is otherwise presented in the standard bulleted format (Figure 6-19). You can start the conversion by removing the bullets.

FIGURE 6-19

3. In the **CSS Styles** panel, make sure you're in **All** mode and select **#nav ul**. In the Properties pane, click **Add Property**. Enter **list-style** and press Tab; enter **none** and press **Enter** (Windows) or **Return** (Mac).

Next, you change the orientation of the list items from vertical to horizontal by applying a float property. You also space the items apart with a margin-right and align the text labels to the center.

4. In the **CSS Styles** panel, select **#nav li**. Enter the following three new properties by clicking Add Property for each:

- **float: left**

- **margin-right: 10 pixels**

- **text-align: center**

With the additional properties and values in place (Figure 6-20), your vertical list becomes horizontal and is almost ready for the background images. However, the background images must be applied to an <a> tag, so you need to add links to each of the list items first.

FIGURE 6-20

5. Click in the text HOME and from the **Tag Selector** choose **<li>**. In the Property inspector's **Link** field, enter **home_nav.htm**. Repeat this operation with each of the three remaining list items to insert these links, respectively: **solo.htm**, **group.htm**, and **contact.htm**.

The text turns a dark shade of blue, the default browser color for links; you correct the color a bit later in these steps. First, however, you add the background graphic to represent the up state of the navigation.

178   PART **01**   PART **02**   PART **03**   PART **04**   APPENDIX

Photoshop to Dreamweaver   Fireworks to Dreamweaver   Flash to Dreamweaver   Photoshop to Bridge to Fireworks to Dreamweaver   Additional Workflows

6. In the **CSS Styles** panel, select **#nav a**. Click **Edit Style** and when the CSS Rule definition for #nav a appears, switch to the **Background** category. Click **Browse** next to the **Background image** field and navigate to the **Chapter 6 ▶ Images** folder to select **nav_btn_unselected.gif**; click **OK**. From the **Repeat** list, choose **no-repeat**. Switch to the **Block** category and, from the **Display** list, choose **block**. Click **OK** to apply the changes.

Now, all four list items have a button background (Figure 6-21). Next, you can add a little color to the match your Fireworks comp.

FIGURE 6-21

7. In the **CSS Styles** panel, select **#nav a:link, #nav a:visited**. Click **Add Property** in the Properties pane and enter **color**. Press **Tab** and enter **#AFC6FF**.

This rule includes two selectors—one for the link's initial state and one for the visited state. By grouping them, you're assuring that the navigation buttons won't have different colors after they've been clicked. Now you can set the hover color.

8. In the **CSS Styles** panel, select **#nav a:hover, #nav a:active**. Click **Add Property** in the Properties pane and enter **color**. Press **Tab** and enter **#FFFFFF** (Figure 6-22).

FIGURE 6-22

You won't see the effect of this rule change until you preview the page in your browser, but you've just set the hover and active states to white for each list item label.

The last CSS Styles modification brings in the selected state graphic exported from Fireworks. This background image is applied to the button with the ID of #current.

9. In the CSS Styles panel, select **#current a:link**, **#current a:visited**, **#current a:hover**, **#current a:active**. Click **Edit Style** and when the CSS Rule definition for **#current a:link**, **#current a:visited**, **#current a:hover**, **#current a:active** dialog box appears, click the **Color** swatch and sample the body background color, **#000064**. Switch to the **Background** category and click **Browse** next to the Background image field. Navigate to the **Chapter 6 ▶ Images** folder to select **nav_btn_selected.gif** and click **OK**. From the **Repeat** list, choose **no-repeat**. Click **OK** when you're done.

    Although you've set up the style, you won't see a change on the page until you set one of the buttons to #current.

10. Place your cursor in the **HOME** text. From the **Tag Selector**, right-click (Windows) or Control-click (Mac) on <li> and choose **Set ID ▶ current**.

    Congratulations, you've successfully created tabbed navigation from an unordered list in Dreamweaver with graphics sliced and exported from Fireworks.

    Now you can try it out.

11. Save your page and press **F12** to preview it in your primary browser. Move your mouse over any of the navigation buttons to see the rollover effect (Figure 6-23). Click on SOLO or GROUP to visit their respective pages.

PART **01**   PART **02**   PART **03**   PART **04**   APPENDIX

Photoshop to Dreamweaver   Fireworks to Dreamweaver   Flash to Dreamweaver   Photoshop to Bridge to Fireworks to Dreamweaver   Additional Workflows

FIGURE 6-23

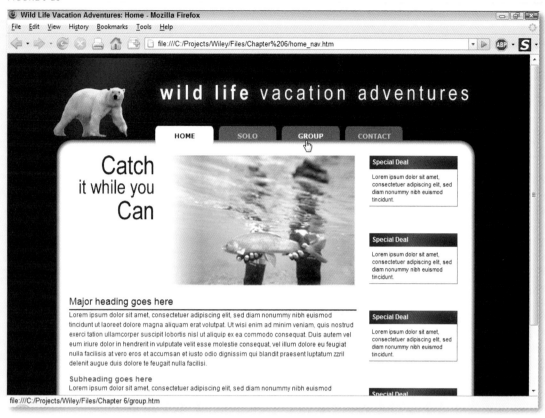

I've taken the liberty of building out these additional pages from the Fireworks comp—Solo and Group—to give you the full interactive effect. Besides switching the graphics, I also set the #current ID for each page appropriately.

Feel free to dive deeper into the HTML or CSS for any of the sample pages. If you don't feel you understand what effect a CSS property has, try removing or changing it temporarily. If you'd like to test your Fireworks to Dreamweaver workflow skills further, comp and build out the final page in the navigation, Contact, with a simple informational page that could include a contact form.

Throughout the three chapters that make up Part II, you've seen how well Fireworks and Dreamweaver work together, from initial design to completed Web pages. Although both programs are true standouts when used by themselves, the Fireworks/Dreamweaver combination is a clear example of the adage "the whole is greater than the sum of its parts."

Debra Wanner Dance

skip intro

PART 03

FLASH TO DREAMWEAVER

Flash and Dreamweaver are a natural fit. Flash is terrific for realizing the designer's imagination without compromise, from the most basic animations to fully realized rich Internet applications to full-screen, high-quality video. However, Flash exports a specialized format that requires a browser plug-in to be seen, and without a Web page to trigger the plug-in, Flash is far from ubiquitous. Although you could use other Web authoring tools, or even a text editor, to create your Flash-ready sites, no tool makes it easier than Dreamweaver.

Inserting a Flash movie into a Dreamweaver page is a snap. In fact, there's almost nothing to it: Just choose the Flash object from the menu or toolbar and choose your Flash file. Dreamweaver automatically reads the Flash metadata, sets the file dimensions, and presents other options. Best of all, Dreamweaver writes out all the necessary code that, in recent years, has become quite complex because of changes in Internet Explorer. The fact that you may not be aware of these code changes is a testament to the smooth integration of Flash and Dreamweaver.

There are a number of Flash spin-offs in Dreamweaver CS3: Flash Text, Flash Buttons, Flash Elements, FlashPaper, and Flash Video. It has been announced by the Dreamweaver engineering team that all but the last two are on the chopping block for the next version of Dreamweaver; they are intended for the Flash non-user. If you're comfortable working in Flash on even a rudimentary level, you can easily create equivalent and infinitely more flexible movies.

The following chapters illustrate a variety of ways of working with Flash and Dreamweaver. First, you have a chance to explore a pure example of a Flash-only implementation: the Flash intro. Next, you learn how to work with Flash video, prepping it properly for playback on the Web. Finally, you learn how to integrate Flash with Dreamweaver in a variety of ways in a hybrid Flash/HTML design.

THE FLOW: FLASH TO DREAMWEAVER

NOTE

The original design shown here is the basis for the exercises in Part III.

Incorporating Flash movies onto your Web pages—whether as the sole content or integrated into an area—is a very straightforward process (Figure III-1):

1. In Flash, set the stage dimensions to the desired final output size by choosing Modify ▶ Document.

   Dreamweaver automatically picks up the width and height of the Flash movie.

2. Choose File ▶ Publish Settings and make sure that the Flash (.swf) option is selected and the HTML (.html) option is not.

   Because you're making a Web page file in Dreamweaver, you don't need the additional HTML page.

3. In Dreamweaver, choose Insert ▶ Media ▶ Flash and select the published SWF file.

   Dreamweaver displays a placeholder within the page with a custom Property inspector for adjusting key parameters like loop and autoplay; additional parameters can be added. Click Preview to play the Flash movie in Dreamweaver.

FIGURE III-1

To edit the Flash movie directly from within Dreamweaver, follow these steps (Figure III-2):

1. In Dreamweaver, select the Flash movie you want to modify.

2. From the Property inspector, choose Edit.

3. When Flash opens the original source file, make any desired changes.

4. Click Done to return to Dreamweaver.

FIGURE III-2

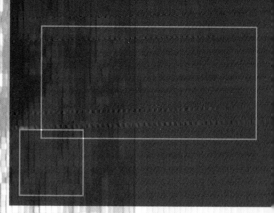

Flash is a key player in almost all of the Adobe Creative Suite configurations, particularly the Web-related ones. As such, it integrates smoothly with much of the Adobe product line. You can easily move images into Flash from Photoshop or Fireworks; you can even import the properties you'd like from either image-based tool. The workflow from Flash to Dreamweaver and back is just as elegant and well defined.

There are many different ways to use Flash on the Web. A Flash intro typically consists of a single Flash movie contained in a site's home or gateway page. While nowhere near as popular as they once were, Flash intros are occasionally requested by clients. However, that is not the reason this design choice is covered in this book. For the purpose of this book, the standard Flash intro is included because it incorporates many fundamental Flash techniques—such as working with timelines and incorporating images—and demonstrates the workflow of integrating a Flash movie in a Dreamweaver Web page.

In the following exercises, you'll learn these core Flash techniques:

- Importing images
- Manipulating the timeline
- Creating navigation buttons

And this Dreamweaver technique:

- Inserting Flash movies

CHAPTER
07
BUILDING FLASH INTROS

SETTING THE STAGE

While Flash has expanded its repertoire to rich Internet applications and telephones and has even spun off a product or two (like Adobe Flex), at its heart Flash remains a program for creating animations. Flash's primary interface is referred to as a *stage*, whose elements are controlled by a *timeline* and whose output is a *movie*. To help you better work in Flash, the following series of steps explores this environment while you set up the work environment needed for the intro.

1. From Flash, choose **File ▶ New**. When the **New Document** dialog box appears, select **Flash File (ActionScript 3.0)** and click **OK** (Figure 7-1).

FIGURE 7-1

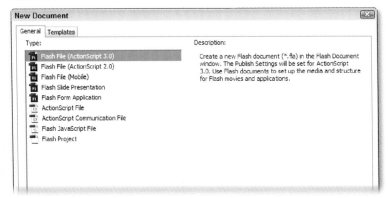

Although you could easily accomplish the goals of the intro with the earlier version of ActionScript, it's better to get used to working with ActionScript 3.0 if you're just starting out. The coding methodology is quite different between the two, and all future code will be 3.0-based.

Now you can define the properties of the stage to suit your full-screen intro

2. Choose **Modify ▶ Document**. When the **Document Properties** dialog box appears, change the **width** value to **1000** and the **height** to **800**. Click the **Background color** swatch and select **black** with the eyedropper (Figure 7-2). Leave the Frame rate at the default setting and click **OK**.

You'll need to have Flash Player 9 or greater installed to work with the files created in this exercise. To download the current version of the Flash Player, visit www.adobe.com/go/get-flashplayer. Also, if you haven't downloaded and unzipped the exercise files, you can get them from www.wiley.com/go/adobecs3web-workflows.

FIGURE 7-2

Document Properties

Title:

Description:

Dimensions: 1000 (width) Y 800 (height)

Match: ○ Printer ○ Contents ◉ Default

Background color: ■▾

Frame rate: 12 fps

Ruler units: Pixels ▾

Make Default | OK | Cancel

Now with the stage set appropriately, you can turn your attention to the timeline. Layers can be easily renamed, added, and organized.

3. In the timeline, double-click Layer 1 and rename it **Background**. Press **Enter** (Windows) or **Return** (Mac) to confirm the change.

4. Click Insert Layer, the first icon at the bottom of the timeline on the left (Figure 7-3). Double-click the new Layer 2 and rename it **Image 1**.

FIGURE 7-3

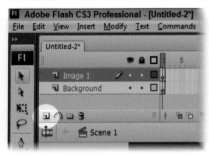

New layers are always inserted above the currently selected layer; you can, of course, modify their placement by dragging them into position.

5. Repeat step 4 three more times and name the layers **Image 2**, **Image 3**, and **Image 4**, respectively.

As in Photoshop or Fireworks, the layers add up quickly in Flash. Because of the timeline's limited screen real estate, it's especially important that you organize your layers into folders whenever possible.

188 | PART **01** | PART **02** | PART **03** | PART **04** | APPENDIX

Photoshop to Dreamweaver | Fireworks to Dreamweaver | Flash to Dreamweaver | Photoshop to Bridge to Fireworks to Dreamweaver | Additional Workflows

6. With the Image 4 layer selected, click **Insert Layer Folder**, the third icon from the left on the timeline. Double click **Folder 1** and rename it to **Images**. Shift-select Images 1 through 4 and drag them into the Images folder (Figure 7-4).

FIGURE 7-4

Now you add one more layer at this time—a special one to hold your ActionScript code.

7. Select the **Images** folder and click **Insert Layer**. Double-click Layer 6 and rename it **actions**. To the right of the name, click in the Lock column.

By locking the actions layer, you're prevented from accidentally adding any objects to its timeline. You can, however, insert code into the layer as you'll learn later in this chapter.

8. Choose **File ▶ Save**. When the **Save As** dialog box appears, navigate to the **Chapter 7** folder and, in the **File name** field, enter **intro**. Click **Save**.

Now that your document is prepped and saved, you're ready to start adding the images that form the base of the intro.

IMPORTING IMAGES

Flash is chock-full of drawing tools for the construction of original, often animated, artwork. Quite often, however, the materials Flash is called upon to animate are externally created images. To meet this need, Flash is quite adept at importing a wide range of graphic formats, including Photoshop PSD, Illustrator AI, and Fireworks PNG, along with a host of non-program specific file types such as JPEG, GIF, and PICT.

You have a number of options when importing images. You can bring them into your library for placement at your convenience or you can import them directly onto the stage—which automatically places a copy in the library and an instance in the document. You get an opportunity to try both of these methods in the following exercise.

1. In the timeline, select the **Image 1** layer (Figure 7-5).

FIGURE 7-5

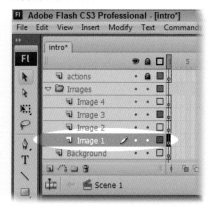

You can start by bringing an image onto the stage. The key benefit to this method is to place the image exactly where you want it—which, in this case, is the first frame of the Image 1 layer.

2. Choose **File ▶ Import ▶ Import to Stage**. When the **Import** dialog box opens, navigate to the **Chapter 7 ▶ images** folder and select **IMG_01.jpg**. Click **Open**.

   Flash is quite savvy when it comes to handling multiple images and recognizes that the chosen file has a similar filename as others in the same folder. Therefore, you get the option to bring in all the related images or just the selected one.

3. When Flash asks if you'd like to import all the image in what appears to be a sequence, click **No**.

   Flash puts the graphic in the center of the stage. While you could drag it where you'd prefer it to go, it's better to use the Property inspector for more precise positioning.

190 PART 01 PART 02 PART 03 PART 04 APPENDIX

Photoshop to Dreamweaver   Fireworks to Dreamweaver   Flash to Dreamweaver   Photoshop to Bridge to Fireworks to Dreamweaver   Additional Workflows

4. Select the image and in the Property inspector change the **X** value to **0** and press **Tab** (Figure 7-6).

FIGURE 7-6

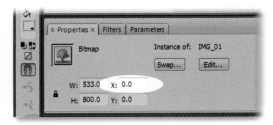

Flash automatically formats your zero entry to one decimal place, thus revealing one of Flash's strengths: extremely precise positioning, up to four decimal places.

Now, you can bring all the remaining images into the library in one operation.

5. Choose **File ▶ Import ▶ Import to Library**. When the Import to Library dialog box opens, Shift-select **IMG_02.jpg**, **IMG_03.jpg**, and **IMG_04.jpg** and click **Open**.

There's no indication that the operation was successful, so take a look for yourself.

6. From the panel dock, click **Library**. If the library is not available in the dock, choose **Window ▶ Library**. To see previews of any imported image, select its entry (Figure 7-7).

FIGURE 7-7

FL CORE TECHNIQUES

IMPORTING IMAGES

Flash is capable of importing a wide range of media, from static graphic to movie files. The primary interface for importing is located under the **File ▶ Import** menu; the degree of control over imported files varies from file type to file type. Within the Adobe Creative Suite Web product line, you have the following options:

- **Fireworks**—With Fireworks PNG files, you're given the option to either import objects or text as bitmaps to maintain appearance or as vectors to retain editability. You also have the option to import all or individual pages into new frames or scenes as movie clips. A Fireworks file can also be inserted into Flash as a single flattened bitmap. Of the three graphics programs in CS3, only Fireworks offers the import options when a selection copied to the clipboard is pasted in Flash.

- **Illustrator**—When importing Illustrator CS3 files, you have the ability to choose which layers to import and whether to convert them to Flash layers, keyframes, or a single Flash layer. Other options include placing objects in their original position, matching the Flash document size to the Illustrator artboard, importing unused symbols and importing the file as a single bitmap image. It is also possible to generate a report listing the incompatible items, which will not come into Flash properly.

(continued)

Note that not only are the three images just imported in the Library, but also the initial file is imported to the stage.

7 Choose **File ▶ Save**.

In the next series of exercises, you begin to explore the timeline and put the imported images to work.

WORKING WITH THE TIMELINE

The timeline, Flash's defining interface, is composed of a series of frames. When a Flash movie is played, the frames are displayed at a particular rate; by default, the playback rate is 12 frames per second. A frame in which something in the layer changes is called a *keyframe*. To automatically create smooth transitions from one keyframe to the next, a *tween* is added. There are two types of tweens: one for changing shapes and another for altered motion and other properties.

To achieve all of these effects, you first need to convert your graphic to a special symbol called a *movie clip*. In essence, a movie clip is a self-contained Flash movie, with its own timeline.

 PART **01**
Photoshop to Dreamweaver

 PART **02**
Fireworks to Dreamweaver

 PART **03**
Flash to Dreamweaver

 PART **04**
Photoshop to Bridge to
Fireworks to Dreamweaver

 APPENDIX
Additional Workflows

In this exercise, you establish keyframes for each of the image layers at different points in the timeline. Here, the desired effect is to fade the images in and out, sequentially. To achieve this, the alpha value for each image is modified on the keyframes and motion tweens inserted in the frames in-between.

1. Select the image on the stage and choose **Modify ▶ Convert to Symbol**. When the **Convert to Symbol** dialog box opens, change the **Name** to **first_image**. Make sure the **Type** is set to **Movie clip** and click **OK** (Figure 7-8).

FIGURE 7-8

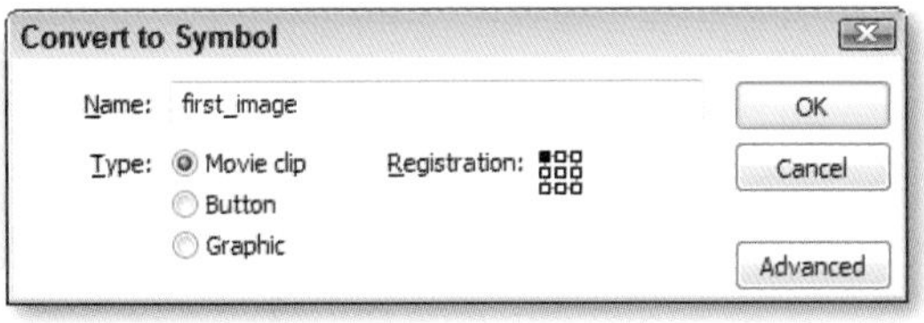

Convert to Symbol

Name: first_image

Type: ● Movie clip   Registration: ⬚⬚⬚
       ○ Button
       ○ Graphic

OK
Cancel
Advanced

You get an opportunity to work with the Button type of symbol later in this chapter.

2. In the Property inspector, choose **Alpha** from the **Color list** and set the value to **10%**. Press **Enter** (Windows) or **Return** (Mac) to confirm the change.

The image dims almost to the point of imperceptibility. Why not set the alpha to zero percent? From a design perspective, I want a hint of the image to be seen at all times. From a practical standpoint, it's much less taxing on the client's processor to fade from 10 percent to 100 percent than it is to fade from zero.

3. In the Image 1 layer, place your cursor in **frame 20**. Choose **Insert ▶ Timeline ▶ Keyframe**.

Note that Flash automatically fills in the frames between 1 and 20. Now, it's time to make a change to the graphic in your new keyframe.

(continued)

- **Photoshop**—As with Illustrator, you have complete control over which Photoshop layers are imported; additionally, you can choose whether the layer is converted to a movie symbol or remains a bitmap graphic. Graphics may retain their editable layer styles or be flattened. Moreover, you can set the publication settings at import and choose between lossy and lossless with a default or custom quality setting.

4. On the stage, select the image. From the Property inspector, change the **Alpha** value to **100%** (Figure 7-9).

FIGURE 7-9

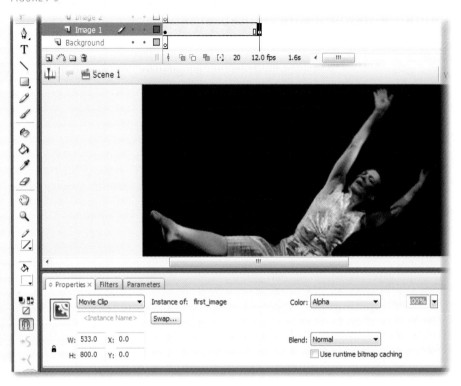

If you were to test your Flash movie now, you'd notice a big jump when the second keyframe was reached. You can smooth out that transition with a motion tween.

5. **Right-click** (Windows) or **Control-click** (Mac) any standard frame from 2 to 19 and choose **Create Motion Tween**. Drag the playhead, the red frame indicator at the top of the timeline, to the left and right to see the interpolated frames.

The left-to-right arrow in the frames indicates a tween.

Next, you can follow a similar series of steps to fade out the image.

6. In the Image 1 layer, place your cursor in **frame 40**; **right-click** (Windows) or **Control-click** and choose **Insert Keyframe**. Select the image on the stage and, in the Property inspector, change the **Alpha** value to **10%**. Press **Enter** (Windows) or **Return** (Mac). **Right-click** (Windows) or **Control-click** (Mac) any standard frame from 21 to 39 and choose **Create Motion Tween**.

Congratulations—you've just completed your first Flash animation! Now you can check out the results.

194   PART **01**   PART **02**   PART **03**   PART **04**   APPENDIX

Photoshop to Dreamweaver   Fireworks to Dreamweaver   Flash to Dreamweaver   Photoshop to Bridge to Fireworks to Dreamweaver   Additional Workflows

7. Choose the first keyframe and press **Enter** (Windows) or **Return** (Mac). The image should first fade smoothly in and then smoothly out (Figure 7-10).

FIGURE 7-10

The next series of steps adds the other imported images in a similar way, but progressively down the timeline.

8. In the timeline, select the **Image 2** layer and place your cursor on **frame 20**. **Right-click** (Windows) or **Control-click** (Mac) and choose **Insert Keyframe**. From the Library panel, drag **IMG_02** onto the stage. In the Property inspector, set the **X** value to **80** and **Y** to **0**.

With your second image on the stage, it's time to set up its transition by first converting it to a movie clip symbol.

9. **Right-click** (Windows) or **Control-click** (Mac) on the image and choose **Convert to Symbol**. Change the **Name** to **second_image** and set the **Type** to **Movie Clip**; click **OK**.

10. From the Property inspector, choose **Alpha** in the **Color** list and make sure that the value is set to **10%**. In the timeline, place your cursor on **frame 40** of the Image 2 layer. **Right-click** (Windows) or **Control-click** (Mac) and choose **Insert Keyframe**. Select the image on the stage and, in the Property inspector, change the **Alpha** value to **100%**. **Right-click** (Windows) or **Control-click** (Mac) any standard frame from 21 to 39 and choose **Create Motion Tween**.

If you drag the playhead now between frames 20 and 40, you can see the first image cross-fading with the second (Figure 7-11). This is exactly the type of effect you are looking for. Now you can complete the transition for the second image.

FIGURE 7-11

PART **01**   PART **02**   PART **03**   PART **04**   APPENDIX

Photoshop to Dreamweaver   Fireworks to Dreamweaver   Flash to Dreamweaver   Photoshop to Bridge to Fireworks to Dreamweaver   Additional Workflows

11. In the Image 2 layer, place your cursor In **frame 80**, right-click (Windows) or Control-click and choose **Insert Keyframe**. Select the image on the stage and, in the Property inspector, change the **Alpha** value to **10%**. Press **Enter** (Windows) or **Return** (Mac). **Right-click** (Windows) or **Control-click** (Mac) any standard frame from 41 to 59 and choose **Create Motion Tween**.

Two down, two to go! Are you feeling ready to solo? See if you can follow through with just an overview of the steps for incorporating the next image into the movie.

12. To incorporate the third image into the movie, follow these steps:

   • On Layer 3, frame 40, create a keyframe.

   • Drag **IMG_03** onto the stage and position at **X: 160 pixels**, **Y: 0 pixels**.

   • Convert the image to a movie clip symbol called **third_image** and set the **Alpha** to **10%.**

   • Create a **keyframe** on **frame 60** with the **Alpha** at **100%;** add a **motion tween**.

   • Create another **keyframe** on **frame 80** with the **Alpha** set to **10%** and again, add a **motion tween**.

If you preview your movie at this point, you see three images fading in and out, one after the other (Figure 7-12).

FIGURE 7-12

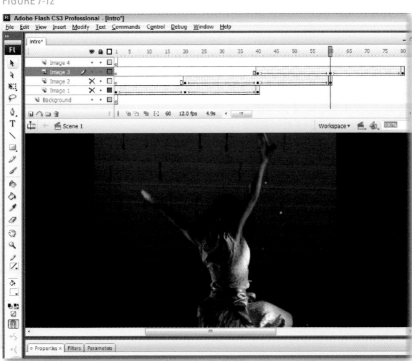

Fl CORE TECHNIQUES

MANIPULATING THE TIMELINE

The essence of any animation—including Flash animation—is movement over time. The timeline is Flash's primary interface for establishing what happens when and for how long. The playback rate (frames per second) is set in Document Properties dialog box, which is displayed by choosing **Modify ▶ Document**. The higher the playback rate, the smoother the animation—but higher playback is also more processor intensive. The key components of the timeline are:

- **Layers**—The Layer is Flash's main compositional element. Objects can be placed on separate layers to appear at different points or places in the movie. As is the case in Photoshop or Fireworks, Flash layers are hierarchical in nature: An object in the uppermost layer appears to be in front of all other object in other layers. Layers can be moved from one position in the stack to another by dragging; layers can also be hidden, locked, or just shown as outlines by using the associated toggle controls.

(continued)

You can now finish it with the fourth image; the one difference here is that the final image does not fade out as the others did.

13. To incorporate the fourth image into the movie, follow these steps:

- On Layer 4, frame 60, create a keyframe.

- Drag **IMG_04** onto the stage and position at **X: 240 pixels**, **Y: 0 pixels**.

- Convert the image to a movie clip symbol called **fourth_image** and set the **Alpha** to **10%.**

- Create a **keyframe** on **frame 80** with the **Alpha** at **100%;** add a **motion tween**.

  With all of your images properly placed, you can save the page and preview it properly.

14. Choose **File ▶ Save** to store the file and then choose **Control ▶ Test Movie**. To prevent the automatic looping, choose **Control ▶ Loop**. Close the movie window when you're done.

Now you can get a full sense of the rhythm and flow of your animated intro (Figure 7-13). Next, you add some text to present site title.

198   PART **01**   PART **02**   PART **03**   PART **04**   APPENDIX

Photoshop to Dreamweaver   Fireworks to Dreamweaver   Flash to Dreamweaver   Photoshop to Bridge to Fireworks to Dreamweaver   Additional Workflows

FIGURE 7-13

INSERTING TEXT

Flash text is extremely flexible. It can be entered and edited as with any other graphics authoring program, and then, once input, it can be animated like nothing else. Because Flash text is vector-based, it renders crisply and scales beautifully—and what's more, you're not restricted to fonts common to PCs and Macs; you can use any font on your own system.

In this exercise, you add some basic title text, convert it to a symbol and then animate it, much as you did the graphics. The first step is to add a new layer to contain the text.

1. In the timeline, select the **Images** folder and click **Insert Layer**. Double-click the new layer name and rename it **Text**.

   Although you built the basic layer structure at the start of this chapter, it's important to keep in mind that you can add layers at any time, in any location.

2. Select **frame 70** in the Text layer (Figure 7-14). **Right-click** (Windows) or **Control-click** (Mac) and choose **Insert Keyframe**.

(continued)

- **Layer folders**—Layer folders are organizational aids, very useful in layer intensive projects. Layer folders can be nested and, like layers themselves, hidden, locked, or outlined.

- **Frames**—Frames are the building blocks of the timeline. To make an object visible in a layer, it must be on a frame.

- **Keyframes**—A keyframe is a frame where something is set to change, such as the position of an object or its Alpha (transparency) value.

- **Tweens**—A tween is a series of frames between two keyframes. There are two types of tweens: A shape tween is used when a vector object changes shape while a movement tween is applied when the object moves or changes color or Alpha values.

FIGURE 7-14

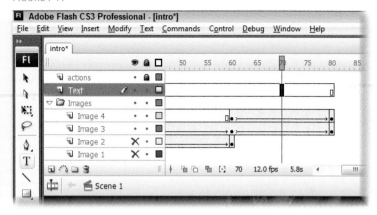

This design calls for the text to appear to the right of the final image just after the image is completely faded in. Because the text fades in as well, it's best to start it a bit before the final keyframe of the graphic.

3. From the **Tools** panel, select the **Text** tool. In the Property inspector, choose **Tahoma** from the **Font list** and set the **size** to **36**. Click the **Color swatch** and choose **white** from the pop-up color picker. Finally, set the **letter spacing** to **12** (Figure 7-15).

FIGURE 7-15

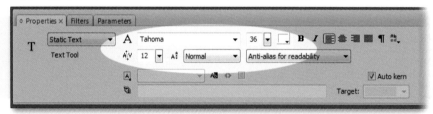

Flash has a number of different text types. Here, you're using the default, Static Text, because the text will neither be changed programmatically (Dynamic Text) nor interactively (Input Text).

4. Place your cursor to the right of the final image, about 2/3 from the top of the image and enter **Debra Wanner Dance** with two line returns after each word, except the last. Choose the **Selection** tool from the **Tools** panel when you're done.

You can always use the Property inspector to fine-tune your text placement.

5. In the Property inspector, change the **X** value to **790** and press **Tab**. Change the **Y** value to **150** and press **Tab** (Figure 7-16).

FIGURE 7-16

Now, you can set up the animated fade.

6. **Right-click** (Windows) or **Control-click** (Mac) on the text and choose **Convert to Symbol**. Change the **Name** to **title_text** and set the **Type** to **Movie Clip**; click **OK**.

The procedure for fading in text is the same as it was with the graphics.

7. From the Property inspector, choose **Alpha** in the **Color** list and make sure that the value is set to **10%**. In the timeline, place your cursor on **frame 100** of the Text layer. **Right-click** (Windows) or **Control-click** (Mac) and choose **Insert Keyframe**. Select the image on the stage and, in the Property inspector, change the **Alpha** value to **100%**. **Right-click** (Windows) or **Control-click** (Mac) any standard frame from 71 to 99 and choose **Create Motion Tween**.

Notice that while the text is now vibrantly clear, the final image has disappeared. Because the design calls for the image to stay visible, you need to add frames to the image layer.

8. Place your cursor on **frame 100** of the Image 4 layer. **Right-click** (Windows) or **Control-click** (Mac) and choose **Insert Frame.**

Flash fills in the missing frames automatically (Figure 7-17).

FIGURE 7-17

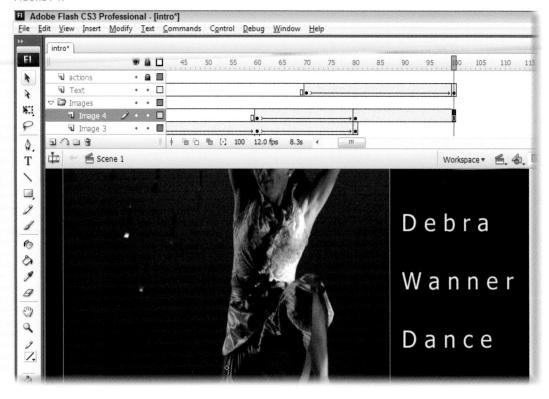

9. Choose **File ▶ Save** to store the file and then choose **Control ▶ Test Movie**.

Technically, your Flash intro is now complete, and you could publish and bring it into Dreamweaver for deployment. However, not every site visitor wants to view the intro each time they visit the site, and it is considered a best practice to always include a way to skip the movie and proceed directly to the site. In the next series of exercises, you learn how to provide that option with a navigational link, complete with ActionScript coding.

CREATING NAVIGATION BUTTONS

Interactivity is a key aspect of many Flash movies. Whether you're designing effects that follow the user's cursor or going for an immersive game environment, Flash interactivity depends on two primary elements: symbols and ActionScript.

In this exercise, you get a taste of what's possible through Flash scripting, with a very practical example: the skip intro link. As the name implies, this type of link has a very clear purpose: to break out of the current animation and redirect the visitor to the site's main page. In HTML, this type of link is extremely straightforward with rollover effects easily achieved through CSS. In Flash, you need to apply both button symbols and ActionScript code to get the same effect.

MAKING THE BUTTON SYMBOL

As you've seen, there are a number of options when converting a selection to a Flash symbol: movie clip, button, and graphic. All of the previous exercises converted the images to movie clip symbols. The button symbol is, in a sense, a specialized form of movie clip with four distinct frames. Three of the frames are used to display the button states (up, over, and down) and the fourth defines the button's interactive area or hit state. Button symbols can be created from graphics with text labels or, as in this case, straight text.

1. Choose **View ▶ Rulers** and from the vertical ruler drag out a guide to line up with the left edge of the title text.

   A guide helps you make sure the link is properly placed.

2. In the timeline, choose **frame 1** in the **Background** layer (Figure 7-18).

   FIGURE 7-18

   You want the skip intro link to be available throughout the movie, so it must be in place from frame 1 onward.

3. Select the **Text** tool and in the Property inspector change the **Font Size** to **10**; click the **Color swatch** to sample the **light gray** color (#CCCCCC); and set the **Letter Spacing** value to **1**.

   These properties are intended to keep the link in the same style as the title text, but with a far less pronounced impact.

4. Place your cursor in alignment with the vertical guide near the bottom of the stage and enter **skip intro**. Choose the **Selection** tool and in the Property inspector change the **Y** value to **735** and press **Tab**.

Here's another circumstance where you need to add frames make sure the text is visible to the end of the movie.

5. **Right-click** (Windows) or **Control-oliok** (Mac) on **frame 100** in the Background layer and choose **Insert Frame**.

Your text is now on the stage at the proper position (Figure 7-19)—time to turn it into a button symbol.

FIGURE 7-19

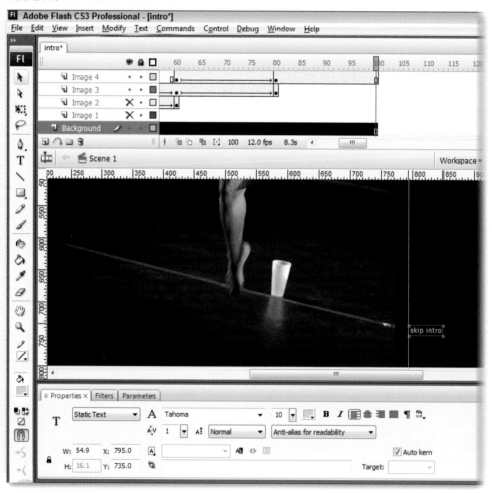

6. **Right-click** (Windows) or **Control-click** (Mac) the just inserted text and choose **Convert to Symbol**. When the **Convert to Symbol** dialog box appears, enter **skip_intro** and choose **Type: Button** (Figure 7-20). Click **OK**. In the Property inspector name field, enter **skip_btn**.

FIGURE 7-20

Notice that the symbol and instance names are distinct. Although names are often arbitrary, here at least part of the instance name is quite significant. The _btn suffix indicates a button symbol to the Flash code editor and makes writing the ActionScript code easier.

With the button symbol created, you're ready to define the various states.

7. Double-click the newly created button symbol on the stage to enter into editing mode.

Flash allows symbol editing in place, so you can keep track of the other stage elements, such as the graphic, although it is dimmed and obviously not the focus. The other indicator is the breadcrumb trail located at the top of the stage window that now displays Scene 1 followed by your symbol name, skip intro (Figure 7-21). When you're done editing, you click Scene 1 to return to the main timeline.

FIGURE 7-20

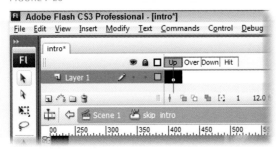

The other key difference that indicates a button symbol comprises the four specialized frames: Up, Over, Down, and Hit. While there is only one keyframe for the Up state when you begin editing, you can easily create the others and modify them as needed.

8. Select the keyframe under the **Up** frame. Press **Alt** (Windows) or **Option** (Mac) and drag a copy of the keyframe to the **Over** frame. Select the **skip intro** text and in the Property inspector change the **Color swatch** to **white** and toggle **Bold** on (Figure 7-22).

FIGURE 7-22

While you could insert other layers here to achieve any number of effects, a simple color change and emboldening is enough to indicate the hover state to the user. You can also keep the same design for the down state.

9. Select the **Over** keyframe. Press **Alt** (Windows) or **Option** (Mac) and drag a copy of the keyframe to the **Down** frame. Repeat this operation to create a copy for the Hit state. Click **Scene 1** at the top of the stage window to leave editing mode.

The interactive design for the skip intro link is now complete, although there are no actions yet attached to the button. You can, however, test the various button states right on stage.

10. Choose **Control ▶ Enable Simple Buttons**. Click anywhere off the stage to clear the selection and then move your pointer over the skip intro text. After you've verified the change (Figure 7-23), choose **Control ▶ Enable Simple Buttons** again to disable the feature and press **Ctrl+S** (Windows) or **Cmd+S** (Mac) to save your document.

FIGURE 7-23

With that done, it's time to pop the hood on Flash and dive into its powerful engine: ActionScript.

206 PART **01**   PART **02**   PART **03**   PART **04**   APPENDIX

Photoshop to Dreamweaver   Fireworks to Dreamweaver   Flash to Dreamweaver   Photoshop to Bridge to   Additional Workflows
Fireworks to Dreamweaver

ADDING ACTIONSCRIPT CODE

ActionScript is the programming language for Flash. The current version, 3.0, is an object-oriented structured language that allows for very sophisticated applications and managements of large datasets. The ActionScript 3.0 engine is utilized in Flash Player 9 as well as Adobe Flex and Flex Builder. The current release is capable of running code generated by the previous versions, but significantly faster overall.

To create a functioning link, your code needs to accomplish three things:

- Set up a link to a specific page with a `URLRequest()` object.

- Establish an event listener to wait for the user's click.

- Navigate to the link when the link occurs.

Although it may appear to be overkill for a simple link, Flash guides you in your coding to simplify the process. You start by taking advantage of the actions layer previously established.

1. In the timeline, select **frame 1** of the **actions** layer. **Right-click** (Windows) or **Control-click** (Mac) and choose **Insert Keyframe**.

    All ActionScript code is embedded in this keyframe, which is processed first when the movie is played in the Flash Player.

2. Choose **Window ▶ Actions**.

    The Actions panel is the built-in ActionScript editor. You can toggle it by pressing F9.

3. Place your cursor in the code editor and enter the first line of code:

    ```
    var link:URLRequest = new URLRequest("homepage.htm");
    ```

    and press **Enter** (Windows) or **Return** (Mac) to create a new line.

    Notice that after you type `var link:` the first code hints appear. Each of the next letters you type narrows the selection in the list; by the time you've typed the first four letters, `URLR`, you see the desired function. To auto-complete the function name, press **Enter** (Windows) or **Return** (Mac). Another type of code hint appears after you've entered the opening parenthesis after `new URLRequest` (Figure 7-24); this hint indicates what is expected for this function.

FIGURE 7-24

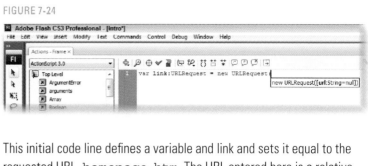

This initial code line defines a variable and link and sets it equal to the requested URL, homepage.htm. The URL entered here is a relative link—you could have just as easily entered an absolute link, for example, www.adobe.com.

4. On the new line, enter the following code:

```
skip _ btn.addEventListener(MouseEvent.CLICK,
   onClick);
```

and press **Enter** (Windows) or **Return** (Mac) to create a new line.

Again, various code hints appear as you type. The first part of this code refers to the instance of the button symbol placed on the stage, skip _ btn. The addEventListener() function tells Flash to wait for a specific interaction, which in this case is the MouseEvent known as CLICK. The final code—onClick—is the name of the function to execute when the click event is detected.

Next, you enter the onClick function in its entirety.

5. On the new line, enter the following code:

```
function onClick(event:MouseEvent):void
{
   navigateToURL(link);
}
```

and press **Ctrl+S** (Windows) or **Cmd+S** (Mac).

208   PART 01   PART 02   PART 03   PART 04   APPENDIX

Photoshop to Dreamweaver   Fireworks to Dreamweaver   Flash to Dreamweaver   Photoshop to Bridge to Fireworks to Dreamweaver   Additional Workflows

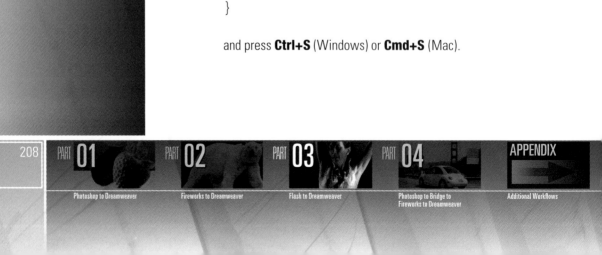

This code (Figure 7-25) creates the function named onClick, which is defined as a MouseEvent function. The Flash function navigateToURL() is used perform the actual browser redirection to the page declared as the variable, link.

FIGURE 7-25

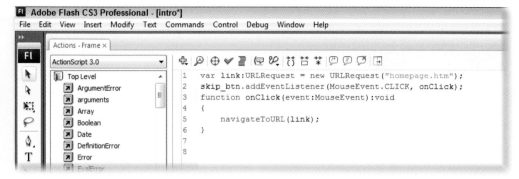

6. Press **F9** to close the Actions panel.

Your Flash intro is now completed, ready to be published, and then deployed in Dreamweaver.

DISPLAYING IN DREAMWEAVER

Before you can integrate your Flash intro into a Dreamweaver page, you need to publish it first. Flash's native source format is the FLA file and published movies, viewable by the Flash Player, are SWF files. While you can also publish a number of other file types, including HTML, PNG, and QuickTime movies, the typical Flash to Dreamweaver workflow requires only the SWF file.

1. Choose **File ▶ Publish Settings**.

    The Publish Settings dialog box allows you to set which formats to export. Every selected export option offers its own tab for specific parameters. By default, the two options are Flash (.swf) and HTML (.html).

2. When the **Publish Settings** dialog box appears. Make sure you're on the **Formats tab** and deselect the **HTML** option. Click the **folder icon** and when the **Select Publish Destination** dialog box appears navigate to the **Chapter 7** folder and click **Save** (Figure 7-26). If Flash asks if you'd like to overwrite the existing file, click **Yes**.

FL CORE TECHNIQUES

CREATING NAVIGATION BUTTONS

Flash offers a full slate of interactivity, not the least of which are navigational buttons. A navigational button may be either a graphical button or text link that when finalized may include a rollover as well as other states. Here are the basic steps for creating a navigational button.

1. Choose basic element.

2. Convert to symbol, button type.

3. Edit button to define Up, Over, Down, and Hit states of button.

4. Give instance on stage a unique name, ending with `_btn`.

5. Create actions layer with single keyframe in frame 1.

6. Insert ActionScript code.

   - Define link variable with `URLRequest()`.

   - Add an eventListener to button instance that calls function on click.

   - Create a function that incorporates `navigateToURL()`.

FIGURE 7-26

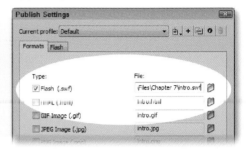

As noted earlier, in this exercise, you create your own HTML page in Dreamweaver, so there is no need to create one here. This is, however, a good option when you just want to quickly show your Flash work to a client on a Web page—although you still need to put the page online somehow.

3. Switch to the **Flash tab** and verify that **Version** is set to **Flash Player 9** and **ActionScript version** to **ActionScript 3.0**. Leave all other settings at their default and click **Publish.** After the publication is complete, click **OK**.

When the SWF file published, you're ready to bring it into Dreamweaver. With designs like the Flash intro, the Flash movie is the only item on the page. In many cases, however, you might still want to style the page with CSS and provide a simple layout to control margins and padding.

1. In Dreamweaver, choose **File ▶ Open** and when the **Open** dialog box appears, navigate to the **Chapter 7** folder. Select **index.htm** and click **Open**.

   Flash intros should be stored in a file with the default folder filename like index.htm or

210   PART **01**   PART **02**   PART **03**   PART **04**   APPENDIX

Photoshop to Dreamweaver   Fireworks to Dreamweaver   Flash to Dreamweaver   Photoshop to Bridge to Fireworks to Dreamweaver   Additional Workflows

default.html. The just-opened file has a black CSS background with a single <div> tag, #outerWrapper, which is styled to center its content.

2. Select the placeholder text, **Content for id "outerWrapper" Goes Here**, and press Delete. From the **Common** category of the **Insert** bar, choose **Flash** under the **Media** menu button. When the **Select File** dialog box opens, navigate to the **Chapter 7** folder and select **intro.swf**.

   The Flash movie placeholder is displayed in Dreamweaver, complete with custom Property inspector.

3. In the Flash Property inspector, clear the **Loop** checkbox and make sure the **AutoPlay** checkbox is selected (Figure 7-27).

FIGURE 7-27

4. Choose **File ▶ Save**. If Dreamweaver reminds you of the files you need to copy to your remote site, click **OK**. Press **F12** to preview the intro (Figure 7-28).

   Unless you're previewing through a Web server, your skip intro link won't work. Flash requires an actual Web server—such as a hosted site—for the ActionScript code to function properly.

FIGURE 7-28

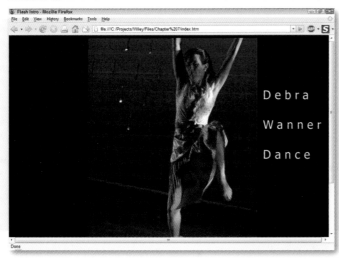

Dw CORE TECHNIQUES

INSERTING FLASH MOVIES

Dreamweaver's Flash movie object makes integrating SWF files as straightforward as possible. The only mandatory step is to choose **Insert ▶ Media ▶ Flash** or, from the Common category of the Insert bar, select **Flash** under the Media menu button. Just select the desired SWF file and Flash does the rest.

Although it's not apparent in design view, Dreamweaver inserts a fair amount of sophisticated code for each Flash movie. The primary JavaScript is contained in an external file, `AC _ RunActiveContent.js`, and is automatically copied to your site in a Scripts folder. This JavaScript file includes Flash detection and redirection code, as well as setting the proper ActiveX call for a variety of Internet Explorer browser versions.

The placeholder Flash movie can be previewed by selecting it and clicking Preview in the Property inspector. Other parameters, such as loop and autoplay, are also settable in the Property inspector.

When publishing your HTML page that contains the Flash file, it's important to remember to upload all dependent files as well, including the SWF and the related JavaScript file.

Working with Flash can be a real eye opener for graphic designers used to dealing with static imagery. While this chapter barely scratched the surface of what's possible with Flash, you'll find the methods and effects covered can be put to good use in many situations

In the next chapter, you'll learn how to work with Flash video so that it can be easily played back in a Dreamweaver Web page.

212

PART **01**
Photoshop to Dreamweaver

PART **02**
Fireworks to Dreamweaver

PART **03**
Flash to Dreamweaver

PART **04**
Photoshop to Bridge to
Fireworks to Dreamweaver

APPENDIX
Additional Workflows

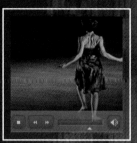
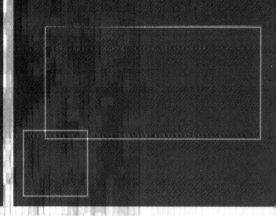

One of the great innovations in the Flash Player in recent years is the support of video. With Flash's ubiquity across browser platforms, it was suddenly possible to publish your video in one format and have it play everywhere. If anything, the popularity of Flash video—and use by YouTube and Google video—has further enhanced the Flash Player's hold on the marketplace.

Video is increasingly integrated into Web pages, both as standalone movies and as elements in Flash animations. In this chapter, you'll learn how to import a Flash video file (FLV) into an existing Flash movie to add an extra bit of sizzle and then bring that composition into Dreamweaver. Additionally, you'll learn how to work with the Flash video components that allow flexible player control with features like full-screen display and onscreen captioning. While it has been possible for Dreamweaver users to easily integrate an FLV into their pages for a number of versions, you have a great deal more power and customizability available when you work within the Flash to Dreamweaver workflow.

In the following exercises, you'll learn these core Flash techniques:

- Importing video
- Using the playback component

And this Dreamweaver technique:

- Inserting Flash movies

CHAPTER

08

SETTING UP FLASH VIDEO

INTEGRATING VIDEO IN FLASH ANIMATIONS

With Flash, video doesn't need to be isolated in a box—you can easily bring the realistic movement of video into standard Flash animations as just another layer. The trick, of course, is to make sure that your video integrates well with the other elements of your composition. Some designers rely on Flash's ability to display alpha channel video—commonly referred to as *green screen*—where the background is removed. Another approach, used in this exercise, is to find video that fits the design in both background color and positioning.

In this exercise, you import a Flash video file into an existing Flash movie. When completed, this Flash design is inserted as a header element in the homepage of a site in Dreamweaver.

1. In Flash, choose **File ▶ Open**. When the **Open** dialog box appears, navigate to the **Chapter 8** folder of exercise files and select **header.fla** and click **OK.**

   This Flash file uses imagery and text design (Figure 8-1) from the Flash intro created in the previous chapter. As designed, the graphics appear immediately, and the title text fades in shortly after.

FIGURE 8-1

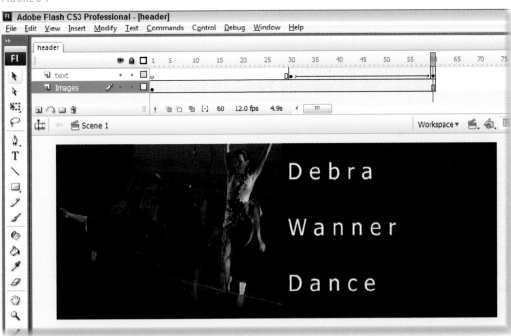

Now you can set up a layer to hold the video.

INTEGRATING VIDEO IN FLASH ANIMATIONS // ENCODING VIDEO // CHAPTER 215

WORKING WITH PLAYBACK COMPONENTS // ADDING CAPTIONS TO FLASH VIDEO //
INSERTING VIDEO INTO DREAMWEAVER // EDITING FLASH FROM DREAMWEAVER //

08

2. In the Timeline, select the **Images** layer and click **Insert Layer**. Double-click the layer name and enter **Video**; press **Enter** (Windows) or **Return** (Mac). Drag the new layer below the Images layer.

To make sure that all the other elements remain visible, you place the video in a layer at the lowest point.

3. Choose **File ▶ Import ▶ Import Video**. When the **Import Video** dialog box appears, make sure the **On your computer** option is selected and click **Browse**. In the **Open** dialog box, navigate to the **Chapter 8** folder and choose **debra_wanner_dance.flv**; click **Open** (Figure 8-2). When you're ready, click **Next**.

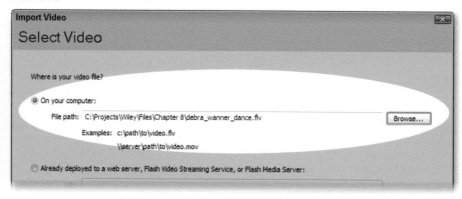

Unless your video has already been deployed, your most likely choice here is a file on your computer.

4. On the Deployment step, choose the **Progressive download from a web server** option and click **Next**.

The basic choices between deploying your Flash video are storing it on a standard server or on a media server. For more short length video files, the standard server using the progressive download works well; media servers such as Flash Media Server are better for longer videos where features such as instant on and seekability are important.

5. On the Skinning step, choose **None** from the **Skin** list (Figure 8-3); click **Next**.

You have a good number of options when it comes to adding player controls to your Flash movie through what is referred to as the skin; however, for this integration, you don't want any to be shown.

216   PART **01**   PART **02**   PART **03**   PART **04**   APPENDIX

Photoshop to Dreamweaver   Fireworks to Dreamweaver   Flash to Dreamweaver   Photoshop to Bridge to Fireworks to Dreamweaver   Additional Workflows

FIGURE 8-3

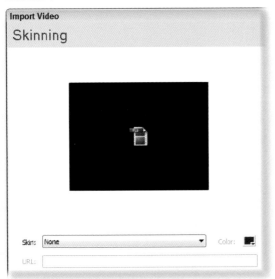

6. On the final screen, review the presented information, especially the reminder to upload your FLV file, and click **Finish**.

   The Flash video is placed on your stage in its original dimensions (720 x 480); you need to reduce the size and position it properly.

7. With the newly inserted video selected, click the **padlock** icon in the Property inspector to lock the aspect ratio. Change the **Width** value to **426.6** and press **Tab**; the **Height** value changes to **284.4** automatically. Press **Tab** again and in the **X** field enter **315**. Press **Tab** and enter **0** in the **Y** field (Figure 8-4).

FIGURE 8-4

Once imported, your video can be quickly rescaled and placed as needed. Next, it's time to check out the completed composition.

8. Choose **Control ▶ Test Movie**. After the movie has played, close the Flash Player window.

   The video plays once and stops as the text fades in (Figure 8-5). The text motion tween loops, which you can correct in Dreamweaver.

   FIGURE 8-5

9. Choose **File ▶ Publish Settings**. When the **Publish Settings** dialog box appears, make sure you're on the **Formats tab** and deselect the **HTML** option. Click the **folder icon** and, when the **Select Publish Destination** dialog box appears, navigate to the **Chapter 8** folder with the filename **header.swf** and click **Save**. If Flash asks if you'd like to overwrite the existing file, click **Yes**.

   Now, you can create a SWF file to use in Dreamweaver.

10. Choose File ▶ Publish.

You've completed one of the three video projects you want to integrate into Dreamweaver. Next, you'll learn how to convert raw video files into FLV format.

218 PART 01 PART 02 PART 03 PART 04 APPENDIX

Photoshop to Dreamweaver   Fireworks to Dreamweaver   Flash to Dreamweaver   Photoshop to Bridge to   Additional Workflows
                                                                                Fireworks to Dreamweaver

CORE TECHNIQUES

IMPORTING VIDEO IN FLASH

Flash includes a feature for converting standard video files to its own video format, FLV, one at a time. With the Import Video feature, you can create either a standalone video, complete with player controls, or a video element to be integrated into a Flash composition.

To import a Flash video, follow these steps:

1. Choose **File ▶ Import ▶ Import Video**.

2. In the first step of the wizard, select the video file to be converted.

   You can select either a local file or a file already published on the Web. Supported file types are QuickTime Movies (.mov), Video for Windows (.avi), MPEG Movie (.mpg), Digital Video (.dv), Windows Media (.wmv), and 3GPP/3GPP2 for Mobile Devices (.3gp). You can also import Flash Video (.flv) without converting the file.

3. In the second step of the wizard, choose how you would like to deploy your video.

   The two most common choices are progressive download and stream from Flash Media Server. The first option allows the video file to be published to a standard Web server while the second option requires the use of a specialized video server. For short videos, progressive download is an adequate solution although the user will notice a short delay while the video is initially downloaded for playback. If your site requires a good deal of video or lengthy videos, the streaming solution is more appropriate. Playback is instantaneous and the seek feature is immediately available throughout the video.

4. Next, set the encoding options, including video and audio quality, cue points, and display size.

   A wide range of video and audio options are available that can determine viewing quality and file size. A cue point is a specific time in the video that is assigned a variable name that can be called in ActionScript coding. On the Crop and Resize tab, you can resize the video to a size more appropriate to your Web page.

(continued)

(continued)

5. In the fourth step of the wizard, you select the skin for your video. The skin contains the various player controls.

Flash CS3 Professional offers two basic skins: one that overlaps the bottom of the video and another that appears below the video. Each skin has a number of variations with different control combinations and can be set to any color desired. Further variations, such as control over the transparency (alpha) of the skin, are available in the Property inspector once the video is on the Flash stage.

6. The final step confirms your choices and starts the import and conversion process.

After the video has been imported, various aspects can be easily modified through the Property inspector.

ENCODING VIDEO

For video to be shown in the Flash Player, it must be in the FLV format. Flash CS3 Professional provides a number of key methods for converting video files in other formats, such as QuickTime MOV or Windows AVI, to FLV. One such tool is the Adobe Flash CS3 Video Encoder. The Video Encoder is the perfect tool to use if you need to convert a number of video clips and is a great addition to the Flash video workflow.

> You need Adobe Flash CS3 Video Encoder installed to complete the following exercise. If you don't have it installed, you can choose File ▶ Import ▶ Import Video in Flash and execute similar steps.

In this exercise, you convert an excerpt from a video that is currently in AVI format to FLV. The converted video is used later in this chapter, first in conjunction with Flash playback components and later in Dreamweaver as a demonstration of full-screen capabilities.

1. From the Adobe CS3 Web applications folder, choose **Adobe Flash CS3 Video Encoder**.

   While the core functionality is available in Flash through the Import Video feature, you can only import one video at a time within Flash. The key advantage of this separate program is its ability to batch process video files.

2. Choose **Add** and, when the **Open** dialog box appears, navigate to the **Chapter 8** folder and select **Surface.avi**; click **Open**.

   While you can proceed with the conversion now that the file is listed (Figure 8-6), typically you need to refine your settings before continuing.

PART **01**   PART **02**   PART **03**   PART **04**   APPENDIX

Photoshop to Dreamweaver   Fireworks to Dreamweaver   Flash to Dreamweaver   Photoshop to Bridge to Fireworks to Dreamweaver   Additional Workflows

FIGURE 8.6

3. Click **Settings**. On the Encoding Profiles tab, choose **Flash 8 - Medium Quality (400bps)** from the list. In the **Output filename** field, enter **surface.flv**.

Flash gives you a great deal of control over the output file with separate video and output options. You can also define cue points that can be later used to trigger ActionScript events. The only modification you make in this exercise, however, is to reduce the video dimensions.

4. Switch to the **Crop and Resize** tab. Select the **Resize video** option and, with **Maintain Aspect Ratio** selected, enter **360** in the **Width** field and press **Tab** (Figure 8-7). Click **OK**.

FIGURE 8.7

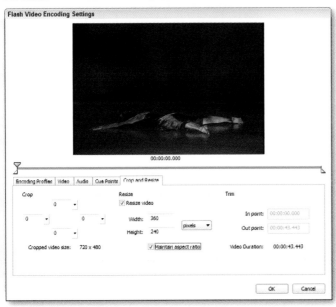

While you could rescale the movie in Flash, you get a much smaller file size if you resize it as part of the encoding process.

INTEGRATING VIDEO IN FLASH ANIMATIONS // ENCODING VIDEO // CHAPTER   221

WORKING WITH PLAYBACK COMPONENTS // ADDING CAPTIONS TO FLASH VIDEO //
INSERTING VIDEO INTO DREAMWEAVER // EDITING FLASH FROM DREAMWEAVER //   08

5. Choose **Start Queue**.

   Depending on the speed of your processor, the conversion should take approximately three minutes.

6. When the process is completed, select the entry and choose **Remove**. Close the application.

   While it's not essential that you delete the queue item, it's a good habit to get into. Otherwise, the same entry is present the next time you open the Video Encoder, and you could rerun the conversion unnecessarily.

In the next exercise, you'll apply your just converted FLV to a new playback component.

WORKING WITH PLAYBACK COMPONENTS

If you're primarily a Dreamweaver user who has integrated Flash video into a site before, you're probably familiar with the Flash Video object. This feature outputs both the video and player controls (a.k.a., the skin) and adds them to your Web page. The Flash Video object approach is very handy if you're using just Dreamweaver and don't have access to Flash itself. However, compared to what's possible with a Flash and Dreamweaver workflow, it is very restrictive—and following the Flash and Dreamweaver workflow is not that much more difficult.

The Flash to Dreamweaver workflow relies on one or more Flash components. A Flash component is, essentially, an object with customizable properties that adds advanced functionality with drag-and-drop ease. For video, the primary one is the FLVPlayback component. Once this is placed on the stage, you can easily set the FLV source file and adjust any necessary parameters, including setting the skin.

In this exercise, you create a new Flash movie, insert an FLVPlayback component, define its parameters, and stylize the skin.

1. In Flash, choose **File ▶ New**. When the **New Document** dialog box appears, select **Flash File (ActionScript 3.0)** and click **OK**. Choose **File ▶ Save**; in the **Save As** dialog box, navigate to the **Chapter 8** folder and enter **surface_movie.fla** in the **File name** field; click **OK.**

   While you could set the properties at this point, it's actually better to wait until the video component is on the stage so you can match the size exactly.

2. Choose **Window ▶ Components**. When the **Components** panel opens, expand the **Video** entry and drag **FLVPlayback** onto the stage (Figure 8-8).

222 PART **01** PART **02** PART **03** PART **04** APPENDIX

Photoshop to Dreamweaver   Fireworks to Dreamweaver   Flash to Dreamweaver   Photoshop to Bridge to   Additional Workflows
                                                                                Fireworks to Dreamweaver

FIGURE 8-8

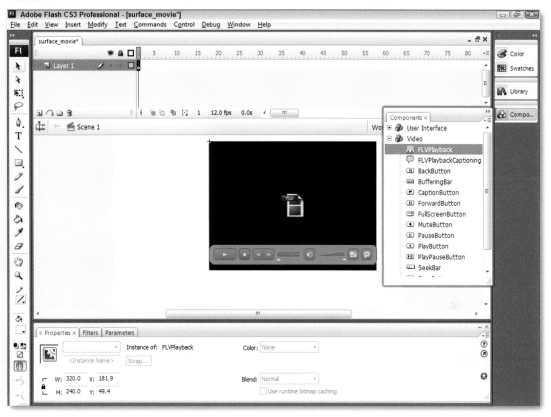

Most of the components in the video section are individual controls such as the BackButton and PlayButton. The FLVPlayback component combines all of the controls in the optional skin.

3. In the Property inspector, choose the **Parameters** tab. Click the entry next to the **skin** property and choose the **Browse** icon. In the **Select Skin** dialog box, choose **SkinOverAll.swf** from the **Skin** list and select a **medium blue** from the color picker, click **OK**. Set the **skinAutoHide** property to **true**.

    You've now chosen a skin that has all the available controls, set a basic color for it, and opted to hide it when the user's mouse is off the movie. With the great number of other parameters you can set, you can see how easily you can customize your Flash movie. It's time to add the video source now.

4. Select the field next to **source** and click the **Browse** icon. When the **Content Path** dialog box appears, click the **folder** icon. In the Browse for FLV file dialog box, navigate to the **Chapter 8** folder and select **surface.flv**; click **Open**. Click **OK** to confirm your choice and close the **Content Path** dialog.

Notice that the movie placeholder changes size slightly; the default FLVPlayback component is a bit smaller than the FLV file that you resized with the Video Encoder in the previous steps. Now it's time to resize the stage to match the component.

5. Choose **Modify ▶ Document**. In the **Document** dialog box, choose **Match: Contents** and click **OK**.

The stage resizes to match the video component (Figure 8-9), ready to be played.

FIGURE 8-9

6. Choose **Control ▶ Test Movie**. After the video begins to play, move your cursor over the movie and try a number of the controls, such as **Pause/Play** and the **seek bar** (Figure 8-10). When you're done, close the window.

Certain controls won't have any apparent effect. For example, neither the full-screen or closed captioning options work right now; you need to do a little more setup to activate these controls.

FIGURE 8-10

224   PART **01**   PART **02**   PART **03**   PART **04**   APPENDIX

Photoshop to Dreamweaver   Fireworks to Dreamweaver   Flash to Dreamweaver   Photoshop to Bridge to   Additional Workflows
                                                                              Fireworks to Dreamweaver

7. Choose **File ▶ Publish Settings**. When the **Publish Settings** dialog box appears, make sure you're on the **Formats** tab and deselect the **HTML** option; click **OK**.

There's no need to set the destination for the SWF because the FLA file was already saved in the desired directory. Now you can output the movie to add to your Dreamweaver page later in the chapter.

8.Choose **File ▶ Publish** and then choose **File ▶ Save**.

In the next exercise, you'll learn how to take advantage of another Flash component to easily add captions to your video.

ADDING CAPTIONS TO FLASH VIDEO

Flash CS3 Professional offers a major advance in video accessibility with the FLVPlaybackCaptioning component. As the name implies, this component adds captions to any Flash video. The captions are then displayed or hidden interactively via a control button built in to a variety of skins.

The captions are tied to the time code of the video; each line begins at a precise time, is displayed for a specific period, and then vanishes at a specifically defined point. The text for the captions—and their exact timings—are

USING THE PLAYBACK COMPONENT

When your video is in FLV format, you can use Flash's playback component to quickly prepare your file for watching. Additionally, the FLVPlayback component is easily modified in the Flash Property inspector.

To add a playback component to your Flash movie, follow these steps:

1. Choose Window ▶ Components.

2. In the Components panel, expand the Video entry.

3. Drag the FLVPlayback component onto the stage.

4. Set the video attributes by selecting the Parameter **t**ab in the Property inspector. Key parameters are:

   • **source**—The path and filename of the FLV file.

   • **skin**—The player controls, if any. Choose whether you'd like the controls to appear on or below the video as well as what controls should be included.

   • **skinAutoHide**—If set to true, hides the controls until the user's cursor is over the movie.

   • **skinBackgroundColor**—Sets the color of the controls.

5. Save and publish the Flash movie as usual.

detailed in an XML file, the format of which is a subset of the W3C's XML Timed Text specification. Captions are styled by declarations within the XML file; you can establish different styles to be displayed at different points. For example, the text can change color from white to red for emphasis.

There are three main sections for a typical Flash Timed Text XML file. The first section, the heading, contains the various required declarations:

```
<?xml version=»1.0» encoding=»UTF-8»?>
<tt xml:lang=»en» xmlns=»http://www.w3.org/2006/04/ttaf1»  xmlns:tts=»http://
   www.w3.org/2006/04/ttaf1#styling»>
```

After the opening XML tag, the `<tt>` tag identifies the file as a Timed Text format with a declared namespace.

The next section contains the style information for the captions. In the following example, a single style with the ID of 1 is defined with five different attributes:

```
<head>
  <styling>
    <style xml:id="1"
       tts:textAlign="center"
       tts:color="white"
       tts:backgroundColor="transparent"
       tts:fontSize="18"
       tts:fontFamily="Arial"
    />
  </styling>
</head>
```

Note the special attribute in the `<style>` tag, `xml:id`. This attribute marks the style in a way so that it can be assigned to one or more captions. Multiple <style> tags can be nested within the <styling> tag; each must have a unique xml:id.

The final section contains the captions themselves. The captions are linked to a defined style by referencing the appropriate `xml:id` in as a `style` attribute in either a surrounding `<div>` tag or individual `<p>` tags. The following example sets all the captions to the same style via the `<div>` tag:

226   PART **01**   PART **02**   PART **03**   PART **04**   APPENDIX

Photoshop to Dreamweaver   Fireworks to Dreamweaver   Flash to Dreamweaver   Photoshop to Bridge to Fireworks to Dreamweaver   Additional Workflows

```
<body>
    <div style="1">
        <p begin="00:00:03.13" end="00:00:05.00">She says</p>
        <p begin="00:00:05.20" end="00:00:06.25">on the subway</p>
        <p begin="00:00:08.03" end="00:00:09.10">she's afraid of most
            of the people</p>
        <p begin="00:00:010.00" end="00:00:11.15">most of the time</p>
    </div>
</body>
</tt>
```

Each caption is contained within a `<p>` tag. The `begin` attribute gives the precise time code to display the caption. Here, the `end` attribute marks when the caption should disappear; it is also possible to use a `dur` attribute to declare the duration of a caption. Another technique is to not use either an `end` or `dur` attribute and allow the next caption to simply replace the current one at the specified time.

The hardest part of adding captions to a Flash video is creating the XML file; an example file is included so you can focus on the setting up the captioning component properly, as described in the following exercise.

1. In Flash, choose **File ▶ New**. When the **New Document** dialog box appears, select **Flash File (ActionScript 3.0)** and click **OK**. Choose **File ▶ Save**. In the **Save As** dialog box, navigate to the **Chapter 8** folder, and enter **sheStories_movie.fla** in the **File name** field; click **OK.**

2. Choose **Window ▶ Components**. When the Components panel opens, expand the **Video** entry and drag **FLVPlayback** onto the stage. In the **Property inspector name** field, enter **sheStories** (Figure 8-11).

FIGURE 8-11

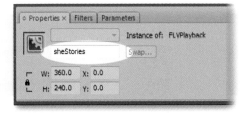

As before, you add a playback component and set the initial parameters. Here, however, you need to refer the caption component to the movie component, so a name is necessary.

3. In the Property inspector, choose the **Parameters** tab. Click the entry next to the **skIn** property and choose the **Browse** icon. In the **Select Skin** dialog box, choose **SkinUnderAll.swf** from the **Skin** list and select a **medium blue** from the color picker; click **OK**.

Because the captions are displayed in the lower portion of the screen (Figure 8-12), it's best to move the player controls below the video.

FIGURE 8-12

4. Select the field next to **source** and click the **Browse** icon. When the **Content Path** dialog box appears, click the **folder** icon. In the **Browse for FLV file** dialog box, navigate to the **Chapter 8** folder and select **sheStories.flv**; click **Open**. Click **OK** to confirm your choice and close the **Content Path** dialog.

Again, you need to match the document size to the size of the video. Unfortunately, Flash doesn't recognize the skin as part of the contents, so you need to adjust the height.

5. Choose **Modify ▶ Document**. In the **Document** dialog box, choose **Match: Contents.** In the **Height** field, change the value to **276** and click **OK**.

The playback component is now properly configured—it's time to add the captioning.

6. From the Component panel, drag the **FLVPlaybackCaptioning** component into the document area, but off the main stage.

228
PART **01**
PART **02**
PART **03**
PART **04**
APPENDIX

Photoshop to Dreamweaver   Fireworks to Dreamweaver   Flash to Dreamweaver   Photoshop to Bridge to   Additional Workflows
                                                                              Fireworks to Dreamweaver

Because there is no visible interface to the FLVPlaybackCaptioning component, you want to keep it off-stage.

7. In the Property inspector, switch to the **Parameters** tab. Set the **flvPlaybackName** property to **sheStories** and the **source** property to **captions.xml** (Figure 8-13).

FIGURE 8-13

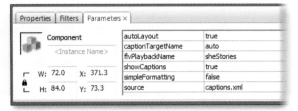

There is no browse functionality for the captioning component's source attribute, so you need to enter the full path and filename of the XML file. The example XML file, captions.xml, is contained in the Chapter 8 folder.

Ready to see your captions in action?

8. Choose **Control ▶ Test Movie**. After the video begins to play and a number of captions have displayed (Figure 8-14), toggle them off and on by selecting the Caption button. When you're done, close the window.

FIGURE 8-14

Now it's time to finish up with this file and get ready to move to Dreamweaver.

9. Choose **File ▶ Publish Settings**. When the **Publish Settings** dialog box appears, make sure you're on the **Formats** tab and deselect the **HTML** option; click **OK**. Choose **File ▶ Publish** and then choose **File ▶ Save**.

All of your Flash video work is completed, and you're ready to begin integrating these elements into Dreamweaver.

INSERTING VIDEO INTO DREAMWEAVER

The beauty of compositing your videos in Flash—whether they are integrated into another Flash movie, like the header created earlier in this chapter, or are like either of the videos created so far—is that adding them to Dreamweaver is a snap. Essentially, all you need to do is insert them as regular Flash movies and check off a couple of options. There are, however, a few parameters you need to add to enable full-screen capability.

1. In Dreamweaver, choose **File ▶ Open**. When the **Open** dialog box appears, navigate to the **Chapter 8** folder and select **homepage.htm**; click **Open**.

   To help you focus on the task at hand, I've constructed a simple page with three placeholders (Figure 8-15), one for each Flash movie you insert.

FIGURE 8-15

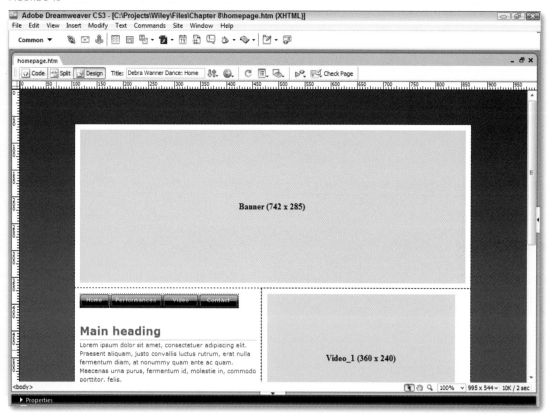

2. Select the **banner** placeholder and press **Delete**. From the **Common** category of the **Insert** bar, choose **Flash** under the **Media** menu button. When the **Select File** dialog box appears, navigate to the **Chapter 8** folder and select **header.swf** and click **OK**.

The Flash file, with the integrated Flash video, fills the header area as expected. You just need to disable a single option to achieve the desired effect.

3. From the Property inspector, deselect the **Loop** option. Click **Play** to review the Flash movie in Dreamweaver (Figure 8-16); after it's over, click **Stop**.

FIGURE 8-16

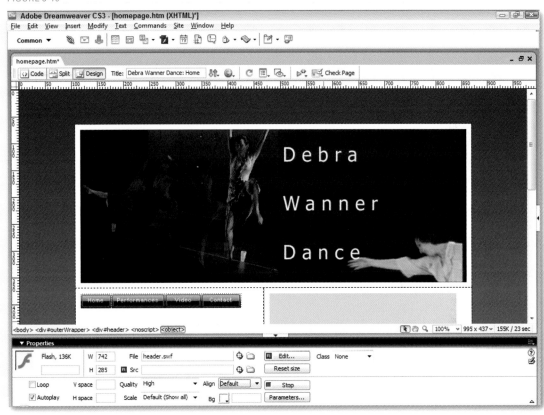

If you hadn't cleared the Loop option, the title (Debra Wanner Dance) would have kept appearing and disappearing; the integrated video, on the other hand, because it is in a movie clip, plays only once. You can bring in the second video now.

4. Select the **Video_1** placeholder and press **Delete**. From the **Common** category of the **Insert** bar, choose **Flash** under the **Media** menu button. When the **Select File** dialog box appears, navigate to the **Chapter 8** folder and select **surface_movie.swf** and click **OK**.

Here, you need to make sure the Flash movie doesn't automatically play or loop. Additionally, you need to add a couple of parameters for the full-screen feature of the Flash Player to work properly.

5. From the Property inspector, deselect the **Autoplay** and **Loop** options. Click **Parameters**. When the **Parameters** dialog box appears, click **Add (+)** and enter **allowFullScreen** in the **Parameter** column. Click in the **Value** column and enter **true** (Figure 8-17). Click **OK** when you're done.

FIGURE 8-17

Now, the video shows just the opening frame and waits for user interaction to play through once—and, if the user so desires, displays in full-screen mode. Now it's time to add the third and final Flash movie.

6. Select the **Video_2** placeholder and press **Delete**. From the **Common** category of the **Insert** bar, choose **Flash** under the **Media** menu button. When the **Select File** dialog box appears, navigate to the **Chapter 8** folder and select **sheStories_movie.swf** and click **OK**. Repeat step 5 to set the proper parameters.

With your page completed, you're ready to take it for a test drive.

7. Choose **File ▶ Save** and press **F12** to preview your page. Note the integrated video that runs in the header. Play the video in the top of the right column and at some point select the **Full Screen** button; press **Esc** to return to standard view. After the video has finished, play the video in the bottom of the right column and toggle the **Caption** button to hide and display the captions (Figure 8-18). When you're done, close your browser and return to Dreamweaver.

232 PART 01 PART 02 PART 03 PART 04 APPENDIX

Photoshop to Dreamweaver   Fireworks to Dreamweaver   Flash to Dreamweaver   Photoshop to Bridge to   Additional Workflows
                                                                                  Fireworks to Dreamweaver

FIGURE 8-18

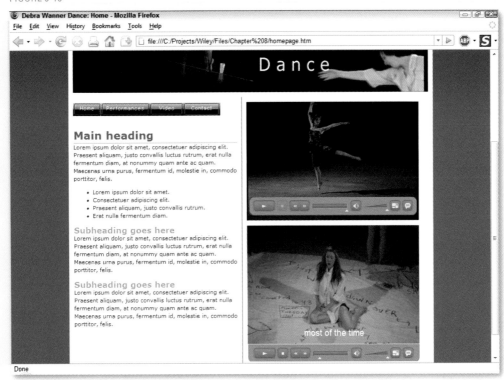

Although the page is apparently completed, in the next exercise, you take a look at what happens when the inevitable request for change comes in—and see how easy it is to modify your Flash movies from within Dreamweaver.

EDITING FLASH FROM DREAMWEAVER

Once you've inserted a SWF file in your Dreamweaver page, updating the related FLA file in Flash is extremely straightforward. While there are a number of options you can control from Dreamweaver, such as autoplay or looping, there are a great number of variables you cannot. For example, with Flash video, you might want to:

- Change to a different FLV source file.

- Modify the player controls.

- Add ActionScript functionality.

- Embed the video in an outer frame of a Flash movie.

Dw CORE TECHNIQUES

INSERTING FLASH VIDEOS

There are two techniques for inserting Flash videos in Dreamweaver. If you only have access to the FLV file, but not Flash, you can use the Dreamweaver Insert Flash Video feature. If you've already imported your video or used the FLVPlayback component in Flash, you would use Dreamweaver's Insert Flash feature.

To use the Insert Flash Video option, follow these steps:

1. Choose **Insert ▶ Media ▶ Flash Video**.

2. When the **Insert Flash Video** dialog box opens, choose between progressive download and streaming.

3. Choose the location of the FLV file, either a local file for progressive download or a URL path for streaming.

4. Select the desired skin.

   Please note that the choices available in Dreamweaver are significantly different than those in Flash.

5. Set the video size and options like auto play and auto rewind.

6. If desired, you can prompt users to download the correct version of the Flash Player and set the displayed message.

Dreamweaver copies all the necessary files to your site and reminds you that they need to be published along with the movie and skin SWF files.

To use the Insert Flash option, choose **Insert ▶ Media ▶ Flash** and select the SWF file. All modifications are made through the Property inspector.

PART **01**
Photoshop to Dreamweaver

PART **02**
Fireworks to Dreamweaver

PART **03**
Flash to Dreamweaver

PART **04**
Photoshop to Bridge to
Fireworks to Dreamweaver

APPENDIX
Additional Workflows

In the following exercise, you call on Dreamweaver and Flash's round-trip editing ability to bring the video skins more in line with the rest of the page design.

1. Select the Flash movie **surface_movie.swf** on the Dreamweaver page. In the Property inspector, click the **Browse for File** icon next to the **Src**. When the **Select Flash Source File** dialog box appears, navigate to the **Chapter 8** folder and choose **surface_movie.fla** (Figure 8-19) and click **OK**.

FIGURE 8-19

By identifying the source file for the current SWF file, you make it possible to invoke the Dreamweaver/ Flash round-trip feature.

2. In the Property inspector, click **Edit**.

If Flash is not open, it launches and displays surface_movie.fla. If Flash is already open, the source file is loaded.

3. In Flash, select the **FLVPlayback** component and in the Property inspector switch to the **Parameters** tab. Change the **skinBackgroundAlpha** value to **.5** and the **skinBackgroundColor** to a medium gray, **#999999**. When you're done, click **Done** (Figure 8-20).

FIGURE 8-20

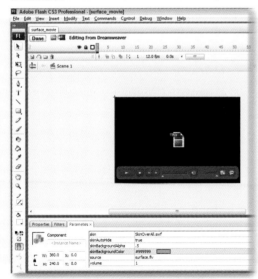

Flash publishes the file anew, closes the FLA file in Flash, and returns control to Dreamweaver. Now run through the process one more time to make the same adjustments to the other Flash video on the Dreamweaver page.

4. In Dreamweaver, select the Flash movie **sheStories_movie.swf** on the Dreamweaver page. In the Property inspector, click the **Browse for File** icon next to the **Src**. When the **Select Flash Source File** dialog box appears, navigate to the **Chapter 8** folder and choose **sheStories_movie.fla** and click **OK**.

5. In the Property inspector, click **Edit**. In Flash, select the **FLVPlayback** component and in the Property inspector switch to the **Parameters** tab. Change the **skinBackgroundAlpha** value to **.5** and the **skinBackgroundColor** to a medium gray, **#999999**. When you're done, click **Done**.

Congratulations! You've completed and modified your Flash video in Dreamweaver page. You can easily verify your changes without even previewing in a browser.

6. Choose **View ▶ Plugins ▶ Play All**. In each of the two Flash videos, select the **Play** button on the respective control bars (Figure 8-21). After you've finished reviewing the page, choose **View ▶ Plugins ▶ Stop All**. Choose **File ▶ Save** to store your page.

FIGURE 8-21

Integrating Flash into your Web workflow can be totally exhilarating, especially when you're working with exciting technology such as Flash video and innovative features such as captioning and full-screen capabilities. The ability to preview your Flash movies in Dreamweaver and, if necessary, edit the source in Flash, makes it possible to fine-tune your Flash integration.

In the next chapter, you begin to explore a more complex workflow that showcases the best features of Photoshop, Bridge, Fireworks, and Dreamweaver.

PART **04**

All Rules
- <style> (all)
- SpryValidationTextField.css
- SpryValidationCheckbox.css
- SpryValidationSelect.css
- mySpry.css
  - .textfieldRequiredState .text
  - .textfieldValidState input, inp
  - input.textfieldRequiredState, inp
  - .checkboxRequiredState .che

Digital R

HOME   **SERVICES**

The before image on the left is tilted down giving a sinking feeling. The after image has been magically straightened.

Midas was asked to repostion this artwork front and center from its only known image. Just a magic touch was required to meet the customer needs.

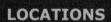ching

OLIO   **LOCATIONS**   **TESTIMONIALS**   **CONTACT US**

PHOTOSHOP TO BRIDGE TO FIREWORKS TO DREAMWEAVER

When Adobe acquired Macromedia, there was great interest—and some downright concern—about how Fireworks would be treated in the home of Photoshop. Somewhat surprisingly, the answer is "exceedingly well." Not only has Fireworks thrived under Adobe's management; it turns out that Photoshop and Fireworks are excellent workflow partners. Photoshop definitely plays well with others.

Although Fireworks is beyond decent at manipulating bitmaps, Photoshop is the true champ. With more tools and a longer history of shaping digital information, Photoshop is better equipped at correcting and cleaning up digital photographs that make up much of the modern Web. Fireworks, for its part, excels at optimization and maintaining editability—something that Photoshop picked up from Fireworks's talent pool.

Adobe Bridge provides a much needed conduit between the two graphic programs. While Fireworks can import native Photoshop files and vice versa, a more frequently used workflow is for Fireworks to incorporate digital images after they have been adjusted by Photoshop. With Bridge, you can easily tag such images with custom keywords that, in turn, can be browsed and filtered from Fireworks. The aptly named Bridge can also be launched and taken advantage of from Dreamweaver.

Fireworks's rich symbols, with 9-slice scaling such as Adobe Illustrator, are another differentiator from Photoshop. Fireworks offers several libraries of rich symbols including two (one for Mac and the other for PC) for comping forms and their wide range of form elements. When bringing your form comp pages to life, Dreamweaver adds its own bit of power with Spry form widgets, which combine multistate validation with drag-and-drop ease.

The chapters in Part IV explore the workflow from Photoshop to Bridge to Fireworks and onto Dreamweaver, highlighting key features in each program that can ramp up your efficiency and broaden your available toolset.

THE FLOW: PHOTOSHOP TO BRIDGE TO FIREWORKS TO DREAMWEAVER

All three core programs—Photoshop, Fireworks, and Dreamweaver—can call Bridge directly. Consequently, output from one is easily transported to the others (Figure IV-1):

1. In Photoshop, choose File ▶ Browse to launch Bridge.

2. Once Bridge opens, double-click any related image to open it in Photoshop.

   Initially, Photoshop is the default program for many file formats, including Bitmap (`.bmp`), CompuServe GIF (`.gif`), JPEG (`.jpg`), and TIFF (`.tif`). You can change these settings in Bridge Preferences.

3. Choose File ▶ Place ▶ In Photoshop to create a linked file from Bridge.

4. A selection of images in Bridge can be processed in Photoshop by choosing Tools ▶ Photoshop. Options include Batch, Contact Sheet II, Image Processor, and Merge to HDR among others.

FIGURE IV-1

Fireworks has a similar connection to Bridge (Figure IV-2):

1. In Fireworks, choose File ▶ Browse to launch Bridge.

2. Double-clicking PNG files opens them in Fireworks.

   If you work more with Fireworks than with Photoshop, you might want to adjust the default file associations as described in Chapter 9.

3. Certain Fireworks tools are available to act on a selection of images in Bridge, regardless of their format by choosing Tools ▶ Fireworks: Convert to Grayscale, Convert to Sepia, Invert Selection Color and Batch Process.

FIGURE IV-2

Locate images in Bridge quickly for use in Dreamweaver (Figure IV-3):

1. In Dreamweaver, choose File ▶ Browse in Bridge to launch Bridge. Place your cursor where you'd like the image(s) to appear.

2. HTML files are also displayed in Bridge and open, by default, in Dreamweaver.

3. To move a Web-ready file to your site from Bridge, choose File ▶ Place ▶ In Dreamweaver. Bridge will copy the files to your site's default image folder.

FIGURE IV-3

NOTE

The original design shown here is one of several pages that serve as the basis for the exercises in Part IV.

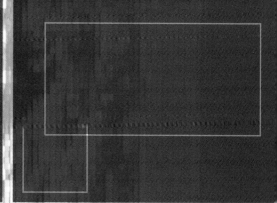

To some extent, both Photoshop and Fireworks cover the same territory. For example, both are great at compositing images in multiple layers and both apply nondestructive effects well. However, each program definitely has its own core competencies: Photoshop is the quintessential bitmap manipulation program, capable of adjusting photographs so effectively that "to Photoshop" has become an accepted verb for altering imagery. Fireworks, on the other hand, excels at image optimization and preparing pages for the Web.

In this chapter you'll work with both programs, emphasizing the strengths of each and learn how to use them together in a coherent workflow. You'll also engage with another component of the Adobe Creative Suite 3 Web bundle, Adobe Bridge. The appropriately named Bridge acts as a conduit from one Adobe program to another through an efficient workflow as you create your Web sites.

In the following exercises, you'll learn these core Photoshop techniques:

- Realigning bitmaps
- Healing photographs

This critical Bridge technique:

- Tagging images

And this essential Fireworks technique:

- Automating with commands

CHAPTER
09
ASSET CREATION
AND COMPING

STRAIGHTENING PHOTOS

No photographer is perfect, and often photographs appear perfect for use—if only they were tilted a bit this way or that. And sometimes the image is completely at the wrong angle: for example, in perspective when what is needed is a straight-on view. Photoshop has the power to easily make corrections like these to ensure that your photographic assets are seen just the way you think they should be.

ALIGNING CROOKED SHOTS

No one will ever laud me for being the world's greatest photographer, but I do try to take pictures with a sense of composition. Unfortunately, I'm not always spot on—occasionally my landscape images are noticeably crooked, a characteristic immediately evident to even the most casual viewer. Luckily, Photoshop has a simple, yet powerful mechanism for straightening such photographs.

As you can see in the following exercise, the overall process requires three steps. First, the Ruler tool identifies the desired angle. Next, a special Rotate Canvas command adjusts the image to the exact position. Finally, the Crop tool is applied to eliminate unneeded portions of the image.

1. In Photoshop, choose **File ▶ Open**. When the **Open** dialog box appears, navigate to the **Chapter 9 ▶ source** folder and select **tiburon.jpg** (Figure 9-1).

   The image appears to tilt slightly down and to the right, which might give your site visitors a sinking feeling if left uncorrected.

STRAIGHTENING PHOTOS // MOVING ASSETS INTO FIREWORKS VIA BRIDGE // CHAPTER 243
INCREASING PRODUCTIVITY WITH COMMANDS //
COMPING FORMS WITH RICH SYMBOLS //

09

FIGURE 9-1

2. From the Tools palette, select the **Ruler** tool, the second icon from the top of the last group.

    Normally, the Ruler tool is used to display measurements. Here, you use it to get the desired angle that Photoshop uses for realignment.

3. Click the Ruler tool once where the distant shore meets the lake on the left of the image. Drag the cursor to the right side of the image along the shoreline and release (Figure 9-2).

    Now that you've defined which line should be perpendicular, you can bring a little Photoshop magic into play.

FIGURE 9-2

PART **01**   PART **02**   PART **03**   PART **04**   APPENDIX

Photoshop to Dreamweaver   Fireworks to Dreamweaver   Flash to Dreamweaver   Photoshop to Bridge to   Additional Workflows
                                                                                      Fireworks to Dreamweaver

4. Choose **Image ▶ Rotate Canvas ▶ Arbitrary**. When the **Rotate Canvas** dialog opens, click **OK**.

   Photoshop takes the angle of the line drawn and uses that to rotate the picture into position, expanding the canvas as needed. Now your task is to crop the image to restore the rectangular appearance; you use guides to make sure you have the largest possible image.

5. If necessary, choose **View ▶ Ruler** to display the vertical and horizontal rulers. Drag a guide from the horizontal ruler so that it aligns with the upper-left image of the rotated photograph; drag a second horizontal guide to align with the bottom-right corner. From the vertical ruler, drag one guide to align with the lower-left corner and another to meet the top right.

   When you're done, you have mapped out the maximum area of the photo that can appear unrotated (Figure 9-3).

FIGURE 9-3

6. From the Tools palette, select the **Crop** tool, the fourth icon from the top of the first group. Drag out a selection from the upper left of the intersecting guides to the lower right. Press **Enter** (Windows) or **Return** (Mac) to confirm your selection.

The Crop tool snaps to the guides for a no-guesswork operation. Finally, save your modified image in a different location in case it is ever necessary to return to the source file.

7. Choose **File ▶ Save As**. Navigate up a folder level and into the **images** folder. Click **OK**; when the **JPEG Options** dialog box appears, click **OK** to accept the defaults.

The final file, while now rotated into a straighter appearance (Figure 9-4), is quite large in both dimensions and file size; you have an opportunity to optimize it for the Web later in the workflow with Fireworks.

FIGURE 9-4

REMOVING PERSPECTIVE

Not only can Photoshop rotate images in two-dimensional space; it also has the ability to work with the third dimension, depth. In this exercise, you learn how you can take a portion of a photo shot in perspective and rotate the Z-axis so that the image appears straight on. The Crop tool, in a special mode, is the central player in this operation, with an assist by the Image Sizing feature.

1. In Photoshop, choose **File ▶ Open**. When the **Open** dialog box appears, navigate to the **Chapter 9 ▶ source** folder and select **tilted_lady.jpg** (Figure 9-5).

FIGURE 9-5

This image is of a piece of art in my home called *Lady Lazarus* by Leavenworth Jackson. One practical aspect of this technique is that it eliminates the glare that typically comes from photographing a glass-enclosed artwork head-on.

2. From the **Tools** palette, choose **Crop**. In the **Options** bar, select the **Perspective** option.

   Once the Crop tool Perspective option is chosen, you can adjust the corners of the Crop tool.

3. Drag a rectangle that encompasses the entire print inside the frame. Select the top-right corner of the cropping rectangle and Shift-drag it down to the upper-right corner of the print. Shift-drag the lower-right corner of the cropping rectangle to the lower-right corner of the print (Figure 9-6).

FIGURE 9-6

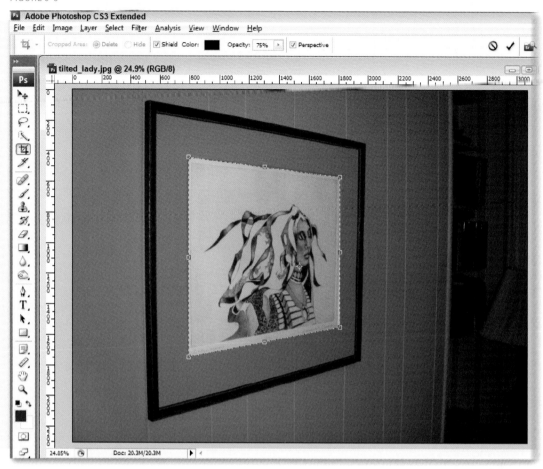

It's important to press Shift while you drag the corners into perspective to constrain the vertical angles.

4. Press **Enter** (Windows) or **Return** (Mac) to confirm the crop.

    While Photoshop does a terrific job of rotating the newly cropped image in three-dimensional space, it is disproportionately tall. You can use the Image Size feature to correct that problem.

5. Choose **Image ▶ Image Size**. In the **Image Size** dialog box, make sure that the **Resample Image** option is selected and the **Constrain Proportions** option is not. Change the **Height** value to **80 percent** and click **OK** (Figure 9-7).

FIGURE 9-7

Image Size

Pixel Dimensions: 3.08M (was 3.85M)

Width: 100   percent ▼

Height: 80   percent ▼

OK

Cancel

Auto...

Document Size:

Width: 14.347   inches ▼

Height: 14.489   inches ▼

Resolution: 72   pixels/inch ▼

☐ Scale Styles
☐ Constrain Proportions
☑ Resample Image:
   Bicubic (best for smooth gradients) ▼

Your artwork is now extracted from a perspective view, correctly proportioned and ready to be stored as an asset for future Web work (Figure 9-8).

FIGURE 9-8

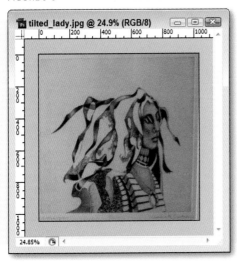

tilted_lady.jpg @ 24.9% (RGB/8)

24.85%

6. Choose **File ▶ Save As**. Navigate up a folder level and into the **images** folder. Change the **File name** to **lady_lazurus** and click **OK**; when the **JPEG Options** dialog box appears, click **OK** to accept the defaults.

In the next series of exercises, you'll learn how to use Photoshop's Healing tools to provide a more polished look to your image assets.

Ps CORE TECHNIQUES

REALIGNING BITMAPS

Photoshop includes some very specific tools for realigning bitmapped images in both two and three dimensions. You can adjust a photograph to compensate for a crooked shot or take a portion of a picture out of perspective.

To straighten a bitmap in two-dimensional space, follow these steps.

1. With the **Ruler** tool, drag out a segment along the line in the bitmap you want to be horizontal or vertical.

2. Choose **Image ▶ Rotate Canvas ▶ Arbitrary**.

3. Crop the image to remove nonrectangular portions of the bitmap.

To move an image from a perspective view to a straight-on view, follow these steps.

1. Select the **Crop** tool and, in the **Options** bar, enable the **Perspective** option.

2. Drag out a rectangle surrounding the entire image in perspective.

3. Adjust the crop corners to align with the perspective points. Press the Shift key while moving the crop corners to constrain the adjustment horizontally or vertically.

4. Press **Enter** (Windows) or **Return** (Mac) to confirm your cropping choice.

5. Choose **Image ▶ Image Size**. Disable the **Constrain Proportions** option and enter new width and/or height values to correct for distortion. The values you enter depend on the angle and degree of original perspective.

250

PART **01**
Photoshop to Dreamweaver

PART **02**
Fireworks to Dreamweaver

PART **03**
Flash to Dreamweaver

PART **04**

Photoshop to Bridge to
Fireworks to Dreamweaver

APPENDIX
Additional Workflows

In Photoshop parlance, removing scratches from scanned-in photographs or blemishes from digital photos is known as *healing*. Photoshop has three different healing tools:

- **Spot Healing Brush tool**—Automatically samples an area around the brush to match the texture, lighting, transparency, and shading of the sampled pixels to the pixels being repaired.

- **Healing Brush tool**—Similar to the Spot Healing Brush tool, except you must designate the area to be sampled manually.

- **Patch tool**—Works with a selection made by the tool in a way that is similar to the Healing Brush tool; once your selection is made, you drag the selection to the area you wish to sample.

Which tool you choose depends largely on the size of the area to be repaired and availability of the compatible areas to be sampled. In many situations, all three tools may come into play: The Spot Healing Brush tool is initially used to clear up a few areas; the Healing Brush tool is then applied to target a larger section; and finally the Patch tool relies on the newly healed portion of the image as the sampled area for a larger section.

In the following exercises, you have an opportunity to explore both the Spot Healing Brush tool and the Healing Brush tool.

AUTOMATIC SPOT HEALING

Imperfections in images can take many forms. Often, as in the case of the example used in this exercise, the problems are in the photograph itself rather than the subject of the photo. Regardless of where the issue stems from, the Spot Healing Brush tool is a great way to remove unwanted image blemishes.

1. In Photoshop, choose **File ▶ Open**. When the **Open** dialog box appears, navigate to the **Chapter 9 ▶ source** folder and select **bridge_car.jpg** (Figure 9-9).

    The two prominent UFO-like gray spots in the blue sky are the most obvious glitches in need of healing. On closer inspection you find a number of others closer to the cloudbank.

FIGURE 9-9

2. From the Tools palette, choose the **Spot Healing Brush** tool, the first icon in second group from the top.

   The primary benefit of this tool, introduced in Photoshop CS3, over the older Healing Brush tool; is that Photoshop does all the initial sampling for you.

3. Press the right bracket key (**]**) to increase the size of your brush to 100 pixels, as shown in the Options bar. Click once on each of the large image problems in the main sky area (Figure 9-10); if the healed spot is more noticeable than you like, press **Ctrl+Z** (Windows) or **Cmd+Z** (Mac) to undo the operation and try again.

FIGURE 9-10

You'll notice a black circle when you first apply the Spot Healing Brush tool; Photoshop temporarily applies this mask while sampling and recalculating the appropriate pixels to paint. Because Photoshop automatically selects the area to sample, you will face occasions where an improper selection is made and the effect is not as desired. In these circumstances, you can also undo and redo the operation.

4. Press the left bracket key([ ) to reduce the Spot Healing Brush tool size to **50** and heal the smaller blemishes along the cloudbank and above the sign by clicking on them once.

   After you've repaired the photograph to your own satisfaction, it's often a good idea to take a look at how far you've come from the original before saving your changes.

5. Press F12 to revert to the unmodified image. When you're done, press **Ctrl+Z** (Windows) or **Cmd+Z** (Mac) to return to your altered photo (Figure 9-11).

FIGURE 9-11

Finally, you can store your newly cleaned-up asset for later use.

6. Choose **File ▶ Save As**. Navigate up a folder level and into the **images** folder. Click **OK.** When the **JPEG Options** dialog box appears, click **OK** to accept the defaults.

The Spot Healing Brush tool was quite appropriate for this image because of the large expanse of sky available for sampling. In the next exercise, you'll work with an imperfect subject (that would be me) and the Healing Brush tool.

Although the Spot Healing Brush works remarkably well much of the time, there are situations that require more control. As noted earlier, the Healing Brush tool requires that you select a sample point before painted over the damaged area.

1. In Photoshop, choose **File ▶ Open**. When the Open dialog box appears, navigate to the **Chapter 9 ▶ source** folder and select **joe.jpg** (Figure 9-12).

FIGURE 9-12

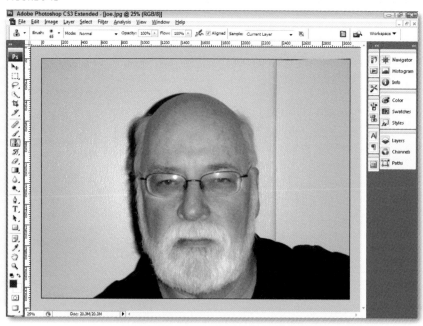

Now you can see if you can help polish my image a bit with the Healing Brush tool.

2. From the Tools palette, select the **Healing Brush** tool, which is in the same tool pop-up list as the Spot Healing Brush tool.

You've got a fair amount of work to do here, so start with the blemishes below my glasses.

3. **Alt-click** (Windows) or **Opt-click** (Mac) on the left side of the image adjacent to the red mark next to my nose and then click on the mark itself. Perform the same two-step operation to remove a similar blemish on the right side of the image, near the cheekbone.

For best results, set the sample point in tonal area similar to the section you're trying to repair with the Healing Brush tool. If your results are not as desired, undo the action and try again with a different sample point.

254   PART 01   PART 02   PART 03   PART 04   APPENDIX

Photoshop to Dreamweaver   Fireworks to Dreamweaver   Flash to Dreamweaver   Photoshop to Bridge to Fireworks to Dreamweaver   Additional Workflows

4. Continue using the Healing Brush tool on the forehead area to achieve a smoother skin appearance. When you're ready, press F12 to temporarily revert the image and note the differences between original and modified image. Press **Ctrl+Z** (Windows) or **Cmd+Z** (Mac) to restore your changes (Figure 9-13).

FIGURE 9-13

You may have noticed that other than selecting the sample point, you don't have a great deal of control over the results. However, Photoshop does offer you the ability to set the opacity of a Healing Brush stroke, which is useful when you want to de-emphasize a portion of the image without hiding it altogether.

5. **Alt-click** (Windows) or **Opt-click** (Mac) in the neck area on the right side of the image and then draw with the Healing Brush tool over the uppermost neck line. Choose **Edit ▶ Fade Healing Brush**. When the **Fade** dialog box appears, set the **Opacity** value to **50%** and click **OK** (Figure 9-14).

FIGURE 9-14

The Healing Brush tool can also be used to mask more obvious image elements. Now it's time to see if you can remove the obvious border behind my headshot.

6. Press the right bracket to increase the brush size to **100**. **Alt-click** (Windows) or **Opt-click** (Mac) to the right of the dark line at the top of the image to set the sample area. Click once with the Healing Brush tool at the top of the dark line and then Shift-click at the bottom.

   The background now has a more seamless appearance (Figure 9-15): almost as smooth as my complexion! Now you can complete this series of exercises by saving the revised image as an upcoming asset.

FIGURE 9-15

7. Choose **File ▶ Save As**. Navigate up a folder level and into the **images** folder. Click **OK.** When the **JPEG Options** dialog box appears, click **OK** to accept the defaults.

Next, you switch to Fireworks and learn how to work with Bridge to place your cleaned-up assets properly in the workflow as well as how to comp a form.

256
PART **01**
PART **02**
PART **03**
PART **04**
APPENDIX

Photoshop to Dreamweaver   Fireworks to Dreamweaver   Flash to Dreamweaver   Photoshop to Bridge to Fireworks to Dreamweaver   Additional Workflows

MOVING ASSETS INTO FIREWORKS VIA BRIDGE

Bridge is Adobe's dedicated asset manager and a key component of the Adobe Creative Suite 3 Web bundle. Bridge provides a flexible, quickly navigated interface that not only displays a great deal of information about any selected file, but also allows you to tag any image or set of images with a custom keyword—which can be immediately filtered for virtually instantaneous searching.

Although Bridge is not as tied into Fireworks as it is Photoshop or Dreamweaver, there are numerous pathways between the two programs. Fireworks has a direct command for opening Bridge, the **File ▶ Browse** menu option. Once Bridge is open, there are three ways to open selected files in Fireworks:

- Copy/paste
- Drag
- Open with...

The Open with... option can be found under the File menu as well in as in the context menu that appears when you right-click (Windows) or Control-click (Mac) an image.

Ps CORE TECHNIQUES

EALING PHOTOGRAPHS

Photoshop provides a dedicated toolset for removing small portions of a photograph and blending in the surrounding area. There are four tools in the Healing group, each of which is applied somewhat differently:

- **Spot Healing Brush tool**—Size your brush to cover the blemish and click once to automatically sample similar areas. Because the sampling is automatic, you may need to undo and redo to achieve the desired results.

- **Healing Brush tool**—Using the Healing Brush is a two-part process. First Alt-click (Windows) or Opt-click (Mac) the point from which you want to sample and then paint over the section to heal. Short strokes often work best.

- **Patch tool**—Make a selection with the Patch tool, which works exactly like the Lasso tool; you can adjust your selection using any of the standard techniques. Then, designate the sample area with Alt-click (Windows) or Opt-click (Mac) and drag the selection to the area you wish to sample. A preview of the sample is displayed over the image.

- **Red-eye tool**—While not as multipurpose as the other tools in the Healing group, the Red-eye tool can be useful for quick removal of the red-eye effect caused by camera flash. After you select the Red-eye tool, drag a rectangle around the entire eye. If the effect is not as desired, undo and adjust the Pupil Size and/or Darken tool options.

NOTE

If you use Bridge with Fireworks more than you use it with Photoshop, you can make Fireworks the default program for certain file types. Choose Edit ▶ Preferences and then select File Type Associations from the category list and change the preferences for JPEG and GIF to Fireworks CS3.

1. In Fireworks, choose **File ▶ Browse**.

   The Browse command opens Bridge, if necessary, and brings it to the front.

2. When Bridge opens, choose the **Folders** tab in the upper-left corner and navigate to the exercise files on your system. Locate and select the **Chapter 9 ▶ source** folder (Figure 9-16).

FIGURE 9-16

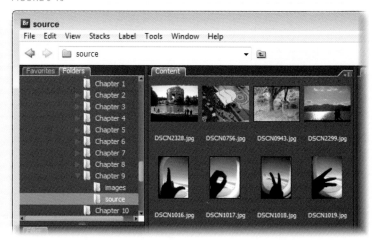

   You find a number of images in the folder in addition to the ones that were used in this chapter's earlier exercises. You can make it easy to identify those figures regardless of how many files might be in a folder.

3. Select the Keywords tab in the lower right and click **New Keyword Set**, the first icon from the left at the bottom of the panel. Change Untitled Set to **Chapter 9**. With the Chapter 9 keyword set selected, click **New Keyword**, the second icon from the left. Enter **Unmodified** for the keyword name and press **Enter** (Windows) or **Return** (Mac) (Figure 9-17).

   You can quickly add as many keyword sets and keywords as necessary. Once created, they are just as easy to apply and use.

258   PART **01**   PART **02**   PART **03**   PART **04**   APPENDIX

Photoshop to Dreamweaver   Fireworks to Dreamweaver   Flash to Dreamweaver   Photoshop to Bridge to Fireworks to Dreamweaver   Additional Workflows

FIGURE 9-17

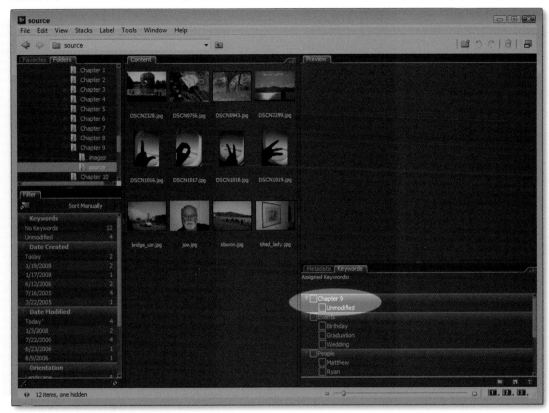

4. Select the four files previously referenced: **bridge_car.jpg**, **joe.jpg**, **tiburon.jpg**, and **tilted_lady.jpg**. In the Keywords tab, select **Unmodified**.

   Once files have been tagged with a keyword, they can be retrieved instantly through the Filter tab. The primary benefit here may not be so evident if you've been working through the chapter at a steady pace. However, most workflows are not so lucky to proceed uninterrupted; quite often, you're returning to a project after a lengthy delay.

5. In the Filter tab, on the lower left of the screen, select **Unmodified**. Note that the four files with this keyword are the only files now displayed.

   Now that your files have been identified, you can bring them into Fireworks for modification.

6. Choose **Edit ▶ Select All** or drag a selection marquee around all four thumbnails (Figure 9-18). Choose **File ▶ Open with ▶ Fireworks CS3**.

Br CORE TECHNIQUES

TAGGING IMAGES WITH BRIDGE

To quickly find a set of images within a folder, it's a good idea to add one or more keywords to the image. With Bridge, you can quickly create grouped keywords and apply them as needed. Once applied, you can use the Filter panel to display the results on a keyword-by-keyword level.

Bridge comes with a few preset keyword sets like Events, People, and Places. Within each keyword set is a list of keywords; Places, for example, includes New York, Paris, and San Jose. The real power of Bridge tagging is the ability to create your own custom keyword sets easily. Choose **New Keyword Set** to generate an untitled set. Rename the keyword set and then choose **New Keyword** to add tags in the newly created category. A general keyword set, Other keywords, is provided for individual tags that are unrelated to any specific grouping.

To apply a keyword, select one or more images and then click the keyword checkbox. You can apply multiple keywords individually or an entire keyword set to an image. Once a keyword is applied, it appears in the Filter tab. To display images with a particular keyword, select it in the Filter tab; the Filter is cumulative so you can select multiple tags.

FIGURE 9-18

The selected files open in Fireworks, ready to be modified.

INCREASING PRODUCTIVITY WITH COMMANDS

For most designers, working on the Web fluctuates between detail creation and production duty. One day all of your creative juices are flowing as you are focused on getting a single aspect of a new comp just right, and the next you're faced with converting 75 catalog images to a specific format with exact dimensions and layered effects. While I'd like to pretend I love both sides of the business equally, it just isn't so; grunt work is always grunt work. What does give me great pleasure, however, is finding ways within Fireworks and other programs to lessen the workload with built-in productivity mechanisms, like Fireworks commands and batch processing.

260

PART **01** Photoshop to Dreamweaver

PART **02** Fireworks to Dreamweaver

PART **03** Flash to Dreamweaver

PART **04** Photoshop to Bridge to Fireworks to Dreamweaver

APPENDIX Additional Workflows

In this exercise, you'll modify a single image brought into Fireworks in the previous exercise from Bridge—and then convert those modifications to a command that can be reapplied at will.

1. In Fireworks, switch to **tiburon.jpg**, one of the four files opened from Bridge. If necessary, choose **View ▶ Fit All** to reduce the magnification of the image and choose **Select ▶ Select All**.

   These source images are all taken from a digital camera at a relatively high resolution and are typically over 2000 to 3000 pixels in width and height. The next step is to change the image size to something more suitable for the Web.

   > *Although you could select the image with your cursor, the menu option is a better choice because it can be used in an automated command and a mouse selection cannot.*

2. With the bitmap selected, choose **Modify ▶ Transform ▶ Numeric Transform**. In the **Numeric Transform** dialog box, choose **Resize** from the list. Make sure that the **Constrain Proportions** option is selected and enter **243** in the Width value; press **Tab** to confirm your change. Click **OK** (Figure 9-19).

   FIGURE 9-19

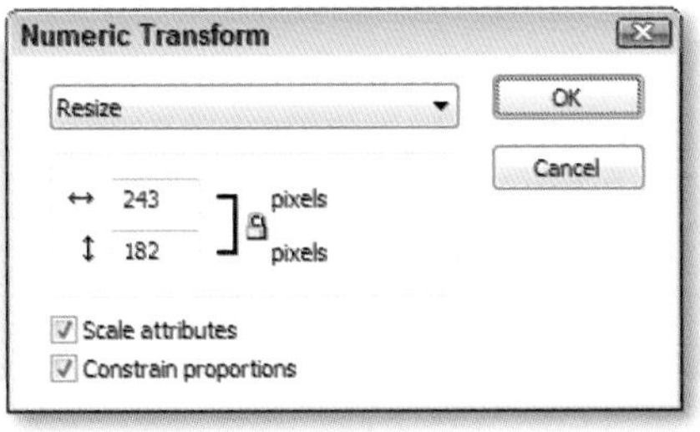

   Now you can adjust the view to work more effectively with the image. This next step changes the magnification and also brings the modified image into view.

3. Choose **View ▶ Fit** Selection.

   Although you could bring this image into the Fireworks comp as it is and then add the effect, you eventually need to incorporate the exact same graphic in Dreamweaver. The better course is to add the effects in the separate file, as you're about to do.

4. Select the image and, from the Property inspector, click **Effects Add (+)** and choose **Bevel and Emboss ▶ Outer Bevel**. In the Outer Bevel properties pop-up, set the **Color** to **white**. Choose **Ruffle** from the top list and **Raised** from the bottom. Set the **Distance** to **9**, the **Opacity** to **75**, and the **Softness** to **3**. Leave the **Angle** at **135** and click outside of the pop-up on the Property inspector to confirm your choices (Figure 9-20).

FIGURE 9 20

Now that you've added a subtle frame to the image, you can punch it up just a bit.

5. From the Property inspector, click **Effects Add (+)** and choose **Shadow and Glow ▶ Drop Shadow**. In the Drop Shadow properties pop-up, set the **Color** to **black** and the **Distance** to **6**. Leave the **Opacity** set to **65**, the **Softness** to **4**, and **Angle** to **315**. Click outside of the pop-up on the Property inspector and then choose **Edit ▶ Crop Document**.

Your image has now been transformed to one more suitable for inclusion on a Web page (Figure 9-21). Because the same modifications need to be applied to other source photos, take a look at how you can easily consolidate all of those steps into a single command through the History panel.

FIGURE 9-21

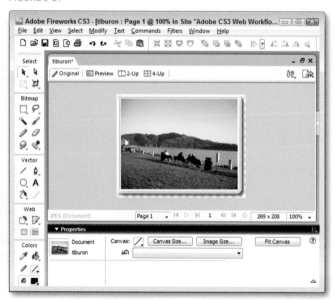

PART **01**   PART **02**   PART **03**   PART **04**   APPENDIX

Photoshop to Dreamweaver   Fireworks to Dreamweaver   Flash to Dreamweaver   Photoshop to Bridge to Fireworks to Dreamweaver   Additional Workflows

6. Choose **Window ▶ History**.

   The History panel lists every action taken for the current document that does not involve the mouse; because they cannot be tracked, mouse selections and movements are not included. All of the steps in this current exercise, however, used menu commands and are represented (Figure 9-22). You can, if you like, drag the step indicator up and reverse each step in turn to quickly undo each of the actions. Or, you can—as you are about to—store the steps as a custom command to be quickly applied when needed.

   FIGURE 9-22

   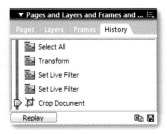

7. From the History panel, Shift-select all of the steps. Click **Save steps as a Command**, the icon on the right at the bottom of the panel. When the **Save Command** dialog box appears, enter **Modify Image** and click **OK**. Choose **Commands** and verify that your new command has been added to the list; do not select it at this time.

   Your new command is added instantly and is ready for use. Now it's time to try it out on one of the other images.

8. Select **bridge_car.jpg** from the open Fireworks documents. Choose **Commands ▶ Modify Image**.

   The resulting image is immediately displayed (Figure 9-23); pretty quick and easy, right? Notice that the History panel only has one entry in it, Command Script. Rather than listing all the steps separately, the application now has them represented by a single combined command. Now, you can save these files in another folder under different names.

FIGURE 9-23

9. Choose **File ▶ Save As**. When the **Save As** dialog box appears, navigate to the **Chapter 9 ▶ images** folder and enter **bridge_car_orig.jpg** in the File name field and click **OK**. Select the **tiburon.jpg** document and repeat the process, saving the file as **tiburon_orig.jpg**.

To get a sense of how these images might be used in a comp—and save you the labor of inserting them— you can take a look at an example design.

10. Choose **File ▶ Close All**. When asked if you'd like to save any of the files, click **No**. Next, choose **File ▶ Open** and, from the **Chapter 9** folder, select **midas_comp.png**. If necessary, choose **View ▶ Slice Guides** to hide them.

The idea behind this sample site is that before-and-after images are shown on the Portfolio page to give visitors a sense of what is possible (Figure 9-24).

FIGURE 9-24

In the next exercise, you'll learn how to use Fireworks's rich symbols to comp a key component in soliciting information from site visitors: the form.

COMPING FORMS WITH RICH SYMBOLS

Forms are ubiquitous on the Web. Virtually any organization whether commercial or nonprofit, small or large, uses one or more forms to establish communication with their site library. A form typically comprises two types of elements: form elements and labels. For easy readability, form elements are aligned with labels in an adjacent column. The most commonly used form elements are text fields, text areas, checkboxes, radio buttons, lists/menus, and buttons.

The appearance of form elements varies according to the operating system and browser in which they are viewed. A list form element, for example, looks quite different on a Mac than it does on a PC. To represent forms in their comp,

Fw CORE TECHNIQUES

AUTOMATING WITH COMMANDS

The Fireworks History panel maintains a list of each action executed in Fireworks except for mouse movements and selections. The steps can be stored as a command that can be applied at any time. To create a command, select a series of History panel steps and choose **Save as Command**. You can name your command whatever you'd like and the entry appears instantly at the bottom of the Commands menu. Here are a few pointers for more effectively creating commands:

- Always use keyboard and menu commands. As noted, the History panel cannot track mouse movements or mouse selections.

- If you're working with the entire image, choose **Select ▶ Select All** to start.

- Use the arrow keys to move an object as part of the command.

- You can create your command from a subset of the History panel steps; you don't have to select them all.

- Once your command has been created, you can rename or delete it by choosing **Commands ▶ Manage Commands**.

- Custom commands are also available in the Batch Process feature, which you can combine with any standard options, such as resize.

designers have often taken a screenshot of a form rendered in a browser and then extracted the various elements for reuse. This practice is, to say the least, tedious and inefficient. Fireworks has eliminated the need for this technique with the introduction of rich symbols for the full complement of form elements in both Mac and XP formats. Better still, these rich symbols all make use of Fireworks' 9-slice scaling technology, which makes it possible to quickly size the form elements as needed without distorting the shape.

In this exercise, you create a comp for a form that includes text fields, checkboxes, radio buttons, menus, and a submit button, along with the necessary labels.

1. In the Fireworks document previously opened, **midas_comp.png**, switch to the Pages panel and choose **Page 2**.

   The second page in the document has the initial elements for the form page—everything, in fact, except the form (Figure 9-25).

   In HTML, forms are typically laid out in a table with the labels in one column and the form elements in another, each combination of label and form element on its own row. While there is no table available as a design aid in Fireworks, you can leverage the grid—with a little bit of set-up—to formally structure your form layout.

266
PART 01 Photoshop to Dreamweaver
PART 02 Fireworks to Dreamweaver
PART 03 Flash to Dreamweaver
PART 04 Photoshop to Bridge to Fireworks to Dreamweaver
APPENDIX Additional Workflows

FIGURE 9-25

2. Choose **View ▶ Grid ▶ Edit Grid**. Choose the **Show Grid** option and make sure the **Snap to Grid** option is selected. In the left-to-right grid lines field, enter **14** and press Tab; in the top-to-bottom grid lines field, enter **28** and click **OK**.

   Tighter left-to-right grid lines are necessary to line up the labels with the form elements. Next you set up the text Property inspector for your labels.

3. From the Tools panel, click the **Text** tool. In the Property inspector, choose **Verdana** from the **Font** list and set the **Size** to **12**. Select the **color** swatch and sample the deep red in the navigation bar (**#891C1A**). Set the **leading** to **240** and **Alignment** to **Right** (Figure 9-26).

FIGURE 9-26

The leading—also known as line height—is set to a high value to emulate the separation between rows of a table. One production technique when comping forms is to enter as many of your labels as you can in a single text block separated by line returns. This keeps the spacing consistent and eliminates the need to manage numerous text objects.

4. Place your cursor so that it aligns with the top of the two text blocks on either side of the page and to the right of the Portfolio navigation button. Enter **Name:** and press **Enter** (Windows) or **Return** (Mac). Continue to enter the following labels, each followed by a line return: **Company:**, **Email:**, **Phone:**, and **Contact by:**.

When you're done, you should have five separate labels, one below the other in a right-justified column (Figure 9-27). Now, you can add the text form elements.

FIGURE 9-27

5. Choose **Window ▶ Common Library**. In the Common Library panel, expand the **WinXP** or **Mac** folders depending on your operating system; Vista users should expand WinXP. Drag the **TextField** rich symbol onto the page, to the right of the Name label.

Fireworks includes a full range of form elements for both Windows and Mac platforms. Because I'm working on a PC, I'll be using the WinXP rich symbols, but they are functionally the same. One of the key advantages of using rich symbols is the 9-slice scaling feature; you can use it to widen the text field.

6. From the Tools panel, choose the **Scale** tool. Select the right-center sizing handle on the form element and drag it until the edge is under the second "t" in Testimonial; the width of the rich symbol should be about 180 pixels (Figure 9-28).

268

PART **01** Photoshop to Dreamweaver   PART **02** Fireworks to Dreamweaver   PART **03** Flash to Dreamweaver   PART **04** Photoshop to Bridge to Fireworks to Dreamweaver   APPENDIX Additional Workflows

FIGURE 9-28

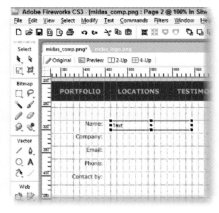

If 9-slice scaling were not in effect, the text within the rich symbol would be elongated as well as the outer edge of the text field.

Now use the Symbol Properties panel to remove the unneeded placeholder text.

7. Choose **Window ▶ Symbol Properties**. In the Symbol Properties panel, select **Text** and press **Delete**.

The TextField rich symbol just has two properties: enabled and text. Other rich symbols are much more intricate.

Now it's time create the other text fields needed for the form.

8. Select the rich symbol on the page and **Alt-drag** (Windows) or **Opt-drag** (Mac) a copy out and place it next to the **Company** label. Repeat this step to create text fields for the next two labels, **Email** and **Phone** (Figure 9-29).

FIGURE 9-29

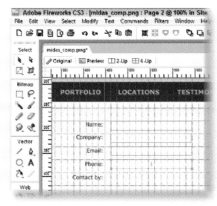

Radio buttons are used for the next set of form elements to offer the site visitor a mutually exclusive choice.

> *If you don't want to copy rich symbols to make new ones, you'll need to open the Library panel and drag them onto the page from there. A rich symbol from the Common Library can only be placed on the document once.*

9. From the Common Library panel, expand the **WinXP** or **Mac** folder and drag a **RadioButton** onto the document in alignment with the Contact by: label. **Alt-drag** (Windows) or **Opt-drag** (Mac) a copy out to the right of the first radio button.

   RadioButton rich symbols have a few more properties. You typically want to set one as selected.

10. Select the leftmost RadioButton rich symbol and, in the Symbol Properties panel, change **Label** to **Email**. From the **selected** list, choose **true**. Choose the second RadioButton rich symbol and change **Label** to **Phone**. Leave **selected** set to **false** (Figure 9-30).

FIGURE 9-30

Now you can draw a line to separate the top area of the form, where basic information is gathered, from the bottom, where questions about the intended job are asked.

11. From the Tools panel, choose the **Line** tool, the first icon on the left of the Vector group. In the Stroke area of the Property inspector, click the **color** swatch and sample the dark red navigation area (**#891C1A**). Select **Pencil ▶ 1-Pixel Hard** from the **Stroke category** list and change the **Tip size** to **2**.

Make sure to choose your stroke type before you set the tip size; otherwise the size reverts to 1, and you have to change it again.

12. Drag a line from below the Contact by: label to just beyond the width of the text fields while pressing Shift to constrain your line to be straight (Figure 9-31).

FIGURE 9-31

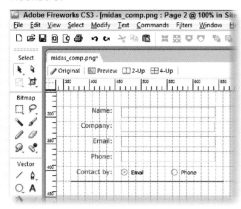

Next, you add the labels for the bottom portion of the form.

13. From the Tools panel, select the **Text** tool. Click below the just-drawn line, aligned with the right side of the previously entered labels. Enter **Types of photos**: and press **Enter** (Windows) or **Return** (Mac) twice. Enter **Number of photos**:, add another line return, and enter **Due date:** (Figure 9-32).

FIGURE 9-32

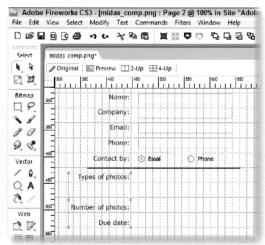

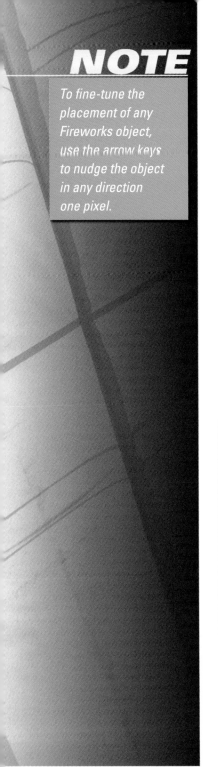

In the next step, you add two rows of checkboxes, which is why two line returns were added after the first of the new labels.

14. From the Common Library panel, expand the **WinXP** or **Mac** folder and drag a **CheckBox** onto the document in alignment with the **Types of photos:** label and the first RadioButton rich symbol. **Alt-drag** (Windows) or **Opt-drag** (Mac) a copy of the checkbox to the right, aligned with the second radio button. Repeat the copy operation twice more to add two more checkboxes.

As with the RadioButton rich symbol, the CheckBox has a range of properties, including ones to change the label and the selected state.

15. Select the leftmost CheckBox rich symbol and, in the Symbol Properties panel, change **Label** to **B & W**. From the **selected** list, choose **true**. Choose the CheckBox rich symbol to the right and change **Label** to **Color**. Leave **selected** set to **false.** Change the **Label** values for the remaining two CheckBox symbols to **Digital** and **From video**; do not change the selected value for either (Figure 9-33).

FIGURE 9-33

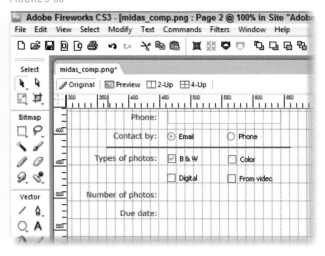

The list is another commonly used form element; in Fireworks, a list (or menu) is called a ComboBox. The next steps add two to the form.

16. From the Common Library panel, expand the **WinXP** or **Mac** folder and drag a **ComboBox** onto the document in alignment with the **Number of photos:** label aligned with the left side of the form elements. **Alt-drag** (Windows) or **Opt-drag** (Mac) a copy of the combobox below the just-added one.

    The ComboBox rich symbols also benefit from being 9-slice enabled. This means I can show you a technique for rescaling multiple objects at the same time.

17. Shift-select both comboboxes and then, from the Tools panel, select the **Resize** tool. Drag the middle-right sizing handle to extend the width of the objects so that they align with the text fields (Figure 9-34). Double-click the comboboxes to confirm your change.

FIGURE 9-34

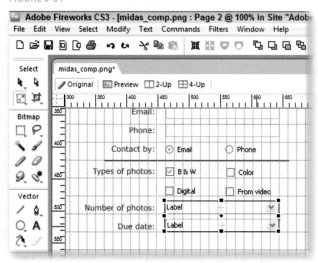

Notice how the down arrow does not get elongated regardless of how wide you stretch the comboboxes. Now adjust the properties to change the initial value for each of the elements.

18. Select the top combobox and in the Symbol Properties panel enter **Less than 5** in the **label** field. Select the bottom combobox and enter **As soon as possible** for the **label** value.

    Just one more form element to go, but it's a key one. The button in a form performs the essential function of submitting the form to whatever page holds the server-side code to process the data.

19. From the Common Library panel, expand the **WinXP** or **Mac** folder and drag a **Button** below and in alignment with the final combobox element. In the Symbol Properties panel, change the **label** value to **Request Information**. From the Tools panel, select **Resize** and drag the middle-right sizing handle so that the new label can be easily read. Choose **View ▶ Grid ▶ Show Grid**.

Congratulations, your form comp is now complete (Figure 9-35)!

FIGURE 9-35

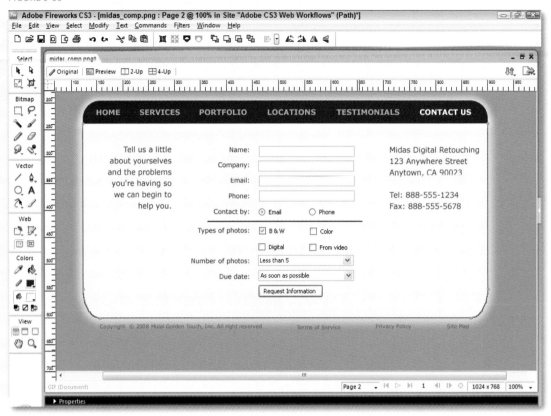

20. Choose **File ▶ Save** to store your file.

Asset production is a key aspect of any Web designer's workweek. This chapter explored a number of the tools and techniques—from three different programs in the Adobe Creative Suite 3 Web bundle—to make your asset production more productive and efficient.

In the next chapter, you'll learn how to transform this comp into an actual form in Dreamweaver.

  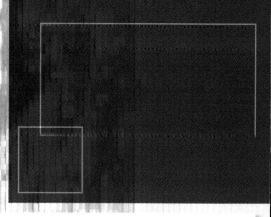

Forms are among the most commonly used page elements on the Web—and among the most misunderstood. What many beginning designers don't comprehend is that a form is the front end to a Web application and requires some type of server-side code to be useful. Once the forms have been filled out and the submit button clicked, the information is passed to code that can store it or send it to an administrator. While it's beyond the scope of this book to detail the server-side code necessary for processing forms, in this chapter you will learn how to create superlative forms with one of the coolest technologies in Dreamweaver: Spry.

What makes the best form? First, it must be easy to use. If site users are confused by an overly complicated form, they'll pass it by, whereas a well-styled, attractive form has a much better chance of attracting people to complete it. Spry form elements are built from the ground up with CSS styling in mind, so you have complete control over the look-and-feel of the form.

Moreover, for the information entered in the form to be useful, it must be in the proper format. The data, in other words, is validated to ensure that it is truly applicable. Spry form elements provide built-in validation, complete with error messages. With a Spry form element, if a user enters a letter in an all-number field—such as a U.S. zip code—an alert is instantly displayed.

In the following exercises, you'll have an opportunity to dive fully into Spry form functionality and, along the way, learn these core Dreamweaver techniques:

- Setting form validation
- Styling Spry elements

CHAPTER

10

ADDING INTERACTIVE
FORMS IN DREAMWEAVER

APPLYING SPRY AND STANDARD FORM ELEMENTS

Spry *elements*—also known as *widgets*—are extremely easy to insert: basically, drag and drop. To get them to conform with the Fireworks-created comp and to accessibility guidelines, however, you need to take a few additional steps. Of the four available Spry form elements, all but one (text area) are called for by the comp, and one of the form elements used (radio button) is not available as a Spry element. Each of the next series of exercises focuses on a combination of Spry and standard form elements: text field, radio button, checkbox, and select list.

INSERTING SPRY TEXT FIELDS

Text fields are, arguably, the most commonly used form field. Typically, a *text field* is used for gathering short strings of alphanumeric characters, which can range from a name to a telephone number.

In this exercise, you insert the top form fields in your comp—all of which are text fields. You are also introduced to Dreamweaver's accessibility options, a highly valued and often necessary feature among modern Web designers.

1. In Dreamweaver, choose **File ▶ Open**. When the **Open** dialog box appears, navigate to the **Chapter 10** folder and open **contact.htm**.

   The basic page has been created so you can focus on adding the form elements properly (Figure 10-1). However, before you can begin, you need to make sure that the proper preferences are set.

FIGURE 10-1

2. Choose **Edit ▶ Preferences** (Windows) or **Dreamweaver ▶ Preferences** (Mac). When the **Preferences** dialog box opens, switch to the Accessibility category and enable the **Show attributes when inserting: Form Objects** option. Click **OK**.

   To make sure that your site visitors who use assistive technology such as screen readers can properly navigate your form, it's important to use Dreamweaver's Accessibility feature. Now you're ready to add two major structural elements: the form itself and a table to contain the form elements.

3. Place your cursor to the right of the text block, under the Portfolio navigation element. Choose **Insert ▶ Form ▶ Form**.

   If Dreamweaver warns you that you won't see element unless View ▶ Visual Elements ▶ Invisible Elements is enabled and the option for this element (the form delimiter) is checked in Preferences, click OK and then turn on those options.

4. With your cursor inside the red dotted border that indicates the `<form>` tag, choose **Insert ▶ Table**. In the **Table** dialog box, set the **Rows** to **10** and **Columns** to **2** with a **Table width** of **530 pixels**. Enter **0** for **Border thickness**, **Cell padding**, and **Cell spacing**. Leave all the other options at their default (Figure 10-2) and click **OK**.

FIGURE 10-2

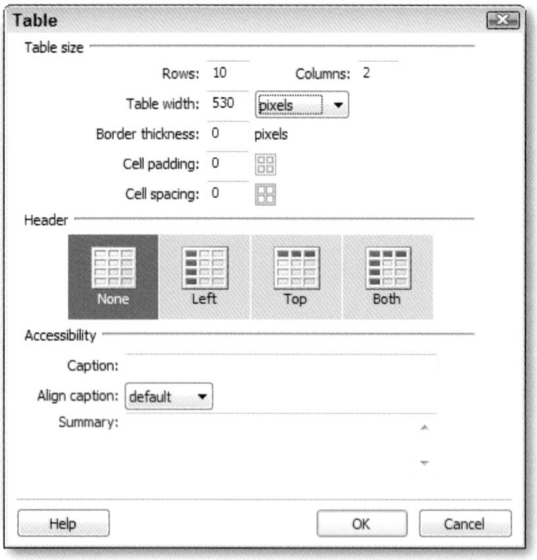

If you remember the comp developed in Fireworks in the previous chapter, the first set of form fields are all text fields. You can enter the first one now to get a handle on how it's done.

5. Place your cursor in the first row, second column of the table. In the Insert bar, switch to the **Forms** category or tab. Click the **Spry Validation Text Field**, the leftmost icon in the last group (Figure 10-3).

FIGURE 10-3

Because you've enabled the Forms accessibility option, a dialog appears before the text field is inserted.

6. When the **Input Tab Accessibility Attributes** dialog box appears enter **nameTxt** in the **ID** field and press **Tab**. Enter **Name:** in the **Label** field. Choose **Style: Attach label tag using 'for' attribute** and make sure **Position** is set to **Before form item**. For **Access key**, enter **n** and, for **Tab Index, 10** (Figure 10-4). Click **OK**.

FIGURE 10-4

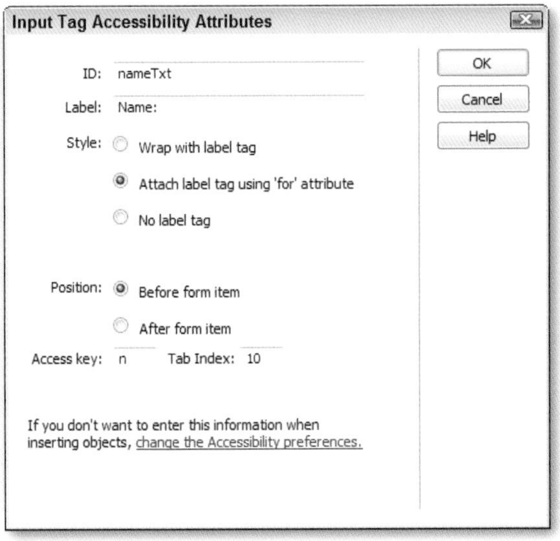

Input Tag Accessibility Attributes

ID: nameTxt	OK
Label: Name:	Cancel
Style: ○ Wrap with label tag	Help
◉ Attach label tag using 'for' attribute	
○ No label tag	
Position: ◉ Before form item	
○ After form item	
Access key: n Tab Index: 10	

If you don't want to enter this information when inserting objects, change the Accessibility preferences.

There's a lot going on in this dialog box, so I want to take it section-by-section. The ID field corresponds to the ID of the form element; it's good coding practice to include the type of form field as part of the name as well as a unique identifier, hence, *nameTxt*. The Label field is self-explanatory, and it relates to the next option, Style. The second Style option is best when using tables to contain your form elements: this method allows the `<label>` tag to be placed in a different table cell. The Position choice is just a matter of preference—it's typical for a text label to appear before the field.

In the final section, two accessibility attributes are exposed. If an Access key is specified, the form field is highlighted when a keyboard combination (modifier key plus specified access key) is pressed. The modifier key—typically Alt/Option or Ctrl/Control—varies according to browser. The Tab Index specifies the order in which the field receives focus when the user tabs through the form. I typically separate these values by 10 to allow for the easy expansion of the form.

The next step is to place the `<label>` tag in the first column of the table, a simple drag-and-drop operation.

7. Place your cursor in the **Name:** text. In the Tag Selector, choose **<label>**. Drag the highlighted element into the first column of the table, in the current row (Figure 10-5).

FIGURE 10-5

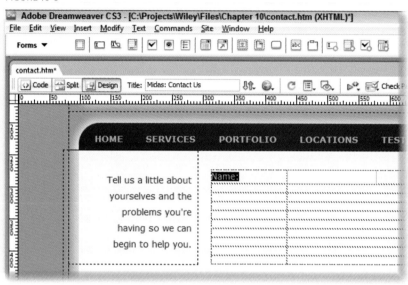

You'll be able to style all the labels in one step a bit later so that they are right-aligned and otherwise properly styled. Right now it's time to get the rest of the text fields in place.

8. Repeat steps 6 and 7 for three more text fields: **Company**, **Email,** and **Phone**. Use the following properties in the Input Tab Accessibility Attributes dialog box:

- Company

  - **ID: companyTxt**

  - **Label: Company:**

  - **Access key: c**

  - **Tab Index: 20**

- Email
  - **ID: emailTxt**
  - **Label: Email:**
  - **Access key: e**
  - **Tab Index: 30**
- Phone
  - **ID: phoneTxt**
  - **Label: Phone:**
  - **Access key: p**
  - **Tab Index: 40**

Leave the **Style: Attach label tag using 'for' attribute** and **Position: Before form item** options at their default settings for each. Make sure that you drag the `<label>` tag for each field to the first column (Figure 10-6).

FIGURE 10-6

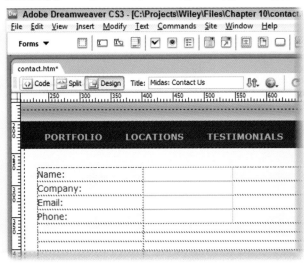

Next you can add a touch of style to both labels and form fields. I've taken the liberty of creating the CSS classes; all you'll need to do is apply them.

9. Click the **Name:** label and drag down the entire first column. From the Property inspector, choose **labels** from the **Class** list. Next, click each text field and from the **Class** list choose **formField** in the Property inspector.

10. Choose **File ▶ Save**. When Dreamweaver alerts you to files that need to be published to your Web server, click **OK**.

Rather than embedding all the necessary JavaScript and CSS files in the current document, Dreamweaver keeps them external and includes or links to them. The files are stored in a folder created for you in the site root called SpryAssets; there are different files for every Spry form element you place on your page. As the alert notes, you must make sure to transfer these files to your live server when you publish your site. You can do this most easily by opting to publish the dependent files when the time comes.

The .labels class aligns the text to the right, adjusts the vertical alignment, and makes sure that the labels don't wrap. When you apply the .formField class, notice that the input field lengthens and a bit of spacing is added with the specified margin (Figure 10-7). What isn't evident until you test the page is that the color of the input text is also changed to match the red of the labels and other text on the page.

FIGURE 10-7

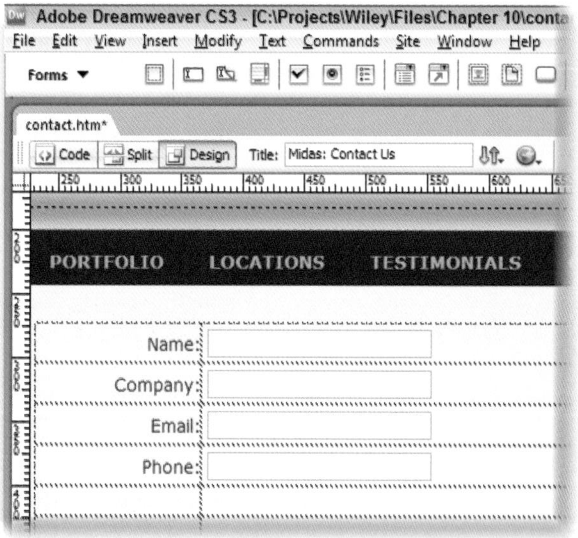

Next, you give your site visitors an either/or choice with radio buttons.

282   PART 01   PART 02   PART 03   PART 04   APPENDIX

Photoshop to Dreamweaver   Fireworks to Dreamweaver   Flash to Dreamweaver   Photoshop to Bridge to Fireworks to Dreamweaver   Additional Workflows

ADDING STANDARD RADIO BUTTONS

As I noted earlier in the chapter, there is no Spry radio button form element. Why? The key reason is that there is very little validation applicable to a group of radio buttons. By their very nature, *radio buttons* offer the user a series of mutually exclusive options, and typically, one of the choices is preselected. Therefore, the user either goes with the default selection or chooses another: no validation required.

The standard Dreamweaver radio button form element is perfectly suitable to the remaining tasks.

1. Place your cursor in the first column, in the cell below **Phone:** label and enter **Contact by:**. From the Property inspector's **Style** list, choose **labelsTop**.

   Unlike the other entries in the first column, there's no need to wrap this bit of text with a `<label>` tag; the labels for radio buttons are typically to their right and are inserted in the next step.

2. From the **Forms** category of the Insert bar, drag the standard **Radio Button** into the cell below the Phone text field. When the **Input Tab Accessibility Attributes** dialog box appears, enter **email** in the **ID** field and press **Tab**. Enter **Email** in the **Label** field. Choose **Style: Attach label tag using 'for' attribute** and make sure **Position** is set to **After form item**. For **Access key**, enter **m** and for **Tab Index**, **50** (Figure 10-8). Click **OK**.

FIGURE 10-8

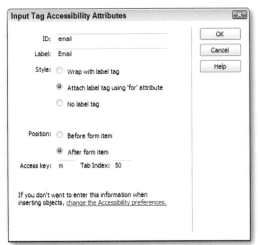

Dreamweaver inserts the radio button with the adjacent label. Before you can add the second radio button, you need to split the current table cell so you can match the layout specified by your Fireworks comp.

3. In the Property inspector, click the **Split** icon, located under the word Cell on the left. When the **Split Cell** dialog box appears, choose the **Spit Cell into: Columns** option and set the **Number of columns** to **2**. Click **OK**. Drag the border between the two columns so that it aligns with the end of the navigation element, **Locations**.

   The current cell is split into two columns. Because there are no other split cells, you can move the division wherever you need it.

4. Press **Space** and repeat step 2 to add another radio button to the right of the first one. Enter the following properties:

   - **ID: phone**
   - **Label: Phone**
   - **Access key: h**
   - **Tab Index: 60**

   There's one last task to handle for the radio buttons: setting the default option.

5. Select the **Email** radio button form field. In the Property inspector, choose the **Initial State: Checked** option.

   Recall from the Fireworks comp that the Email option was initially checked, which is now replicated in your Dreamweaver Web page (Figure 10-9).

FIGURE 10-9

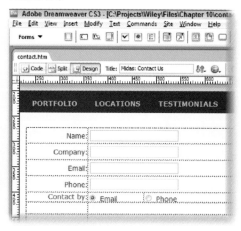

6. Choose **File ▶ Save**.

284
PART 01 Photoshop to Dreamweaver
PART 02 Fireworks to Dreamweaver
PART 03 Flash to Dreamweaver
PART 04 Photoshop to Bridge to Fireworks to Dreamweaver
APPENDIX Additional Workflows

> *How does the browser know which radio buttons are part of the same group? The name attribute needs to be the same value to group the radio buttons; Dreamweaver automatically sets name to "radio."*

You've now completed the top part of the form. Next up: Spry checkboxes.

INCLUDING SPRY CHECKBOXES

When you want to offer your site visitors a range of choices, use *checkboxes*. Unlike radio buttons, checkbox options are nonexclusive. As you can see later in this chapter, with Spry checkboxes you can require both a minimum and maximum number of checkboxes, if desired. However, you need to follow a specific procedure—mixing Spry and standard checkboxes—to get the desired effect. Before the checkboxes are added, it's time to drop in the horizontal rule that's called for in the comp.

1. Shift-select both cells in the row below the radio buttons and in the Property inspector click **Merge**, the icon to the left of the Split icon. Click into the merged cell and choose **Insert ▶ HTML ▶ Horizontal Rule**.

   The horizontal rule expands to span both columns (Figure 10-10). Now you're ready to bring in the Spry checkbox.

FIGURE 10-10

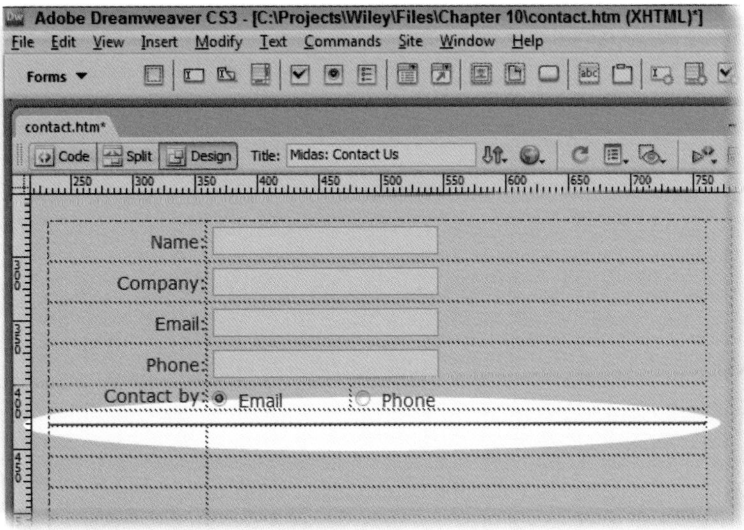

2. Place your cursor in the right column cell beneath the horizontal rule. From the **Forms** category of the Insert bar, choose the **Spry Validation Checkbox**. When the **Input Tab Accessibility Attributes** dialog box appears, enter **bwCB** in the **ID** field and press **Tab**. Enter **B & W** in the **Label** field. Choose **Style: Attach label tag using 'for' attribute** and make sure **Position** is set to **After form item**. For **Access key**, enter **b** and for **Tab Index**, **70**. Click **OK**.

As with other text fields, you want to identify the type of form element in the ID, so for checkboxes the initials CB are appended, for example, bwCB.

Next, you add three more checkboxes, but they need to be Dreamweaver standard ones and not Spry widgets.

3. Place your cursor just after the W in the B & W label and make sure that the tab **Spry Checkbox: sprycheckbox1** is displayed. If <label> is displayed in the Tag Selector, press the right arrow once. The last element on the Tag Selector should now be <span#sprycheckbox1> (Figure 10-11).

FIGURE 10-11

Code placement here is critical: Your additional checkboxes must be contained within the <span> tag that defines the Spry Checkbox but be outside the <label> tag of the initial checkbox.

4. From the Insert bar, choose the **standard Checkbox**. When the **Input Tab Accessibility Attributes** dialog box appears, enter these properties and click **OK**:

286   PART 01   PART 02   PART 03   PART 04   APPENDIX

Photoshop to Dreamweaver   Fireworks to Dreamweaver   Flash to Dreamweaver   Photoshop to Bridge to Fireworks to Dreamweaver   Additional Workflows

- **ID: colorCB**

- **Label: Color**

- **Access key: o**

- **Tab Index: 80**

Two down, two to go! Now you can add a line break and insert the remaining checkboxes.

5. Press **Shift-Enter** (Windows) or **Shift-Return** (Mac) to insert a line break. From the Insert bar, choose the **standard Checkbox**. Enter these properties and click **OK**:

- **ID: digitalCB**

- **Label: Digital**

- **Access key: d**

- **Tab Index: 90**

Press the **right arrow** to move past the selection and then press **Space**. Again, choose the **standard Checkbox** from the Insert bar and enter these properties:

- **ID: videoCB**

- **Label: From Video**

- **Access key: v**

- **Tab Index: 100**

While all four checkboxes are now on the page—properly placed within the Spry Checkbox area—you might notice the two on the right don't quite line up correctly (Figure 10-12). You can take care of that with little bit of styling.

FIGURE 10-12

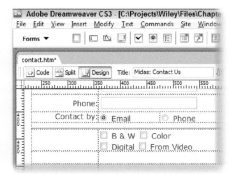

6. Select the **color** checkbox form element and switch to **Code** view. Expand the selection to include the `<label>` tag that immediately follows the current selection. From the Property inspector **Style** list, choose **secondColumn**. Return to Design view and select the **video** checkbox form element. Again, switch to Code view and expand the selection to the subsequent `<label>` tag. From the Property inspector **Style** list, choose **secondColumn2**. Switch back to Design view.

   Now, both elements are in alignment (Figure 10-13) as comped in Fireworks. The two classes used, `secondColumn` and `secondColumn2` add a bit of padding to the left of the automatically inserted `<span>` tag. Two classes are used so the correct amount of padding can be added for each.

   FIGURE 10-13

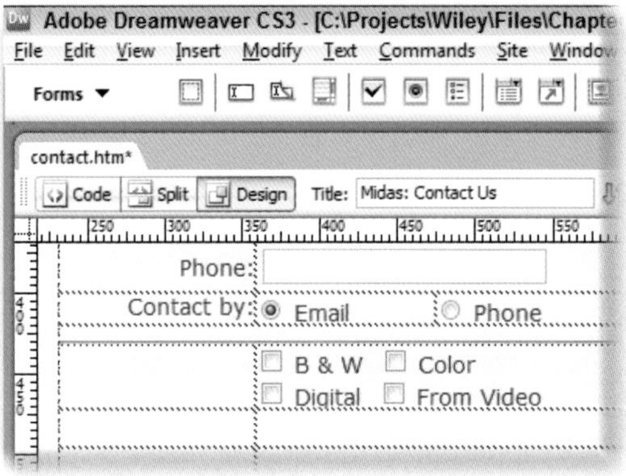

   Last task with the checkboxes: labeling the entire block.

7. Place your cursor in the first column next to the checkboxes and enter **Types of photos:**. From the Property inspector **Style** list, choose **labelsTop**.

   Because the checkboxes section incorporates a line break, the default vertical position forces the overall label to the middle. The `labelsTop` class corrects the appearance (Figure 10-14).

FIGURE 10-14

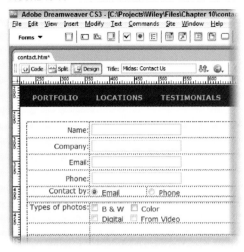

8. Choose **File ▶ Save**. When Dreamweaver alerts you to files that need to be published to your Web server, click **OK**.

The final form element, drop-down lists, is added to the page next.

SETTING UP SPRY LISTS

A *select list* offers a series of mutually exclusive options in a compact format. The options in lists have two parts: a label (what the site visitor sees) and a value (what is submitted by the form). You can enter as many options in a select list as you'd like—Dreamweaver provides an easy-to-use interface from the Property inspector for this very purpose.

In the following exercise, you set one list to find out how many photos the site visitor has to submit and another to determine how quickly the job needs to be done. Both use the Spry select list widget.

1. Place your cursor in the right column cell underneath the checkboxes. From the **Forms** category of the Insert bar, choose the **Spry Validation Select**. When the **Input Tab Accessibility Attributes** dialog box appears, enter **numberList** in the **ID** field and press **Tab**. Enter **Number of photos:** in the **Label** field. Choose **Style: Attach label tag using 'for' attribute** and ensure that **Position** is set to **Before form item**. For **Access key**, enter **u** and, for **Tab Index**, **110**. Click **OK**.

   Like text fields, labels for select lists typically are placed to the left of the form element. You can move the `<label>` field now.

2. Place your cursor in the text Number of Photos and select **<label>** from the Tag Selector. Drag the selection to the adjacent first column.

   Initially, the select list appears collapsed (Figure 10-15). You can add some options to make it grow.

FIGURE 10-15

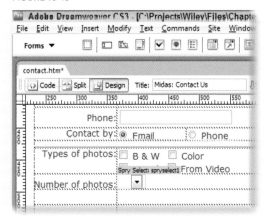

3. Choose the list and from the Property inspector select **List Values**. When the **List Values** dialog box appears, click **Add (+)** and enter **How many do you have?** in the **Item Label** column; press **Tab** and enter **-1** in the **Value** column. Click **Add** (+) once more for each of the following label/value pairs:

ITEM LABEL	VALUE
Less than 5	5_or_less
6 to 20	6_to_20
21 to 50	21_to_50
Over 50	Over_50

   Click **OK** when you're done.

   The value of the first entry, -1, is intended to be unique and indicates an invalid choice; you use this value later when validation is applied. All entries are now displayed in the Property inspector; next you can make sure folks see the one you want them to see when the page loads.

4. In the Property inspector's **Initially Selected** list, click the top entry, **How many do you have?** From the **Class** list, choose **formField** (Figure 10-16).

290
PART **01** Photoshop to Dreamweaver
PART **02** Fireworks to Dreamweaver
PART **03** Flash to Dreamweaver
PART **04** Photoshop to Bridge to Fireworks to Dreamweaver
APPENDIX Additional Workflows

FIGURE 10 16

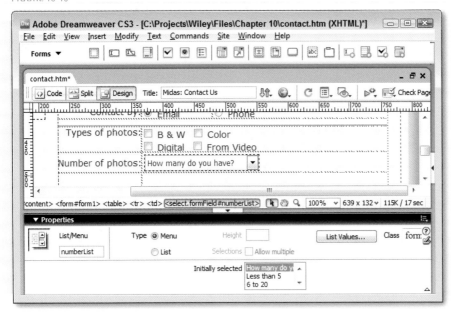

Now it's time to add the second list.

5. Place your cursor in the right column cell under the first list element. From the Forms category of the Insert bar, choose the **Spry Validation Select**. When the **Input Tab Accessibility Attributes** dialog box appears, enter the following properties and click **OK**:

- **ID: dueList**

- **Label: Due Date:**

- **Access key: a**

- **Tab Index: 120**

6. Place your cursor in the text Due Date and select **<label>** from the Tag Selector. Drag the selection to the adjacent first column.

Now you're ready to add the options for this list.

7. Choose the list and, from the Property inspector, select **List Values**. When the **List Values** dialog box appears, click **Add (+)** and enter **When do you need them?** in the **Item Label** column; press **Tab** and enter **-1** in the **Value** column as before. Click **Add (+)** once more for each of the following label/value pairs (Figure 10-17):

ITEM LABEL	VALUE
As soon as possible	asap
1 – 2 days	1_to_2_days
Within the week	this_week
Anytime	anytime

FIGURE 10-17

8. In the Property inspector's **Initially Selected** list, click the top entry, **When do you need them?** and then from the **Class** list choose **formField**.

   All but one of the form elements are now on the page as the form nears completion (Figure 10-18).

FIGURE 10-18

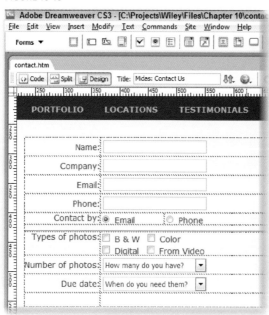

9. Choose **File ▶ Save**. When Dreamweaver alerts you to files that need to be published to your Web server, click **OK**.

The last form element—the all-important submit button—is inserted next.

COMPLETING THE FORM

The submit button has one critical function: to submit the information entered in the form to whatever server-side process is designated to process it. However, despite its strategic importance, it's the simplest of elements to insert. There is no external label, and you have no options to set.

1. Place your cursor in the second column under the final list. From the **Forms** category of the Insert bar, click **Button**. When the **Input Tab Accessibility Attributes** dialog box appears, enter **submit** in the **ID** field and leave the **Label** blank. Choose the **Style: No label tag** option. Enter **r** in the **Access key** field and **130** in Tab Index (Figure 10-19). Click **OK**.

FIGURE 10-19

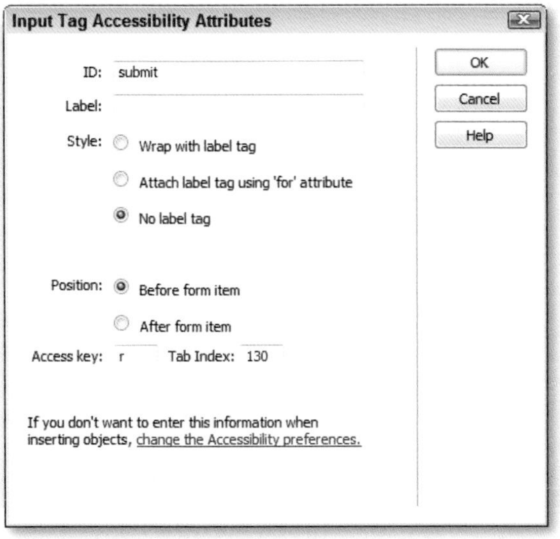

The "r" Access key is for the label that is changed next.

2. In the Property inspector, change the **Value** field to **Request Information** and press **Tab**. From the **Class** list, choose **formField**.

If you were developing this page for production, you'd select the `<form>` tag and enter the *action*, which is the server-side page, or script that the form should be submitted to. For this example's purposes, however, you can consider this first phase of form creation completed.

3. Save your page.

Now that the initial view of the form is done (Figure 10-20), you're ready to move onto what differentiates Spry form elements from standard ones: validation.

FIGURE 10-20

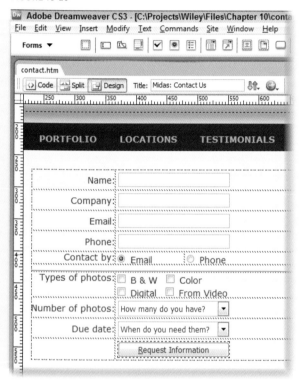

DEFINING VALIDATIONS

Spry form widgets include built-in validation, which is extremely easy to set up and modify. You can, for example, validate a text field against 12 different preset types such as email, credit card, or IP address. The validation function can be triggered when the user tabs away from the field, changes an entry, or submits the form. If an entered value is found to be invalid, an error message—of your choosing—is displayed. All of these properties are easily configured through the Property inspector and in Design view.

PART 01   PART 02   PART 03   PART 04   APPENDIX

Photoshop to Dreamweaver   Fireworks to Dreamweaver   Flash to Dreamweaver   Photoshop to Bridge to Fireworks to Dreamweaver   Additional Workflows

In this exercise, you set the desired validations for each of the Spry form elements and refine the error messages.

1. Hover your cursor over the **nameTxt** form field. When the **Spry TextField** tab appears above the form field, select it.

   Selecting the Spry border is one reliable technique for displaying the relevant Property inspector. You can also click into the field and choose the `<span#sprytextfield>` entry in the Tag Selector.

2. In the Property inspector, choose **Validate on: Blur** and make sure the **Required** option is selected (Figure 10-21).

FIGURE 10-21

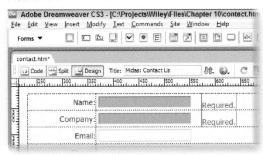

For this text field, there's no need to specify any validation beyond it being a required field.

3. From the Preview states list, choose **Required**. Change the error message from **A value is required** to **Required**.

   The background color applied to the form field is part of the style for this form field state; you'll learn how to modify it later in this chapter. Now, you can apply the same basic steps to the second text field.

4. Hover your mouse over the **companyTxt** form field and click the Spry tab when it appears. In the Property inspector, choose **Validate on: Blur** and make sure the **Required** option is selected. From the Preview states list, choose **Required**. Change the error message to **Required** (Figure 10-22).

FIGURE 10-22

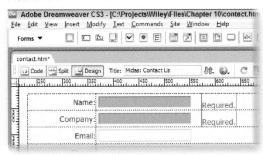

For the next two form fields, you can add a validation to the mix.

5. Hover your mouse over the **emailTxt** form field and click the Spry tab when it appears. In the Property inspector's **Type** list, choose **Email Address**. Select both **Validate on: Blur** and make sure the **Required** option is selected. From the **Preview states** list, choose **Required** and change the error message to **Required.**

Notice that when you add a validation type, a new state is added to the Preview states list, Invalid Format. You could, if desired, change the error message for this state as well

6. Hover your mouse over the **phoneTxt** form field and click the Spry tab when it appears. In the Property inspector's **Type** list, choose **Phone Number** (Figure 10-23); leave **Format** set to **US/Canada**. Select both **Validate on: Blur** and make sure the **Required** option is selected. From the **Preview states** list, choose **Required** and change the error message to **Required.**

FIGURE 10-23

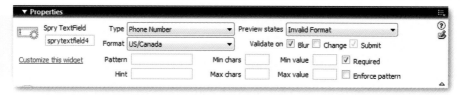

Recall that there is no validation available or necessary for radio buttons, so you can move on to the checkboxes.

7. Hover your mouse over the checkboxes and click the Spry tab when it appears. In the Property inspector, choose **Enforce range (multiple)** and in the **Min # of Selection** field, enter **1**. Leave **Validate on:** set to **Submit** and from the **Preview states** list, choose **Min No. of Selections Not Met**. Change the error message to **Check at least one, please** (Figure 10-24).

FIGURE 10-24

With checkboxes, you have the option to require a certain number of checkboxes to be selected. By setting the minimum to one, you make sure visitors click at least one checkbox.

Next, you can tackle the Spry lists.

296   PART 01   PART 02   PART 03   PART 04   APPENDIX

Photoshop to Dreamweaver   Fireworks to Dreamweaver   Flash to Dreamweaver   Photoshop to Bridge to Fireworks to Dreamweaver   Additional Workflows

8. Hover your mouse over the **numberList** and click the Spry tab when it appears. In the Property inspector, deselect **Blank Value** and select **Invalid Value**; leave the value set to **-1**. Leave **Validate on:** set to **Submit** and from the **Preview states** list, choose **Invalid**. Change the error message to **An estimate, please.**

Remember when you set up the options for each of the select lists and set the initial entry value to -1? Here's where it pays off. This validation makes sure that site visitors give an estimate of how many photos they need fixed. The same basic steps can be followed for the second list.

9. Hover your mouse over the **photosList** and click the Spry tab when it appears. In the Property inspector, deselect **Blank Value** and select **Invalid Value**; leave the value set to **-1**. Leave **Validate on:** set to **Submit** and from the **Preview states** list, choose **Invalid**. Change the error message to **Tell us when, please.**

All the validations have now been set and the error messages clarified (Figure 10-25).

FIGURE 10-25

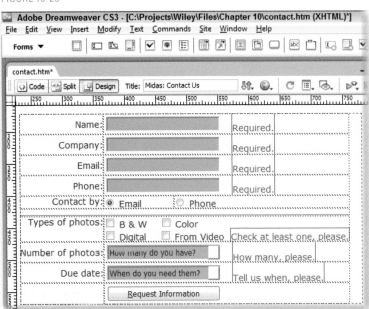

10. Choose **File ▶ Save**.

The last step for working with your Spry form widgets is adjusting their styles. As you'll see in the next exercise, you have complete control over the look-and-feel of these objects.

Dw CORE TECHNIQUES

SETTING FORM VALIDATIONS

Each of the four Spry form widgets includes unique validation capabilities. Once the element is on the page, all validations are set through the Property inspector. Certain validations make additional states available through the Preview states list on the Property inspector. Here's a breakdown of each of the validations and error message types for the Spry form widgets:

- **Text Field**—There are 13 validation types for text fields: Integer, Email Address, Date, Time, Credit Card, Zip Code, Phone Number, Social Security Number, Currency, Real Number/Scientific Notation, IP Address, URL, and Custom. You can set and enforce custom patterns, if desired; for example, you can set the phone number to always be written like (212) 123-4567. Error states include Required, Valid, and Invalid Format.

- **Text Area**—In addition to making text areas required, the Spry widget can set a minimum and/or maximum number of characters. Messages can be displayed to show number of characters entered or left and extra characters can be blocked. Error states include Required, Min. # of Characters Not Met and Max # of Characters Exceeded, and Valid.

(continued)

STYLING SPRY WIDGETS

Recall that each time you initially saved your file after placing a new Spry form element on the page, an alert popped up that listed a number of related files that had been copied to your system and needed to be pushed live when you published your site. A good number of these files are external style sheets. CSS is an integral part of the Spry framework and provides designers with a method for styling the initial appearance of each form field as well as every associated validation state, such as Required or Invalid Format.

While you could change the styles contained in the Spry-generated style sheets, it's better to take a different approach. In this exercise, you create a separate style sheet, duplicate the necessary styles, and modify the copied CSS rules. It's also important to make sure the new style sheet is after the links to the Spry styles so that the cascade is followed properly. This system results in a more streamlined external style sheet that can be easily modified without overwriting the Dreamweaver created source files.

1. Choose **File ▶ New**. When the **New Document** dialog box opens, select **Blank Page** from the main category and **CSS** from the **Page Type**. Click **Create**.

   A new CSS document is generated and opened in Code view.

298   PART 01   PART 02   PART 03   PART 04   APPENDIX

Photoshop to Dreamweaver   Fireworks to Dreamweaver   Flash to Dreamweaver   Photoshop to Bridge to Fireworks to Dreamweaver   Additional Workflows

2. Choose **File ▶ Save**. In the **Save As** dialog box, navigate to **Chapter 10 ▶ styles** folder of the exercise files. Enter **mySpry.css** in the **File name** field and click **Save**. Choose **File ▶ Close**.

   Once you've created your CSS file, there's no need to keep it open; all the style management can be handled through the CSS Styles panel.

3. In the contact.htm file, choose **Window ▶ CSS Styles**. From the CSS Styles panel, make sure you're in **All** mode and click **Attach Style Sheet**. When the **Attach External Style Sheet** dialog box appears, click **Browse** and navigate to the **Chapter 10 ▶ styles** folder. Select **mySpry.css** and click **OK**. Click **OK** once more to close the dialog box (Figure 10-26).

FIGURE 10-26

A new entry has been added to the bottom of the list of embedded and attached styles. This positioning is crucial because styles that are read by the browser last take precedence over styles with the same selector that was encountered earlier.

Now you restyle the Spry text fields first.

4. In the CSS Styles panel, expand the **SpryValidationTextField. css** entry, if necessary. Shift-select the **second, third, and fourth rules** with the following selectors:

(continued)

- **Checkbox**—You can either require that a single checkbox be selected, useful when making sure a legal document is agreed to, or that a range of checkboxes has been selected. Error states include Required, Min No. of Selections Not Met and Max No. of Selections Exceeded, and Valid.

- **Select List**—Validations can be performed to check if an entry with a blank value or specific set value (the default is -1) is not selected. Error states include Required, Valid, and Invalid Format.

```
.textfieldRequiredState .textfieldRequiredMsg,
.textfieldInvalidFormatState .textfieldInvalidFormatMsg,
.textfieldMinValueState .textfieldMinValueMsg,
.textfieldMaxValueState .textfieldMaxValueMsg,
.textfieldMinCharsState .textfieldMinCharsMsg,
.textfieldMaxCharsState .textfieldMaxCharsMsg

.textfieldValidState input, input.textfieldValidState

input.textfieldRequiredState, .textfieldRequiredState input,
input.textfieldInvalidFormatState, .textfieldInvalidFormatState
input,
input.textfieldMinValueState, .textfieldMinValueState input,
input.textfieldMaxValueState, .textfieldMaxValueState input,
input.textfieldMinCharsState, .textfieldMinCharsState input,
input.textfieldMaxCharsState, .textfieldMaxCharsState input
```

You can only see the first couple of selectors in the CSS Styles panel. The selectors listed above are all the ones you'll find in the CSS code.

Press and hold **Ctrl** (Windows) or **Cmd** (Mac) and drag the styles under the **mySpry.css** entry. Your cursor should include a plus sign to indicate the selections are being copied (Figure 10-27).

FIGURE 10-27

If you look over the CSS selectors, you can quickly see that they all are for a specific state like Required or Valid.

300
PART 01   PART 02   PART 03   PART 04   APPENDIX

Photoshop to Dreamweaver   Fireworks to Dreamweaver   Flash to Dreamweaver   Photoshop to Bridge to Fireworks to Dreamweaver   Additional Workflows

Now that the rules are available in your new CSS file, it's time to make some changes, such as getting rid of the border around the error message and switching the background color of the text field in a variety of states.

5. In the CSS Styles panel, under the **mySpry.css** entry, select the first rule where the initial selector is **.textfieldRequiredState**. In the Properties pane, change the **border** value to **none**. Choose the second rule, where the initial selector is **.textfieldValidState**, and in Properties pane change the **background-color** to **white**. Finally, choose the third rule, where the initial selector is **input.textfieldRequiredState**, and again change the **background-color** property to **white**.

The restyled text fields now have, to my eye, a much cleaner appearance (Figure 10-28). You'll note that instead of just deleting the border property for the first rule, you set it to none. This is necessary because of CSS's inheritance quality; if the border is not expressly turned off, it is passed down to the new selectors.

FIGURE 10-28

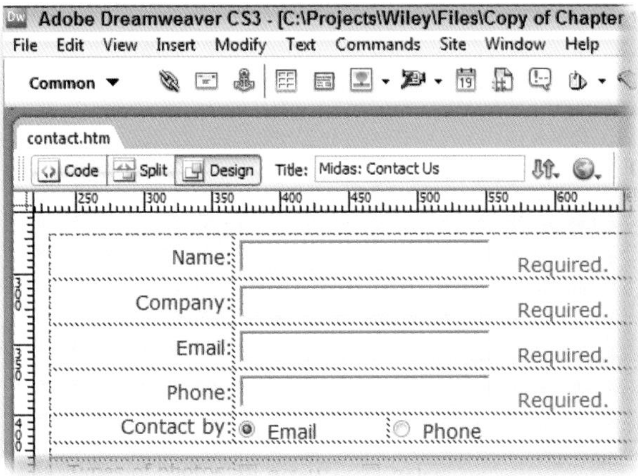

Now skip over the radio buttons and make some style changes for the checkboxes.

6. In the CSS Styles panel, expand the **SpryValidationCheckbox.css** entry, if necessary. Select the **second rule** with the following selectors:

```
.checkboxRequiredState .checkboxRequiredMsg,
.checkboxMinSelectionsState .checkboxMinSelectionsMsg,
.checkboxMaxSelectionsState .checkboxMaxSelectionsMsg
```

Press and hold **Ctrl** (Windows) or **Cmd** (Mac) and drag the style under the **mySpry.css** entry to duplicate it.

Here, all you need to do is remove the border around the error message.

7. In the CSS Styles panel, under the **mySpry.css** entry, select the last rule where the initial selector is **.checkboxRequIredState**. In the Properties pane, change the **border** value to **none** (Figure 10-29).

FIGURE 10-29

There's just one last set of rules to modify, all focused on the select lists.

8. In the CSS Styles panel, expand the **SpryValidationSelect.css** entry, if necessary. Shift-select the **second, third, and fourth rules** with the following selectors:

```
.selectRequiredState .selectRequiredMsg,
.selectInvalidState .selectInvalidMsg

.selectValidState select, select.selectValidState

.select.selectRequiredState, .selectRequiredState select,
.select.selectInvalidState, .selectInvalidState select
```

Press and hold **Ctrl** (Windows) or **Cmd** (Mac) and drag the styles under the **mySpry.css** entry.

Style changes for the select lists are the same as those for text fields.

302   PART **01**   PART **02**   PART **03**   PART **04**   APPENDIX

Photoshop to Dreamweaver   Fireworks to Dreamweaver   Flash to Dreamweaver   Photoshop to Bridge to Fireworks to Dreamweaver   Additional Workflows

9. In the CSS Styles panel, under the **mySpry.css** entry, select the first rule, where the initial selector is **.selectRequiredState**. In the Properties pane, change the **border** value to **none**. Choose the second rule, where the initial selector is **.selectValidState**, and in Properties pane change the **background-color** to **white**. Finally, choose the third rule, where the initial selector is **input.selectRequiredState**, and again change the **background-color** property to **white**.

Congratulations, you've restyled all of your Spry form fields (Figure 10-30) and the page is now complete.

FIGURE 10-30

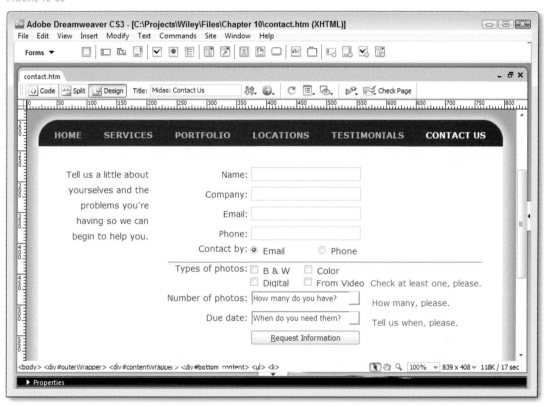

10. Choose **File ▶ Save**.

To make the Web work, you need viable, engaging forms. The AJAX-driven Spry form elements provide an easy way to incorporate highly styled form elements with powerful validation capabilities. It's important to make sure the form elements are accessible as well, which Dreamweaver handles with a simple dialog box, as shown in this chapter.

Dw CORE TECHNIQUES

STYLING SPRY ELEMENTS

All Spry widgets include a full complement of CSS styles that control the initial view of the elements as well as all the various validation states. An external style sheet for each form element is automatically copied to your site when that element is placed on the page. Here are some tips to keep in mind when you are making modifications to your form elements:

- Don't edit the style sheets directly. Because they are copied to your site by Dreamweaver, it's a better idea to regard them as source files and copy styles to a separate style sheet.

- Place the link to your custom Spry style sheet below the links to the Dreamweaver created style sheets. This ensures that your styles take precedence over the earlier referenced styles.

- Copy the entire rule, not just the current selector. One technique for locating which CSS rule to change is to switch to the desired validation state, select the element (such as error message or form field) and then switch to Current mode in the CSS Styles panel. While this pinpoints the exact selector, you want to make sure you cover your bases by altering all the associated selectors in the group at the same time.

- Pay attention to inheritance. If a property such as border is inherited, deleting the property won't prevent it from displaying—you need to explicitly set it to the value none.

I hope this chapter and all the other exercises and information in this book have given you a better sense of the how to use the Adobe Creative Suite 3 Web tools together in a more efficient and smarter workflow. I think you'll find, as I have, the more you work with the various programs, the faster your overall productivity becomes. You'll find more tips on how to use some of the other programs in the Adobe Creative Suite 3 Web bundle in Appendix A.

304 PART 01 PART 02 PART 03 PART 04 APPENDIX

Photoshop to Dreamweaver   Fireworks to Dreamweaver   Flash to Dreamweaver   Photoshop to Bridge to Fireworks to Dreamweaver   Additional Workflows

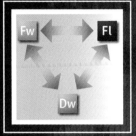
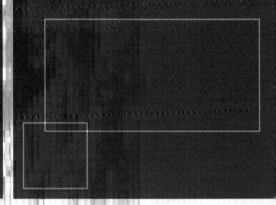

With the seven primary products in the Adobe Creative Suite 3 Web Premium bundle—Photoshop, Dreamweaver, Flash, Fireworks, Illustrator, Acrobat, and Contribute—you have a lot of workflow combinations at your disposal. This appendix is intended to supplement the workflows covered in detail throughout this book's chapters and to give you an idea as to what some of the other workflow combinations might provide.

APPENDIX

A
ADDITIONAL WORKFLOWS

ILLUSTRATOR—PHOTOSHOP—FLASH—DREAMWEAVER

Illustrator and Photoshop are old companions just as Flash and Dreamweaver are. With the Adobe acquisition of Macromedia, these two powerhouse teams can now be used in a single workflow where the sum is definitely greater than its parts.

The Illustrator connection to Flash is particularly strong in Creative Suite 3. While in Illustrator CS3, you can:

- Create Flash-like symbols, including designating the symbol as a movie clip with registration grid location and 9-slice scaling guides. Moreover, the symbol workflow in Illustrator is quite similar to working with symbols in Flash with matching keyboard shortcuts and edit-in-place capability.

- Set up text as you would in Flash and specify it as static, dynamic, or input text. Text attributes and characteristics are carried over to Flash on import, and again, the workflow is similar when working with text in the two programs.

- Export artwork from Illustrator with the preservation of the following attributes: paths and shapes, scalability, masks, stroke weights, gradient definitions, text (including OpenType fonts), linked images, symbols, and blending modes.

- Export SWF files from Illustrator. When exporting from Illustrator, you're given a very robust set of options as well as a Web Preview option (Figure A-1).

FIGURE A-1

You could take any number of paths with this combination of products. You could, for example, develop a vector-based logo in Illustrator and integrate it with bitmapped elements in Photoshop and then send it to Flash for animation and on to Dreamweaver for publication on the Web. However, because of the vector orientation of both Illustrator and Flash, a more frequently taken path is from Illustrator to Flash, with page elements coming to Dreamweaver from both Photoshop and Flash (Figure A-2).

FIGURE A-2

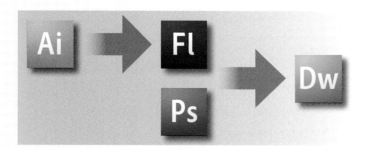

1. In Illustrator, create your static artwork and save in the native format (AI). Export any work intended to be animated as SWF files by choosing **File ▶ Export ▶ Format: Flash (.SWF)**.

2. In Flash, choose **File ▶ Import ▶ Import to Stage** or **Import to Library ▶ Format: Illustrator (.AI)** and deselect unwanted layers or define layers as editable paths, bitmaps, or movie clips (Figure A-3).

   You can also copy/paste from Illustrator to Flash with options for bringing in all or some layers.

3. Publish your work from Flash in SWF format.

4. In Photoshop, save any individual component (primarily foreground images) as a native Photoshop (PSD) file.

5. In Dreamweaver, choose **Insert ▶ Media ▶ Flash** to incorporate Flash movies where desired. Open PSD file in Dreamweaver and convert it to Web-ready format.

308 PART 01 PART 02 PART 03 PART 04 APPENDIX

Photoshop to Dreamweaver   Fireworks to Dreamweaver   Flash to Dreamweaver   Photoshop to Bridge to   Additional Workflows
                                                                                Fireworks to Dreamweaver

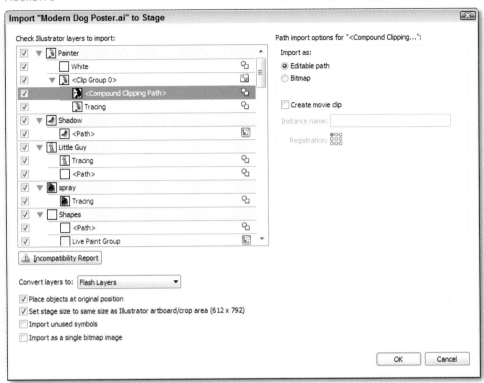

DREAMWEAVER—CONTRIBUTE

Contribute is the perfect tool for content providers such as secretaries, assistants, and writers to manage their Web site's content within the guidelines established by the Dreamweaver designer. The workflow from Dreamweaver to Contribute is a very controlled one. The site is created in Dreamweaver to be Contribute-friendly and gives the Contribute user enough flexibility to edit existing content and add new pages while still retaining the overall look and feel of the site.

It's important to create the site with the Contribute user and the entire organization in mind. Organizing the site by departments makes it possible to limit users' access properly. The Contribute-enabled site can be administered from within Dreamweaver. As an administrator, the Dreamweaver designer continues to maintain comprehensive control of the site while allowing Contribute users to update it.

The Dreamweaver to Contribute workflow (Figure A-4) can be summarized in two words: design and administer.

FIGURE A-4

1. A template-based site is created in Dreamweaver. To create a template, choose **File ▶ Save as Template**.

2. Editable regions are defined in the templates as needed. A best practice is to use multiple editable regions targeting the various page elements, such as headings and text content. If necessary, optional and repeating regions can be employed as well.

3. When the site is ready to be deployed, choose **Site ▶ Manage Sites**, and when the **Manage Sites** dialog box opens, choose **Edit**.

4. In the **Site Definition** dialog box, select the **Contribute** category and choose the **Enable Contribute compatibility** option. If Design Notes have not been enabled, you are notified that they need to be for Contribute compatibility and they are automatically turned on.

5. Make sure the Site Root URL field is correct—press Test to verify—and click **Administer Site in Contribute**.

6. When the **Administer Website** dialog box appears (Figure A-5), begin to define the user roles and settings for the site by selecting the **Administrator** entry and clicking **Edit Role Settings**.

7. Define the desired role limitations and options on the various categories of the Edit Settings available in the dialog box that appears:

    • **General**—Define whether the user can publish files or not. This is a key differentiator among user roles.

    • **Folder/File Access**—Restrict the user to specific folders. Folder access is hierarchical: If you give a user's role access to one folder, the user has access to all the subfolders and files within it.

    • **Editing**—Determine whether the user is to have unrestricted editing access or if editing is to be limited to text editing and formatting (Figure A-6).

310

PART **01** Photoshop to Dreamweaver
PART **02** Fireworks to Dreamweaver
PART **03** Flash to Dreamweaver
PART **04** Photoshop to Bridge to Fireworks to Dreamweaver
APPENDIX Additional Workflows

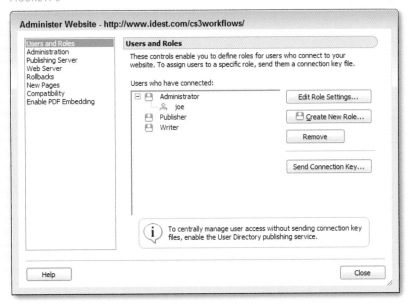

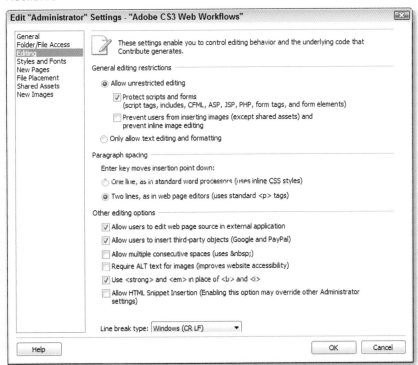

- **Styles and Fonts**—Set whether users can assign styles or not; all style definition is handled by the Dreamweaver designer.

- **New Pages**—Define whether new users can create pages and, if so, how: from a blank page; using the built-in starter pages; creating a new page based on existing, published pages; or created from a template. You can declare which templates can be used as well as which pages can get copied.

- **File Placement**—Specify the file locations for uploaded images and other linked files, such as PDF documents.

- **Shared Assets**—Declare any images, SWF or Dreamweaver Library items you wish to be accessible to the current role or site wide.

- **New Images**—Control how new images are stored and inserted into pages. As administrator, you can set a cap on image size and JPG quality setting.

8. Create and define any new roles needed.

9. Assign users to roles. Users can be assigned manually or, if the Contribute Publishing Server is enabled, through an LDAP or Active Directory service.

10. Set additional parameters, such as rollback strategy, and click **OK**.

11. Publish the site from Dreamweaver. Be sure to include any templates from which the Contribute users create pages.

12. Use Dreamweaver's Check in/Check out system to update any pages beyond the scope of the Contribute users in Dreamweaver.

FIREWORKS—FLASH—DREAMWEAVER

Just as Dreamweaver and Fireworks have a special line of round-tripping communication, so do Flash and Fireworks. Flash can import PNG graphics and retain editability for paths or text or can convert to bitmaps for maximum appearance fidelity. From Flash, you can edit bitmaps in Fireworks for detailed editing, and Flash automatically updates the file, without re-importing.

312

PART **01**
Photoshop to Dreamweaver

PART **02**
Fireworks to Dreamweaver

PART **03**
Flash to Dreamweaver

PART **04**
Photoshop to Bridge to
Fireworks to Dreamweaver

APPENDIX
Additional Workflows

With the interlinking round-trip editing capabilities of Fireworks, Flash, and Dreamweaver, you can make changes at any point in the creative process, even after the Web page is fully developed (Figure A-7).

FIGURE A-7

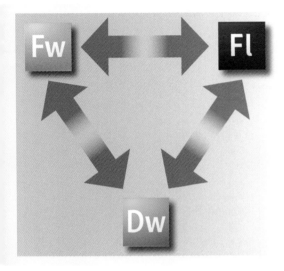

1. In Fireworks, create your comps on different pages and name them appropriately. Save your file as a native PNG file.

2. In Flash, choose **File ▶ Import ▶ Import to Stage** or Import to Library; select the Fireworks PNG file.

   Flash displays a dialog box to control the import (Figure A-8).

   FIGURE A-8

3. In the **Import Fireworks Document** dialog box, choose the **Import as a single flattened bitmap** if you want just the raw graphic; leave this option unselected if you anticipate modifying the image. Other import options include:

- **Import**—Import either all pages or a selected single page.

- **Into**—Choose to either import the page(s) into new frames or new scenes as movie clips.

- **Objects**—Choose between converting the objects to bitmaps or keeping the paths editable.

- **Text**—Choose between converting the text to bitmaps or keeping the text editable.

Elements of the PNG files are added to the library within a Fireworks Objects folder (Figure A-9). Once the graphics are imported, if you opted to retain editability, you can modify paths, effects, and blend modes, among other properties.

FIGURE A-9

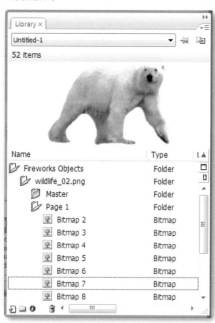

4. To modify individual graphics that have been imported, right-click the entry in the Library panel and choose **Edit with Fireworks**.

5. After the file opens in Fireworks, make any necessary changes and choose **File ▶ Save**.

6. The updates are automatically imported into Flash.

314 | PART 01   PART 02   PART 03   PART 04   APPENDIX

Photoshop to Dreamweaver   Fireworks to Dreamweaver   Flash to Dreamweaver   Photoshop to Bridge to Fireworks to Dreamweaver   Additional Workflows

7. Once your Flash movie is complete, publish the SWF.

8. In Dreamweaver, choose **Insert ▶ Media ▶ Flash** to incorporate Flash movies where desired.

9. If further graphic level changes are desired, select the SWF and locate the source FLA file in the Src field of the Dreamweaver Property inspector.

10. Once the Src has been identified, click **Edit** to reopen the FLA file.

11. Follow steps 5–7 to make changes in Fireworks.

12. Click **Done** to return from Flash to Dreamweaver.

INDEX